The Alchemy of TAROT

The Alchemy of TAROT

Practical Enlightenment through the Astrology, Qabalah, & Archetypes of Tarot

Juno Lucina
Illustrated by Shannon ThornFeather

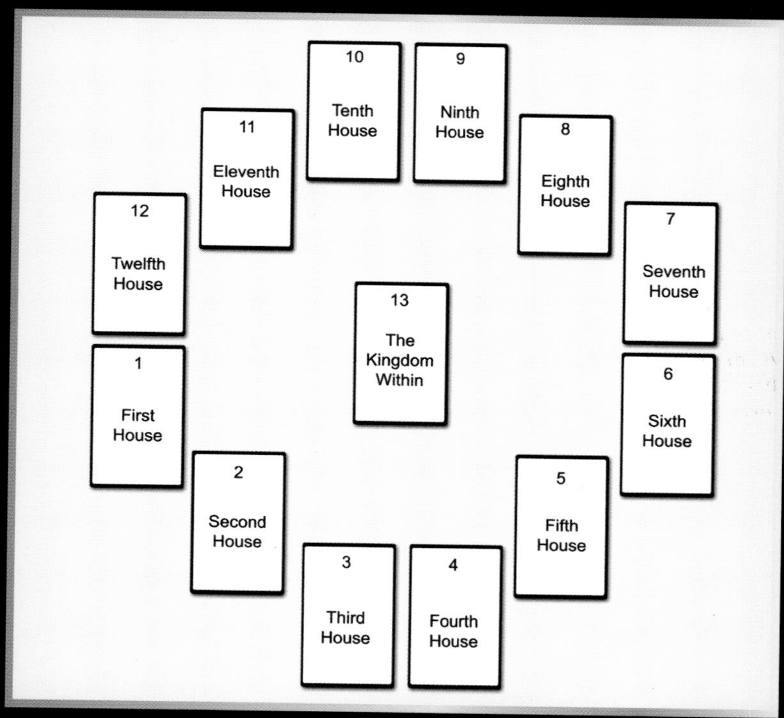

4880 Lower Valley Road, Atglen, Pennsylvania 19310

Text and concepts by Juno Lucina
Illustrations by Shannon ThornFeather

Library of Congress Control Number: 2010942266

Designed by "Sue"
Type set in UnivrstyRoman Bd BT /New Baskerville BT

ISBN: 978-0-7643-3710-9
Printed in China

Schiffer Books are available at special discounts for bulk purchases for sales promotions or premiums. Special editions, including personalized covers, corporate imprints, and excerpts can be created in large quantities for special needs. For more information contact the publisher:

Published by Schiffer Publishing Ltd.
4880 Lower Valley Road
Atglen, PA 19310
Phone: (610) 593-1777; Fax: (610) 593-2002
E-mail: Info@schifferbooks.com

For the largest selection of fine reference books on this and related subjects, please visit our web site at:
www.schifferbooks.com
We are always looking for people to write books on new and related subjects. If you have an idea for a book please contact us at the above address.

This book may be purchased from the publisher.
Include $5.00 for shipping.
Please try your bookstore first.
You may write for a free catalog.

In Europe, Schiffer books are distributed by
Bushwood Books
6 Marksbury Ave.
Kew Gardens
Surrey TW9 4JF England
Phone: 44 (0) 20 8392-8585; Fax: 44 (0) 20 8392-9876
E-mail: info@bushwoodbooks.co.uk
Website: www.bushwoodbooks.co.uk

Dedication

My Tree of Thanks…

To Geoff, who took my hand as I ventured across the Abyss…
To my Father, who demonstrated the virtues of Chesed…
To Jimmy, who shared with me the delights of Geburah…
To Jesus and Shakespeare, who revealed Tiphereth…
To my Mother, who modeled the beauty of Netzach…
To all my Teachers, who passed on to me the mighty sword of Hod…
To Wilson, who dreamed with me the dreams of Yesod…
To Floyd, who initiated me into the lessons of Malkuth…

May all that you have given me,
return to you a hundredfold.

~ Juno Lucina

An Alchemist's Acknowledgments

The crafting of a Philosophers' Stone such as this book requires the transmutation of base metals into an Elixir of Life; there are many who deserve my acknowledgments for this undertaking, just as the base metals did not arise alone in a vacuum—however, I cannot begin to point out the part of every element of existence for its crucial role in this transformation (or publication, to be specific). Thusly, I shall instead simply acknowledge my own seven metals of alchemy, as they were the key metals metamorphosed:

My editor, Dinah Roseberry, and Schiffer Books graciously provided the LEAD by which *The Alchemy of Tarot* was published and presented to the world.

Lon Milo DuQuette—celebrated Occultist, Tarot Expert, and Lover of all things Crowley—provided the TIN through beautifully (and humbly, I might add) writing the resplendent Preface to this tome (which should, in my opinion, serve as introductory primer for all metaphysicians seeking enlightenment about the spiritual history of the Tarot).

The Master Therion provided the IRON for this book, with his martial, world-shattering synthesis and unveiling of Qabalah, Tarot, and the Great Work.

Frater Achad conceived the SILVER for this project, through his groundbreaking works: *Q.B.L.*, *The Egyptian Revival*, and *The Chalice of Ecstasy*.

My daughter, joy of my life and bringer of beauty, embodies for me alchemical COPPER in every movement of her ecstatic being.

My son, Tiphereth of my life and delight of my heart, lends me sunlight and GOLD whenever I need a break from the darker mysteries.

My husband, love of my life and midwife to my spirit, gave the quicksilver (MERCURY) during the many years it took to write this book.

Blessings and abundance to you all!

Contents

Foreword
by Lon Milo DuQuette

For centuries the beautiful and mysterious images of the Tarot have captivated the imagination of western civilization. Earliest examples date from the fourteenth century and (it is commonly believed) were introduced to Europe by nomadic Gypsies who used the cards as a fortune-telling device. Whether or not this is so remains a subject of debate, and ultimately it really doesn't matter. Tarot is what-it-is, no matter what its genesis.

Whatever else Tarot may be, it is in its own way perfection ... or as closely approaching perfection as the human mind can address. Truth reveals itself in perfection. The sublime perfection of nature; the Sun, the Moon, the planets, the stars; each are characters in a cosmic spectacle acted out upon the stage of the cosmos, and directed by perfect universal laws.

Beauty is perfection. In beauty is eternal truth revealed. A glimpse of a dew dappled rose can stun the sensitive heart and inspire the poet to pour forth his soul in verse, each line more truthful than the last.

Mathematics is perfection, and even though algebra and trigonometry may not have seemed so beautiful to us in high-school, the truths revealed (and concealed) in numbers are said to be the music of the spheres. According to the Hebrew mystics, whose holy Qabalah (spelled "Kabbalah" or "Kabbala" by the orthodox, "Cabala" by Christian mystics, and "Qabalah" by modern practitioners of the Hermetic arts) is the womb wherein Tarot was begotten, numbers are the executors of creation and the key to accessing the mind of God.

Tarot is alive; the child of the perfect marriage of beauty and mathematics, of art and Qabalah; and like all healthy children, it lives in a perpetual state of wonder and exuberant growth. The milk that suckles this child is nothing less than the dynamics of the evolving consciousness of humanity, and in the last 150 years our collective consciousness has experienced profound expansion. In five short generations science, technology, and the way we look at the universe around us has changed more than it had in the previous half million. Should it surprise us that Tarot, the mystical barometer of human consciousness, would not also undergo changes in that same 150 years?

In the nineteenth century, the esoteric nature of Tarot came partially out of the shadows largely due to the writings of Eliphas Levi (Alphonse Louis Constant, 1810–1875), Dr. Gerard Encausse (also known as Papus, 1865-1916), and the adepts of the Hermetic Order of the Golden Dawn (founded in England 1888 by Dr. William Robert Woodman, William Wynn Westcott, and Samuel Liddell MacGregor Mathers, esoteric Freemasons and members of Societas Rosicruciana in Angliea). To the mystery school initiate, bound by oaths of secrecy, Tarot was revealed to be the unambiguous expression of classic principles of the Holy Qabalah; its twenty-two trumps assigned to Hebrew letters along with all their elemental, astrological, and magical attachments; its four suits, four court cards assigned to the four letters of the great Name of God, *h w h y*; its four sets of ten pips assigned to the four Qabalistic worlds and the ten Sephiroth of that most perfect of perfect schemas of consciousness, the Tree of Life.

But by the zenith of the Enlightenment, the world was moving too fast for this knowledge to remain the exclusive purview of oath-bound members of secret societies. What poked its nose out of the shadows in the nineteenth century would burst flamboyantly out of the closet at the dawn of the twentieth in the person of Mr. Aleister Crowley (also known as The Master Therion, 1875–1947). Before he drew his last breath on December 1, 1947, esoteric Tarot would not only become the subject of popular study, it would itself undergo a radical facelift; a metamorphosis to match advances in human thought that were by then expanding exponentially with every tick of the clock.

Crowley's *Thoth Tarot* (painted in the late 1930s and early 1940s by his student, Frieda Harris) is a breathtakingly beautiful magical object d'art. It represented for Crowley a synthesis of his vast accumulation of occult knowledge and illumination, and remains for us a testament of Tarot's ability to reflect changes in the magical formulae that determine the magical and spiritual realities of the age. Moreover, the *Thoth Tarot* demonstrates Tarot's living and organic ability to touch, and then make manifest the genius of those who are willing to make it their own; those who offer themselves as the prima mater of their own alchemical transmutation. And the first step in making the Tarot your own ... is making your own Tarot.

It was a requirement of the adepts of the Golden Dawn to paint their own personal deck of cards, copied from a master model that was loaned to them. Today, the modern mystery school, The Builders of the Adytum (BOTA—a group founded in 1922 by Dr. Paul Foster Case for the study of practical occultism), requires each member to color in an uncolored deck provided by the organization; a task that at first glance seems childishly easy, but in reality serves to profoundly engage the student and implant the sacred images and colors deep into his or her subconscious mind.

But painting from a model, or coloring in an existing deck is not the same as creating your own Tarot deck. Simply copying or enhancing an existing deck is like (using a metaphor of the computer age) installing within yourself the Tarot's generic "operating system."

On the other hand, creating your own Tarot deck based on your own knowledge and illuminations is like designing your own unique and personal "program" to run on that operating system; a program that reflects your distinctive and personal grasp of the spiritual universe around you; a program that embodies your own "Qabalah."

Obviously, not every mystic destined for Tarot-induced illumination will end up creating, publishing, and marketing their own deck of Tarot cards (and obligatory accompanying book). But if such enlightenment is to be complete, the *enlightenedee* will nevertheless be required (on one spiritual plane or another) to apply his or her own genius to give life and transform whatever Tarot deck is currently providing the card stock and ink.

No matter what else is said about him, Aleister Crowley was a genius. His Tarot and the magical literature he wrote to explain it demonstrates his profound grasp of magick, Qabalah, Tarot, and the evolving spiritual realities he observed around him. But when all is said and done, his *Thoth Tarot* is precisely that—his. While his work is eminently worthy of perpetual study and meditation (and believe me, after thirty-five years of perpetual study and meditation Crowley remains for me an artesian stream of knowledge, inspiration and insight), I must constantly remind myself that I must digest his work as a series of "upgrades" to my personal program, not as a substitute for it.

Crowley's most promising student (and for a time his heir apparent) Charles Robert John Stansfeld Jones, known in magical literature as Frater Achad (1886–1950: "Achad" d j a Hebrew for "One" and "Unity") did not create a new Tarot deck, but he did develop his own system of Qabalah that appeared to be at odds with both Golden Dawn, and Crowley doctrines. This would eventually lead to a permanent falling out between the two adepts and the formation of two distinct schools of "Thelemic" Qabalah.

Whether or not Achad's new Qabalah represents a more accurate and natural view of the magical formulae that characterize the current age is an argument that must ultimately be weighed by each individual. His work, like those of other masters with whom we might have doctrinal differences nonetheless remains a provocative and valuable tool that can (and I believe should) be used by serious students of every ilk to upgrade their personal programming.

The Kingdom Within Tarot [the companion Tarot deck shown in this book] and *The Alchemy of Tarot* are stunning examples of new Tarot solidly based upon the venerable "operating system" of the Hermetic Qabalah, but offering a new "program" to run on that system; a program created by adepts of the twenty-first century who, while building upon the work of both Crowley and Achad, have applied the touchstone of their own unique genius to transform Tarot.

—Lon Milo DuQuette

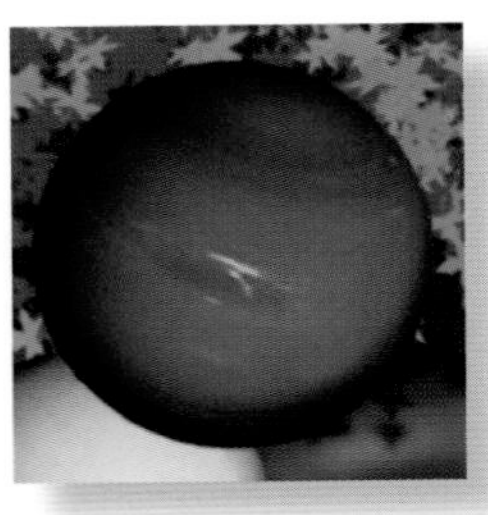

Introduction

The Fool's "Pursuit" of Truth

The Innocence and the Ecstasy

The Fool is Innocence incarnate. Whether we protect it, romanticize it, seek it, or mourn the loss of it, we all seem to value this elusive innocence. Neither a static state of being nor a lost quality of youth, innocence is a faculty, an ability that we can all choose to employ at any time that we are able to escape from our preconceptions. Many children naturally use this innate faculty of innocence to look at a thing in its entirety, correctly perceiving the nature of the object without bias and clearly seeing whatever is presented him…that is, until Mother Culture successfully tutors the child to swallow the prejudices and presuppositions of the adults around him, clouding the child's inner vision.

Innocence is all that is necessary to acquire knowledge (a commodity that is scarce in today's world of rampant emotionalism, propaganda, and misinformation, yet is often considered synonymous with power, attainment, and self-actualization). Innocence is simply approaching each and every new experience with a blank slate or canvas, so that we may see the experience as it is, rather than what we think it should be.

Occultist Aleister Crowley, on the other hand, writes that innocence is empty; instead, he exhorts his readers to seek ecstasy, the bliss of the unencumbered sensual experience of this present moment, as the path to enlightenment. Imagine the pure, unadulterated wonder of a child and puppy playing in abandon, or else those brief moments of orgasmic rapture when you merge with both your partner and the entire universe. Both innocence and ecstasy are the gifts of the Major Arcana's Fool; faculties which, if we but follow the Fool's lead, we can each use to awaken to the truth, that impossibly out-of-reach elixir of life sought by so many in this modern world of pretense.

What is Truth?

Yet many of us, jaded and wearied by this pursuit, do not even know what truth is anymore. Generally puzzled and plagued by this quandary throughout history (and her story), humanity has invested considerable resources to discover the truth—from lie detectors and the courtroom, to multitudinous religious and philosophical traditions, to vast systems of research and education. According to the dictionary, there are two substantively divergent interpretations to the meaning of the word truth: Initially, truth focuses on our day-to-day experience of reality, defined as conformity to fact or actuality, a statement proven to be or accepted as true. In other words, this type of truth is actually based upon the agreement of a particular group of people who decide, together, that something is so. We each have our own reality or interpretation of what we see, regardless of how clear or obscured our vision, and if others agree with our version of reality, we call this "truth."

One of my favorite Buddhist stories regards three blind men who have never encountered an elephant before; each has the opportunity to discover the nature of an elephant through the faculty of touch. The first touches the elephant's trunk, concluding that elephants are long and serpentine, made mostly of wind. The second feels the belly of the elephant, determining that elephants are mighty and round like the Earth itself. The third feels the elephant's legs and decides that elephants are mighty pillars spiraling up into heaven. All of them have correctly based their "truth" of the elephant on their own experiences, yet none of them grasps the entirety of "elephant." They have each perceived a different layer of truth.

Imagine, if you will, that each man decided to form a religion or philosophy based upon his personal knowledge of the elephant. The first might have found "The Church of the Mighty Serpent," the second might call his organization "The Foundation of the Great Earth," and the last might establish "The School of the Heavenly Pillars." Soon others would join, sacred books would be written, all based upon a different layer of truth. Eventually, one group might even fight with another over the "truth of the elephant." Each group has a different interpretation of what is real. From a linguistic standpoint, the very word "real" looks like "re-all," meaning the experiences that the collective has decided shall persist again and again. Reality can actually be seen as one massive loop of existence that all of us are constantly re-creating to be so.

Conversely, the second type of truth (perhaps it would be better to call it "Truth with a capitol *T*") is defined as that which is considered to be the supreme reality and to have the ultimate meaning and value of existence; this Truth is actual, regardless of our own world view, personal experiences, or the agreements about reality held by a particular people group. (After all, regardless of what we say or write about it, the elephant in its entirety actually exists.) I have often heard this Truth referred to as Absolute Truth, which by definition would be *unconditional, pure, complete, and perfect*; however, often attached to this absolutism is the erroneous (and demonstrably dangerous) concept of One Truth, that elusive conviction that has haunted man throughout history, at the root of so much of our civilized lunacies and inhumanities.

Quantum physics inserts a delightful snafu into this concept of Truth, by proving that (at least at the quantum level of existence) matter is not solid or real, but is actually a wave of infinite possibility until we, the observer, focus our attention upon it and make it a momentary particle of reality. From this mind-bending perspective, each individual as both observer and participant plays a role in creating both truth and Truth.

Playing the Game of Truth

Pick up any standard Tarot deck, and within these 78 cards you hold a practical tool that encompasses both definitions of truth. It is an instrument to help regain our innate faculties of innocence and ecstasy, for the truth is everywhere—we need only open our eyes to see it. There is no need to seek outside oneself for truth, for playing the game of the search for truth is really a game of hide and seek with oneself. In fact, whether we seek outside or inside, we are the truth, we are surrounded by the truth, and we meet the truth every day.

Osho, the modern self-proclaimed "irreverent mystic," affirmed this fact when he spoke the following words:

> "...striving towards truth is nothing but creating more confusion. The truth has not to be achieved. It cannot be achieved, it is already the case. Only the lie has to be dropped. All aims and ends and ideals and goals and ideologies, religions and systems of improvement and betterment, are lies. Beware of them. Recognize the fact that, as you are, you are a lie. Manipulated, cultivated by others. Striving after truth is a distraction and a postponement. It is the lie's way to hide. See the lie, look deep into the lie of your personality. Because to see the lie is to cease to lie... In the seeing of the lie, it disappears, and what is left is the truth." (Osho 1973, 124).

Avidyā vs. Vidyā

Seeing the truth forms the foundation of the ancient Eastern practice of yoga—a fairly recent trend in the West—which is one of six spiritual systems of Indian thought known as darśana, derived from the Sanskrit root *drś*, which means to see. According to the Indian sage Patañjali, we are lost in *avidyā*, which is best translated as *incorrect comprehension*. Because of the presence of *avidyā* in our lives, we either act incorrectly because we do not see clearly, or else we do not act correctly because we doubt our ability to see. *Avidyā* is the consequence of the amassed layers of unconscious programming, habits, and actions that have become hidden to us throughout our own existence. The dilemma with clearing the film of *avidyā* from our lives is its concealed nature—once we have begun the downward spiral of not seeing, we lose the awareness that we do not see. Thus the perpetual predicament: If we cannot see our own *avidyā*, then how do we know it is there? By recognizing the four fruits of its existence in our lives: *asmitā* (ego: I am right, special, and more important), *rāga* (attachment: I must keep what I have and get more of what I want), *dvesa* (refusal: I reject any experience in this present moment that is either unknown to me or else has brought me pain in the past), and *abhiniveśa* (fear: I worry about loss, uncertainty, and ending). These four branches of *avidyā* blur our awareness, preventing us from vidyā, or correct comprehension (which leads to knowledge) (Desikachar 1995, 10-11).

Of course, we have disguised our *vidyā* of the truth in a pack of lies. It is no accident that the word lie in the English language has the alternate meaning of remaining still, supine, and unmoving, for to the degree that we resist change and action, we must live in denial and lie to our selves and others in order to avoid confronting the actuality of what is. Subsequent to this refusal, we do not see what is directly in front of us—we see what we think is there, what's been there in the past, what we've decided should be there, and what others have told us is there. We live in a world wherein information is readily available—from so-called "experts," to the media, to the Internet, to bookstores and public libraries—if we want to know about something, the opportunity exists to find out. But to know about something is crucially different than to know it. As a whole, humanity knows about a plethora of subjects. Our heads are filled with facts, half-truths, and other people's truths. We know all about truth, but we are still lost because we still do not know it. We do not recognize it. We do not see it.

The Kingdom Within Tarot

The real question we must ask is, "Why don't I see the truth?" Or perhaps more accurately, "Why did I make the decision to stop seeing?" Helping you divine your own answers to this question is the reason this book was written, as well as the impetus for the creation of the *sui generis* Tarot deck entitled *The Kingdom Within Tarot.* This unique companion deck's title contains an intentional play on words, as it may be read as both The Kingdom *Within* Tarot, implying the Kingdom that may be found within the world of the Tarot deck itself, as well as The *Kingdom Within* Tarot, meaning a Tarot deck that helps us discover the Kingdom that is within our selves. Although this book's comprehensive study of the Tarot may be used with any Tarot deck you choose, the images used throughout this text will be from *The Kingdom Within Tarot* deck, as it visually demonstrates all aspects of the Tarot, making this vital tool accessible to everyone, regardless of prior background or expertise.

The female half of the human race (of which I am currently a member) might wax indignant at the emphasis of a *King*dom, an apparently male-centered view, in contrast to a *Queen*dom or a more deliberately gender-balanced title; all the same, I have intentionally chosen this name for *The Kingdom Within Tarot* deck because of its antiquity of insight, its multi-layered depth of meaning, and finally its basis in Qabalistic symbology. There are male and female bodies, but masculinity and femininity also exist outside the body as two extremes on the spiritual continuum called "gender." The Tarot is intended for neither male nor female bodies, but instead seeks to embrace both masculinity and femininity, uniting and overcoming the limitations of gender, restoring the sovereignty within each one of us.

Ancient Connections

By drawing correlations between the ancient systems of astrology and Qabalah, as well as incorporating the collective archetypes of humanity, the four elements, the cyclical nature of the cosmos, and the fundamental myths of the sacrificial savior and the hero's journey which infuse our holy traditions, the Tarot tenderly helps us begin to remove our own spiritual blindfolds that have hidden the truth from us. Through the synthesis of these essentials we form, not only a practical method of divination to help you reclaim the truth for yourself, but also an accurate map to guide you in remembering and reawakening to Truth, restoring your own Kingdom Within. Tarot is a tool not only for divination, but also to aid you in uncovering these truths.

This search has been the root of all the great religions and philosophies throughout the ages, which characterize humanity as asleep in a world of materiality and matter, unaware of spirit or essence. Plato wrote in his Socratic dialogue entitled *Meno* that the goal of the human spirit is anamnesis, or *to cease to forget*. Just as the New Testament's Gospel of Luke records Jesus Christ's words that "the kingdom of heaven is within you," so Lao-tzu declares in chapter 59 of the Tao Te Ching, "Where there is limitless ability, then the kingdom is within your grasp." Buddha, which means *one who has awakened*, is credited with saying that *everyone has a Buddha within*, whether they know it or not. The Hindu Chandogya Upanishad compares walking unknowing over a buried treasure to all of us who live surrounded by the truth every day (the *city of Brahman*), yet never find it because of *maya*, the veil of illusion that conceals it from us. The Alchemists of old called this most sacred of pursuits the Philosophers' Stone.

Use this guide and the images from *The Kingdom Within Tarot* (or your own Tarot deck) to unlock the mysteries of the Tarot—to discover the Kingdom of Heaven, the Buddha Within, the City of Brahman, the Philosophers' Stone…to unearth the divine secrets that you've, too long, buried within.

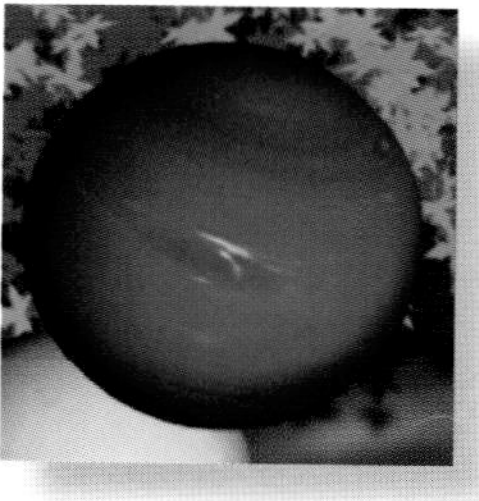

Chapter One
The Major Arcana

What's so Major (and Minor) About the Arcana?

The word *Arcana* is the plural form of the word *Arcanum*, and comes from the Latin *arcere*, "to shut away." Historically, these words were used to suggest occult (literally from the Latin *occultus*, meaning "hidden") mysteries and doctrines of various groups of people. In fact, the earliest recorded usages of the word arcana referred to the religious relics and rituals of mystery religions and secret societies; their arcana were the groups' secrets that were hidden from outsiders. With this in mind, it is obvious that the very titles *Major Arcana* and *Minor Arcana* in the Tarot encompass the idea that hidden within the images upon these cards are the major (and minor) truths of existence that must be protected and guarded from extinction. Another popular interpretation is that these two distinctions reveal the *mysteries* of existence: the Minor Arcana encompassing the *outer mysteries,* exposed to all who seek knowledge, while the Major contain the secrets of the *inner mysteries*, historically concealed from all but a chosen few.

The Major Arcana have traditionally been called the *trumps* from the Italian *trionfi* (also called *tarocchi*). In this card game popularized during the Renaissance, a fifth suit was added to the traditional four suits of a deck of playing cards and called trumps. These trump cards could take (or triumph over) the other four suits in a card game. (This game is still played in parts of Europe even today.) Trionfi was named after a celebratory parade held annually which placed its lowest-ranked participants in the front of the parade, progressing in rank as the highest and noblest brought up the rear, much like the progression of the Major Arcana. Although many occult writers link the Tarot and its secrets to the ancient Egyptians, it was actually only in the late 1700s in France that these twenty-two trumps began to have a verifiable link with the metaphysical and divinatory significance that are ascribed to them today, with the first Tarot deck (the ever-popular Rider-Waite) being published in the English language in 1909.

The Astrological Basis of the Major Arcana

Every Major Arcana card is also the pure expression of a particular astrological planetary or sign energy. Besides our planet Earth, there are ten other "planets" (Pluto, Neptune, and Uranus—the three outer planets; Saturn, Jupiter, Venus, Mars, and Mercury—the five classical planets; and the Sun and Earth's Moon—the two luminaries, also called "planets" to simplify grouping the major orbs together) in our solar system and twelve heavenly constellations in the belt of the zodiac (as well as twenty-two letters in the Hebrew alphabet); this creates twenty-two Major Arcana cards. However, the actual cards usually number zero to twenty-one. (The Fool is either numbered zero or else has no number at all.) In the ten Major Arcana that represent the energy of the planets, you will see the actual image of each planet incorporated into the illustrations of *The Kingdom Within Tarot* card pictures themselves, for easier visual recognition and reference.

The 10 Planets, in order of their average distance from the Sun, are:

Pluto: 20 The *Judgment*
(Although in 2006, astronomers began calling Pluto a "dwarf planet" because of its small size and the fact that it has not yet cleared the Kuiper Belt, for the purposes of astrology it is still referred to as a planet)

Neptune: 12 The *Hanged Man*

Uranus: 0 The *Fool*

Saturn: 21 The *World*

Jupiter: 10 The *Wheel of Fortune*

Mars: 16 The *Tower*

Earth's Moon: 2 The *High Priestess*
(The Moon is called a "planet" in astrology)

Venus: 3 The *Empress*

Mercury: 1 The *Magician*

Sun: 19 The *Sun*
(The Sun is also called a "planet" for the purposes of astrology)

To further visually clarify the Major Arcana's twelve zodiacal sign attributions, **The Kingdom Within Tarot** card images contain both the *actual image* of the planet(s) that rules each sign, as well as the *traditional symbol* associated with its constellation in the zodiac.

The 12 Signs, in order of their progression around the Zodiac are:

Aries (ruled by Mars): 4 The *Emperor*
(The Ram)

Taurus (ruled by Venus): 5 The *Hierophant*
(The Bull)

Gemini (ruled by Mercury): 6 The *Lovers*
(The Twins)

Cancer (ruled by Earth's Moon): 7 The *Chariot*
(The Crab)

Leo (ruled by the Sun): 8 *Strength*
(The Lion)

Virgo (ruled by Mercury): 9 The *Hermit*
(The Virgin)

Libra (ruled by Venus): 11 *Justice*
(The Scales)

Scorpio (ruled by Pluto and Mars): 13 *Death*
(The Scorpion)

Sagittarius (ruled by Jupiter): 14 *Temperance*
(The Archer)

Capricorn (ruled by Saturn): 15 The *Devil*
(The Goat)

Aquarius (ruled by Uranus & Saturn): 17 The *Star*
(The Water Bearer)

Pisces (ruled by Neptune & Jupiter): 18 The *Moon*
(The Circling Fish)

To visually help you further, the images on each card of *The Kingdom Within Tarot* have been carefully crafted to clearly portray the energy of the appropriate planet or sign. Images from all Tarot decks portray these energies to varying extents as well, depending upon the artist's interpretation and creative license.

For those of you who have chosen to work with *The Kingdom Within Tarot,* there is one additional, unnumbered card entitled Kingdom Within All; this card has no planetary or sign attribution, but instead denotes the macrocosm and the microcosm, infinite possibility, and All That Is. (This wholly unique card, and the reason for its addition to the traditional Tarot deck, will be explained in detail later in this chapter.)

How Does "Qabalah" Fit Into All of This?

While the four suits of the Minor Arcana represent the four elements (water, fire, air and earth), the Trumps represent Spirit, the fifth element that forms and pervades the other four. The Major Arcana has also been called the *keys* with regards to its roots in the Jewish Mystic Tradition, called Qabalah (from "QBLH" in Hebrew—also commonly spelled "Kabbalah" by Jewish mystics or "Cabalah" by Christian Medieval Alchemists—from the root QBL, *Qibel*, meaning "to receive"). The trumps represent twenty-two of a total of thirty-two phases or Paths on the Qabalistic map of the cosmos; each is attributed to a Hebrew letter with a corresponding numerical value that is steeped in significance to the Qabalist. In *The Kingdom Within Tarot* examples you will see a colored sphere in the upper left corner (UL) of each Major Arcana card, with a different-colored sphere in the lower right corner (LR). These are each card's correlation to its Path on the Qabalistic Tree of Life: the colored spheres on each card stand for the two of the ten Sephiroth (Hebrew for *Numbers* or *Emanations*) that are joined by the Path of a particular trump. (Please note: it is not necessary to incorporate the Qabalistic Path or the Qabalistic Symbology of the Major Arcana in order to use the cards in a reading. Qabalah has less to do with prediction and more to do with self-discovery and personal progression, although a firm foundation in Qabalah will increase the reader's ability to see clearly and thus advance his or her divinatory skills as well.)

There's Method to This Madness!

At first glance, it seems that the Major Arcana cards are organized sporadically, with no rhyme or reason to their arrangement. Actually, they follow the order of the French Tarot of Marseilles from 1507, and are designed to tell the age-old mythical Hero's Journey. When placed in their numerical order, we see the evolution of our own spiritual progression, our personal hero's rites of passage. (Chapter Six explores this metamorphosis in significantly greater detail.) The order of the Major Arcana also coincides with their attributions to the twenty-two letters of the Hebrew alphabet. The cards are Qabalistically grouped using the following method:

The three mother letters (the generational planets):

Aleph:	The Fool
Mem:	The Hanged Man
Shin:	The Judgment

The seven double letters (the seven planets of classical astrology):

Beth:	The Magician
Gimel:	The High Priestess
Daleth:	The Empress
Kaph:	The Wheel of Fortune
Peh:	The Tower
Resh:	The Sun
Tau:	The World

And the twelve single letters (the zodiacal signs):

Heh:	The Emperor
Vau:	The Hierophant
Zain:	The Lovers
Cheth:	The Chariot
Teth:	Strength
Yod:	The Hermit
Lamed:	Justice
Nun:	Death
Samekh:	Temperance
Ayin:	The Devil
Tzaddi:	The Star
Qoph:	The Moon

Moreover, each Hebrew Letter has an intrinsic definition that corresponds to the meaning of the card, as well as a numerical correlation that is used in Hebrew Numerology. There is an entire study of the hidden meanings of words, phrases, and their connections to each other as derived through the numerical equivalence of letters, called "Gematria" (from the Greek "Geomatria"). The practice of Geomatria (and Arithmancy, its sister study) was a prevalent approach to ascertaining truth in the ancient world: The Greeks, Assyrians, and Babylonians practiced it as well as the Hebrews. Although this book will not delve into this particular aspect of the Major Arcana, the Gematric correlations are given in the card descriptions for those readers who are interested in further pursuance of this fascinating study.

Further Illumination of the "Mother Letters"

The three Major Arcana cards that are associated with the mother letters (the outer, or most distant planets)—the Fool (Uranus), the Hanged Man (Neptune), and the Judgment (Pluto)—are unique in a few ways. Because these three outer planets were discovered much later than the rest of the planets, they "share" their positions of rulership with other planets. Also, they are considered generational planets because of their lengthier orbit around the sun: They affect an entire generation of births as they remain in a particular sign of the zodiac for much longer than those planets that are closer to the sun. When one of these three cards appears in a reading, its energy manifests on a much grander scale, often affecting the querent through national or world events. These three cards may seem negative in their effect on our individual lives, but we are in error to call them "evil;" it would be more correct to say that their energy is too vast for the physical plane; therefore, they seem to wreak havoc in the material world. Each outer planet represents the purest expression of a particular element outside the influence of the solidity and duality of the earth element—the Fool is the pure expression of air, the Hanged Man is the pure expression of water, and the Judgment is the pure expression of fire.

Card Analysis Classification

For each Major Arcana card, you will find the following classification of information:

Name of Card: Planet or Sign Correspondence
Qabalistic Path on the Restored Tree of Life
Qabalistic Letter: Its Meaning / Numerical Value/ English Equivalent

The Astrological Meaning, Title, Personality, Elemental Information, Planetary Rulership, and Minor Arcana Associations

Key Phrases

Qabalistic Symbology (based upon Frater Achad's groundbreaking work)

Understanding Card Placement

As you read the detailed descriptions of the energy of each card, you will often see the terms *well placed* and *poorly placed*. Although Chapter Four thoroughly elucidates this vital aspect of the art of interpretation, the following is a general rule of thumb for determining well vs. poorly placed cards:

A card is well placed when it—

- is surrounded by positive cards.
- neighbors the card (or cards) of a planet or sign that creates a favorable combination (such as the Empress next to the Chariot, creating Venus in Cancer, the Two of Cups).
- with regards to the *Kingdom Within Spread* (Chapter Five), appears in an astrological house in which it is strengthened (like the Empress appearing in the Second House).

A card is poorly placed when it—

- is surrounded by negative cards.
- neighbors the card (or cards) of a planet or sign that creates an unfavorable combination (such as the Empress next to the Star, creating Venus in Aquarius, the Five of Swords).
- with regards to the *Kingdom Within Spread* (Chapter Five), appears in an astrological house in which it is weakened (like the Empress appearing in the First House).

The Qabalah Factor

The final unique aspect of the Major Arcana cards in *The Kingdom Within Tarot* are the colored spheres that you will find on the upper left and lower right corners of each card. Each sphere represents a Sephirah on the Qabalistic Tree of Life. (The meaning of the Sephiroth themselves is summarized in Chapter Three's *Introduction to the Minor Arcana*.) Each of the Tarot's Major Arcana cards represents one of the twenty-two Paths on the Tree of Life, combining with the ten Sephiroth to create a total of thirty-two Paths (called Paths because they represent the Way that must be traveled or the threshold that must be crossed in order to ascend or descend from one Sephirah to another). Therefore, on each card you will find the two corresponding Sephiroth that are connected by the Path attributed to that card. (For example, the Tower has a black sphere in the upper left corner, representing Binah, and a red sphere in the lower right corner, representing Geburah—the Path of the Tower represents the energy of the 28th Path on the Tree of Life, uniting Binah to Geburah.) The Paths represented by these colored spheres apply to the Major Arcana cards of all Tarot decks, but are generally only implied rather than actually visually depicted as they are in *The Kingdom Within Tarot* deck. The unnumbered Kingdom Within All card encompasses the entire Tree of Life rather than just one path connecting two Sephirah.

The *Sepher Yetzirah* (*The Book of Formations* or *Creation*), a foundational text on Qabalah, assigns a certain type of intelligence to each Path, making *Thirty-two Paths of Wisdom*. Qabalists teach that the second through tenth Sephiroth all emanated from the first Sephirah, Kether, by way of what has been called the *Flaming Sword* or *Lightning Flash*; this was followed by the *ascent of the serpent of wisdom* that formed the remaining twenty-two Paths, showing us the way to reclaim our true selves and achieve union with the divine.

Although the origination of Qabalah is attributed to Jewish mystics, its elements are not unique, for the growth of its ideas can be traced historically back to the writings of Plato, and from there to the Stoics, Plotinus, Iamblichus, the Hermeticists, and the Neoplatonists of the Renaissance (Place 2005, 85). Qabalah contains the same mystical basis as the Orphic Mysteries, the Sufis, the Troubadours, and even Christianity itself. The Qabalists, however, succeeded in merging these mystical truths into a holistic, workable model for spiritual progression: The Tree of Life.

The "Restored" Tree of Life

Anyone who has studied Qabalah prior to reading this book will quickly recognize that the Paths that we will be studying and their correlation to the Major Arcana cards do not correspond to the traditional Paths as they are generally taught by many metaphysical texts at present. Almost all contemporary Qabalah and Tarot books are based on the Paths as introduced by a sixteenth-century Jesuit philosopher named Athanasius Kircher (although Kircher's planetary attributions to each Sephirah differ considerably from those that are popularly taught today) and further developed by such famous occultists as S.L. Macgregor Mathers and Aleister Crowley. However, before Kircher's Tree of Life became the common model in the West, there were two alternative placements of the Paths by renowned Jewish mystics, one suggested by Rabbi Luria and the second proposed by Rabbi Eliyahu. Even today, Jewish Kabbalists do not utilize

Kircher's model. In addition, there are two other famous French models whose principle advocates were Papus and Oswald Wirth, as well as an alternate system based upon Jacob's Ladder which was developed by one faction of the Golden Dawn; some Tarot historians suggest that Arthur Edward Waite had this final system in mind when he and Pamela Colman-Smith created their popular Tarot deck.

My purpose in this brief history lesson of the Paths is neither to challenge Kircher's model, nor to suggest a return to an earlier model; I merely point out that Qabalah is neither a dogmatic religion nor a set of strict laws which must be followed in order to attain enlightenment. Instead, it is a spiritual discipline with room for considerable creativity, and there are many equally viable substitutes to the Paths as they are commonly taught today.

These Paths of the Tarot are distinctive in that they are based upon the *Restored Tree of Life* as put forth by Aleister Crowley's star initiate, Charles Stansfield Jones (who wrote under the pen name *Frater* [meaning "brother" in Latin] *Achad* [AChD means "unity" or "one" in Hebrew]) from his two ground-breaking manuscripts: *Q.B.L.* (or *The Bride's Reception*) and *The Egyptian Revival* (or *The Ever-Coming Son in The Light of The Tarot*.) Both may be found on the Internet for the curious scholar; both are public domain.

After achieving high distinction within Crowley's organization for his revolutionary epiphanies and insights into the Tree of Life, Achad (whom Crowley dubbed his "spiritual son") found himself asking a rather obvious question: If Qabalah teaches that the serpent of wisdom *ascends* the tree, how can the Paths begin at the top and *descend*? He began the radical exploration of reordering the paths so that they began at the bottom rather than the top. Among other vital discoveries that I will discuss in a few paragraphs, he found that the pictorial symbolism of the Paths gained substantial importance when placed from the bottom to the top of the Tree, and that the Tree itself gained a universal significance as the reordering of the Paths created the imagery of the Caduceus, the Ankh, and the Holy Grail (along with the already recognized Cross of Elements and the Star of David).

Achad eventually proposed his altered Paths, a reordering that in *Q.B.L.* he called the "Third Order" and suspected to be "the reconstruction of the Original Qabalistic Plan...which may help Humanity to regain the Crown [of Kether] more easily than of yore." These "new" Paths were received by his contemporaries with great accolades and excitement, except for the contradicting opinion of one very important person: Master Therion (Aleister Crowley) himself. Although Crowley admitted the brilliance of the altered Tree, he was unwilling to embrace it, as its acceptance would demand a complete restructuring of the initiatory steps of his Order. Achad was so disturbed by this rift with his teacher that he even chose to begin *The Egyptian Revival* by discussing it in some depth, stating that "...it suggests that there was an Absolute Reason in the Primitive Universal Tradition, though this became Lost to view as time went on." He goes on to assert that, "If this 'New' arrangement is correct, it will prove itself to be so in the minds of those who study it in an unbiased manner" (Achad 1997, *Egyptian Revival*, 2).

Frater Achad entitled this text *The Egyptian Revival* because he believed that the ancient Egyptians best explained the coming of the Kingdom of Heaven to Earth in the inner mysteries of their mythology; with the concurrent discovery of King Tutankhamen's tomb in 1922, he hoped to build upon the resultant renewed worldwide interest in the Egyptians at the time of his writing. In Achad's arrangement, Horus is the "Four-fold Ever-coming Son," Osiris is the Sun of the White Tradition, Isis is the Mother of the Black Tradition, Set is the Adversary, Malkuth is Nuit, and Kether is Hadit.

If you find yourself confused by the previous sentence, you are not alone. Few have the necessary background in Egyptian mythology to understand much of Achad's work, and even less are steeped in the Thelemic lore introduced by Crowley and expanded upon by Achad; thus, much of what Achad (and Crowley, for that matter) has written remains ambiguous to today's seekers. With this in mind, I have created the following crash course for seven Egyptian deities that are crucial to comprehending Achad's conception of the cosmos.

A Crash Course in Egyptian Mythology

Amun-Ra

You have probably heard of the "Eye of Ra" at one time or another (ever seen the movie *Stargate*?) The original sun god, Ra was the patron deity of Heliopolis (literally "city of the sun") in ancient Egypt. Pictorially, the sun was either the entire body of Ra or else simply his eye. During the fifth dynasty (about 2400 BCE), Ra (also called Re) became the sun god of all of Egypt, eventually combining with the Theban god Amun to become Amun-Ra, the supreme deity in the Egyptian pantheon whose symbol was the ram. Even later still, when the Earth god Atum evolved into a god of the setting sun, Atum was subsumed as an aspect of Amun-Ra. Identified with Zeus and Jupiter by the Greeks and the Romans, Amun-Ra remained one of the most important Egyptian gods, except for a brief hiatus during the reign of the Pharoah Akhenaten

(1350-1334 BCE), when monotheistic worship of Aten, the sun disk itself, was imposed upon Egypt. Ultimately the great god Horus, patron deity of Upper Egypt, superceded Amun-Ra in importance, resulting in Amun-Ra becoming simply an aspect of Horus, as Re-Harakhty.

Horus

Falcon-headed Horus, the prime deity in both Achad and Crowley's conception of the Egyptian mythos, held a unique position of honor amongst the gods, evolving right along with Egypt itself. Initially, Horus (also Heru or Har) was the Earth's sky, son of Ra and Hathor (the goddess who was originally the stars which surround the world's sky, the Milky Way), and he was worshipped as patron deity in Upper Egypt.

Around 3000 BCE, when Upper Egypt subjugated Lower Egypt, a new myth concerning Horus arose to explain the conquest: The patron deity of Lower Egypt, named Set, battled Horus for dominance, until eventually the gods sided with Horus. Horus, as the new Lord of Egypt, became known as Horus the Elder, while Set (who purportedly lost one testicle during the battle) became known as the Lord of the Desert, symbolizing infertility and desolation.

As the new supreme god of all of Egypt, Horus' mythos altered to explain both his ascendancy and the changed Egyptian calendar. Horus could no longer be the son of Ra, and so Ra was demoted and demonized in a new myth. Now Ra and his brother Thoth, the god of the moon, became the first children of the god Geb (the Earth) and the goddess Nuit (the starry expanse of the heavens). When Ra saw four more siblings—the deities Osiris, Isis, Set, and Nepthys—forming within Nuit and about to be born, he cursed his mother out of jealous fear, preventing her from giving birth on any day of the year. Wise and far-seeing Thoth gambled with the Moon and won 1/72nd of the moonlight, adding five additional days to the year; thus, the calendar was changed from 360 days to 365, enabling Nuit to give birth on the five extra days.

Osiris presently usurped Ra as Lord of Egypt. Osiris' sister Isis (who in earlier myths was sometimes called the wife of Horus) now became identified with Hathor, instead marrying Osiris and giving birth to Horus. (Later depictions of Horus show him being nursed by Isis, reminiscent of the Madonna and child). Osiris was betrayed and murdered by his brother Set, with Horus being born upon his father's resurrection as Lord of the Dead; therefore, it was said that Horus was the incarnated form of his father, Osiris. After defeating his uncle Set, Horus ruled the land of the living in his father's place while Osiris ruled the land of the dead. Known by scholars of history as Horus-Osiris, this Egyptian myth served as the foundation of the Greek mystery religions, also called Osiris-Dionysus, a myth that historians suggest as the basis for resurrection myths, including that of Jesus Christ.

Crowley (and therefore his disciple Achad) called the merging of Horus and Ra Heru-Ra-Ha ("Horus and Ra Be Praised"), a composite without actual historical basis, whose active aspect is Ra-Hoor-Khuit ("Ra, Horus of the Horizons") and whose passive aspect is Hoor-par-kuit ("Horus the Child"). With the merging of Upper and Lower Egypt, all the prior Lords of Egypt—Amun-Ra, Osiris, Horus the Elder and Horus the Child—also united in one aspect: the great god Horus. Even today, the ever-watchful Eye of Horus can be found upon every U.S. dollar bill.

Osiris

Osiris, husband of Isis and father of Horus, the beloved Lord of Egypt in life and the mighty Lord of the Afterlife following his death and resurrection, governed a realm of primary significance to the ancient Egyptians. Osiris was the Great Father who re-incarnated as Horus, his triumphant Son, and yet remained separate as the god who judged the dead.

The Egyptians attributed an Age of Humanity to many of their principle gods. Just as the worshippers of Horus and his father Osiris were ultimately responsible for the 365-day calendar that, with a few minor adjustments later made by the Romans, we still use to this day, so Egyptian astrologers also envisioned a cosmic calendar called the Great Year, based upon the elliptical orbit of the brightest star in the night sky, Sirius the Dog Star, whose advance through Earth's equinoxes took roughly 26,000 years (also known as the Precession of the Equinoxes); to map this Great Year, they divided the sky into twelve equal arcs (the Zodiac) which Sirius passed through at the Spring Equinox every 2,160 years. Each of these twelve Zodiacal Great Months or Ages (Aions in Greek) marked drastic changes for the Earth and its inhabitants. Around 10,000 BCE, the current Great Year began with the Age of the Lion (our Leo), when humans were primitive hunter-gatherers, followed by the:

Age of the Scarab (or Crab—Cancer): Khepera the Egyptian scarab god of creation and birth; the supremacy of the Mother Goddess.

Age of the Twins (Gemini): Set and Horus the Elder, Biblical Cain and Abel; the beginning of writing systems, accounting, and people groups connecting through trade.

Age of the Bull (Taurus): the sacrificial Bull cults of Osiris (as well as Assyria and Crete); agrarian civilization.

Age of the Ram (Aries): Atum-Ra (also associated with Zeus and Jupiter); war-like civilizations based upon conquest and self-assertion.

Age of the Fishes (Pisces): Kristos or Christ from Egyptian KRST or Karast, meaning "anointed one", sacrificial gods, half mortal and half divine (like Dionysus and Jesus Christ); beginning of world-wide religions and social structures, the plan of sacrifice and redemption, service.

The "New Age" movement, based upon the idea that we have entered (or will soon be entering) the age of the Water-bringer **(Aquarius): the Age of Man**; a time of personal freedom, humanitarianism, one world ideology, and enlightenment.

In addition to the ages outlined above, it is also helpful to understand Crowley's (and thus his disciple, Achad's) view of the Ages of Man (or as Crowley called them, Aeons):

First, **the Age of Isis**, the Mother Goddesses: Matriarchal religions, and natural/ agrarian cultures.

Second, **the Age of Osiris**, the Father Gods: Patriarchal religions, and cultures based upon conquest and industry.

Third, **the Age of Horus** the Ever-coming Son (our present age): Discovery of our own divinity, social upheavals and Great Wars, completion of the Great Work.

(Please note: later in Frater Achad's life, he heralded what he called the dawning of a new age: the Age of Ma'at (the Egyptian goddess of truth, balance, and justice.)

Isis

Wife of Osiris and mother to Horus, Isis was worshipped as the archetypal wife and mother, a manifestation of the Great Mother Goddess; however, there is no record of Isis having a centralized cult in ancient Egypt. Individual worship of Isis did not begin until the thirtieth dynasty, for up until that time she was always worshipped in conjunction with Horus and Osiris. Temples were not dedicated specifically to Isis until much later, in Rome. On the other hand, Isis is the central deity in both *The Egyptian Book of the Dead* and the *Pyramid Texts*. She became known as the "goddess of magic" because of her part in the resurrection of Osiris, and by late Egyptian history she grew into the most powerful magical deity in the Egyptian pantheon; magic became the core of the cult of Isis, rising to prominence in the Hellenistic world only to be banned by the Christian Church in the sixth century. Finally, the Church linked the tradition of the "mistress of magic and witchcraft" with the persona of Satan (of whom Set was the predecessor) to characterize the Black Tradition.

Set

Set, the patron deity of Lower Egypt, was originally a strong, heroic god, but after Lower Egypt was conquered by Upper Egypt, he became associated with the hostility of the desert which surrounded and was married to the fertile land around the Nile (his sister, Nepthys); like the desert he was infertile (and thus homosexual). He was generally depicted as some sort of horrific beast, either a jackal, crocodile, or hippopotamus. As the killer of his brother, Osiris, and therefore the embodiment of evil, he continued to be linked with the immoral gods of foreign nations, such as Baal, Beelzebub, and Sin. The Greeks linked Set with Typhon, the monster who almost destroyed the Greek gods.

Over time, Set's name was distorted to Set-on and eventually the Hebrew Satan (meaning "adversary or accuser"), a being used by God to test humans. Catholic Apocrypha and the New Testament depict Satan as the evil, rebellious leader of the demons, who tempts man, even though it was the Persian prophet Zoraster who (considerably earlier) designated Satan as the "Prince of Darkness." Most Christians today have merged Satan with Lucifer (literally in Latin "the light-bringer," both a fallen Babylonian King described in Isaiah 14:12, as well as one of the Roman names of the planet Venus, the morning star), the Devil (in Latin *diabolus*, "slanderer"), and Beelzebub, the Babylonian demonic Prince of Darkness. The Talmud sometimes calls Satan Samael, and in Islam Shaitan is the chief evil spirit who suffered from pride and refused to bow to Adam at Allah's command. The traditional depiction of Satan as red (the color of Set) with horns and a goat's lower body actually originated from an amalgamation of the Pagan gods Cernunnos and the Horned God, with the Greek god Pan.

Set and Satan are both associated with the Left Hand Path (the way of darkness and individual advancement over all else, through nature and sexual rituals, blood sacrifice, and the eating of flesh) in contrast to the Right Hand Path (the way of light, worship of deity and observance of austere moral restrictions, the unity of all existence, asceticism, and supplication). Interestingly, throughout history many cultures have regarded the left hand as evil. Today, many people think that the Right Hand Path comprises traditional religions, while the Left Hand Path encompasses metaphysics and occultism. Based upon imagery taken from Matthew 25, the goat has become associated with the Left and sheep with the Right. Either both Paths are considered as equally viable approaches to truth, or else the Left views the Right as a repressive, naïve herd of followers while the Right views the left as prideful, immoral, and damned.

Nuit

Nuit (also Nut) was the Egyptian goddess of the heavens and outer space. Daughter of Shu (god of the air), and Tefnut (goddess of moisture), she married the Earth (Geb) and gave birth to the gods and goddesses. Her firstborn, Ra, entered her mouth at sunset and was reborn every sunrise from her vulva. Since Nuit also swallowed the stars every morning and rebirthed them every night, she was regarded as both eternal mother and goddess of resurrection. She was usually depicted as a naked woman, dark blue as the night sky, with her back arched over the heavens, facing Geb who lay with his phallus pointing towards her. According to Crowley and Achad, Nuit is the infinitely vast circle whose circumference is immeasurable and whose center is everywhere. She is the feminine counterpart to the deity, Hadit.

Hadit

In contrast to Nuit, the god Hadit is Crowley's conception of the infinitely small point within the core of each and every part of existence. Hadit is the manifestation of consciousness, while Ra-Hoor-Khuit (Crowley's active aspect of Horus) is the projection of Hadit in the form of the external universe. Hadit represents the infinitely small yet absolutely potent point which, when unifying with the circle of Nuit, animates the manifest universe; he is the spark of individual spirit, which Crowley calls the "flame that burns in the heart of every man, and in the core of every star" (Crowley 1976, *The Book of the Law*, 29). This union of the infinitely small Hadit and the infinitely great Nuit causes an explosive rapture which leads to Samadhi—simultaneous, blissful awareness of both everything and nothing, of both complete, separate individuation as well as intricate interconnectedness with *All That Is*.

Achad's Egyptian Revival

So what does all this Egyptian mythology have to do with Qabalah? According to Frater Achad, when the Sephirah Malkuth (the four-colored circle at the bottom of the Qabalistic Tree of Life) and Kether (the white circle at the top) are united in the Sephirah Tiphereth (the yellow circle in the middle), then Ra-Hoor-Khuit (the active aspect of Horus, the tangible projection of Hadit in the physical universe) takes his throne as the "Ever-coming Holy Son" of the Kingdom Within, resurrecting the fallen individual.

Who, exactly, is this "fallen individual"? It is not the physical body, the emotions, nor the mind, for all these cease. Tarot calls it the Fool, the Romans called it a person's Genius or Juno, Neo-platonists called it the Augoeides, Gnostics called it the Daemon, Christians call it the Spirit, Occultists call it our True Will or Holy Guardian Angel, Scientology calls it the Thetan, Buddhism calls it the Buddha Within or the Watcher, the New Age movement often calls it the True Self. It is the vital spark, the individuated life force, the static with no form, the center seat of consciousness, will, and perception. It exists apart from the realm of dualities (it is neither good nor evil, neither happy nor sad, neither male nor female). For most of humanity, it is obscured and buried beneath layers and layers of *avidyā*, often mistaken for the personality or the ego; sometimes it is even confused with a glorified delusion of our own "true nature" or "higher self," as though the individual we are today is somehow lacking or sinful and awaits unification with what we truly are or meant to be. Actually, the True Self is what we truly are right now—both aside from, and including, our body, emotions, mind, culture, personality, experiences, conditioning, aberration, and trauma; for although these layers are not the essence of our True Self, they are its current state. In its restoration we discover our true sovereign state, our Kingdom Within. It is the process of this restoration that Crowley called the "Great Work."

Frater Achad's Restored Tree of Life reveals the blueprint of this vital restoration. It is a model of classification, a sort of enormous filing cabinet that catalogs and provides crucial insight into the various building blocks of existence. *The Kingdom Within Tarot* specifically provides an image-based system for acquainting oneself with these building blocks; however, Qabalah is the root of *every* Tarot deck. In order to fully understand the Qabalistic Symbology of each Tarot card, it is essential to meditate upon each image of the Major Arcana cards. Their visual imagery has been carefully crafted to guide the spirit to recall through archetypal symbology the higher truths that imperfect words, with the inherent limitation of language, cannot express. (Chapter Six goes into greater depth about various methods that may assist this intuitive approach.) In addition to this innate remembering, the following basic background will aid the reader in understanding the final section of each Major Arcana card, entitled Qabalistic Symbology.

Although students of Qabalah marvel at the genius of the Tree of Life as a basic model of existence, a detailed study of Kircher's Paths often produces confusion and a lack of any practical application to their lives. For many, the Restored Tree of Life supplies a tangible, applicable alternative reordering of the Paths that, quite simply, makes sense. With Achad's new ordering of the Paths, each Major Arcana is united with its logical Sephirah. (For example, the Empress is united with Netzach, the sphere of Venus; the Tower is united with Geburah, the sphere of Mars; and the Magician is united with Hod, the sphere of Mercury.) Also, the middle pillar is aligned so that the outer planets—the purest expressions of the elements—form a direct line leading from Malkuth to Kether, the Crown. (Malkuth represents the earth element, the Fool (Uranus) represents the air element, the Hanged Man (Neptune) represents the water element, and the Judgment (Pluto) represents the element of fire.) In the Qabalistic model of the cosmos, these four elements placed in this exact order create the Tetragrammaton (which literally means "the four letters")—YHVH, the sacred name of the Hebrew God, often pronounced "Yahweh" or "Jehovah"—for the Hebrew letter *Yod* represents fire, *He* is water, *Vau* is air, and the final *Heh* is earth.

The Paths of the Tree of Life have been rearranged for a new era (or, as Frater Achad would claim, they have been restored to the ancient order that was once lost) so that it is no longer a question of *climbing the tree of life* so much as, in Frater Achad's own words, "recognizing how all things have been working together for good so that the Source of All might become manifest in Matter, here on Earth, and the Kingdom...be established" (Achad 1997, *The Egyptian Revival*, Chapter 4). Please understand that the following paragraphs are basically my own modernized paraphrase and distillation of the original conceptions and writings of Frater Achad; all credit is due him for the following ideas.

Decoding the Qabalistic Symbology of the Major Arcana

I recommend that initially the reader study the Qabalistic Symbology of the Devil card in conjunction with the World card, and then the Sun card in conjunction with the Wheel of Fortune card, in that order. Humanity, the incarnation of spirit into matter, is primarily limited by two conceptions: time and space. Einstein introduced the idea that you cannot have space without time or time without space, and thus he called this spectrum of duality the space-time continuum. (Qabalah teaches that all duality is actually an illusion.)

The chief snare of the Devil card is the illusion of time, for just as Saturn (the World card) is the god of time and the progenitor of Satan (the Devil card) or serpent of time, so this illusion begins as we follow Kether to Binah, and is further transmitted from Binah to Tiphereth by the Path of the Devil. This is the Path resulting from the number three, from the Feminine Principle of the Great Mother Binah, from understanding and intuition, from the darkness which conceals the light in its womb of mysteries; it has been called the Black Tradition for, just like the color black, it absorbs all other colors and perceptions. In Egyptian cosmology this was the tradition of Isis and Set, in the Greco-Roman that of Typhon and Diana Lucifera, and in the Judeo-Christian that of Lucifer, Satan, and the Dark Madonna.

On the other hand, the Sun and the Wheel of Fortune cards reveal the alternative route of dualistic mankind. The force of the Primum Mobile of Kether produced the whirling motions of the Wheel of Life, resulting in the star universe and sphere of the zodiac; thus, we have the second great limitation of humanity: space, the focus of the followers of Light. Unfortunately, this conception of space has become narrowed down to the idea of a straight and narrow "only" way. The followers of the tradition of the Light—the followers of the dying and rising Son/Sun as the center of the solar system, whether we call him Osiris, Dionysus, or Jesus Christ—became but a twilight and a reflection of the primal truth, as indicated by the Path of the Moon card. Mankind limited infinite space to the three-dimensionality of the physical universe and the body, worshipping the Son as the Father, and therefore missing the truth of the Father concealed within. Just as the color white reflects all colors, so the White Tradition fell to focusing upon the reflection or persistence of light, rather than recognizing and seeing the *True Light Itself*.

In Tiphereth (the Sun/Son) these limitations of duality are reunited. Chokmah (the Father) is its formal cause and Binah (the Mother) is its material cause. Malkuth (the Fallen Daughter) must unite with Tiphereth (the Son) and be raised to the throne of Binah (the Mother) to re-awaken Chokmah (the Father), so that all things are re-absorbed into Kether (the Crown) and yet continue in their evolving individual state. Rather than the retrogression of Father and the Mother simply reuniting into perfect union and thus returning to a zero state of unity, their consummation gives birth to evolution as they go forth into matter and produce a Son and a Daughter, beginning the progressive cycle of the cosmos (and of mankind) once again in individuation.

Tiphereth is a perfect image of Man, the Beast, the combination of all that is animal, all that is human, all that is spiritual, and all that is god-like; this is the great solar image that much of mankind has worshipped throughout history. However, this is not the highest truth in itself, but instead a harmonious combination and synthesis of light and darkness. Jesus claimed that he was both the Son of Man and the Son of God, as well as stating that "No man comes to the Father but by me;" thus, he is the visible aspect of the invisible and concealed Father, who may never be known because He is the very essence of our being. The followers of the White Tradition have restricted themselves to a narrow way by conceiving their way as "right," making them too proud to perceive the wider and grander spaces and cycles of existence. They dread the ancient, feminine, dark tradition and their subconscious minds hold them back, fearing to enter the darkness of night, lest they lose what little light they have.

If we truly believe in the Son, why should we fear his descent into the Underworld? Jesus did so before he arose again in spirit to his Father in Heaven, thus uniting his true self with the Father, the invisible Central Star of the All That Is. Day and night as we know it only exist on Earth: The Sun, although the Father of life in this solar system, is but the Son of the Great Mother, the star universe. Humanity has missed the truth of the infinitely great Nuit (continuous universe of matter) and the infinitely small Hadit (the inmost essential self, the core of every star). Every point in space is equally the center of the whole, for beingness has no limit; the true Father is invisible, yet is the center of all. Humanity has called him Father Time, but he is really *Father Now*. The

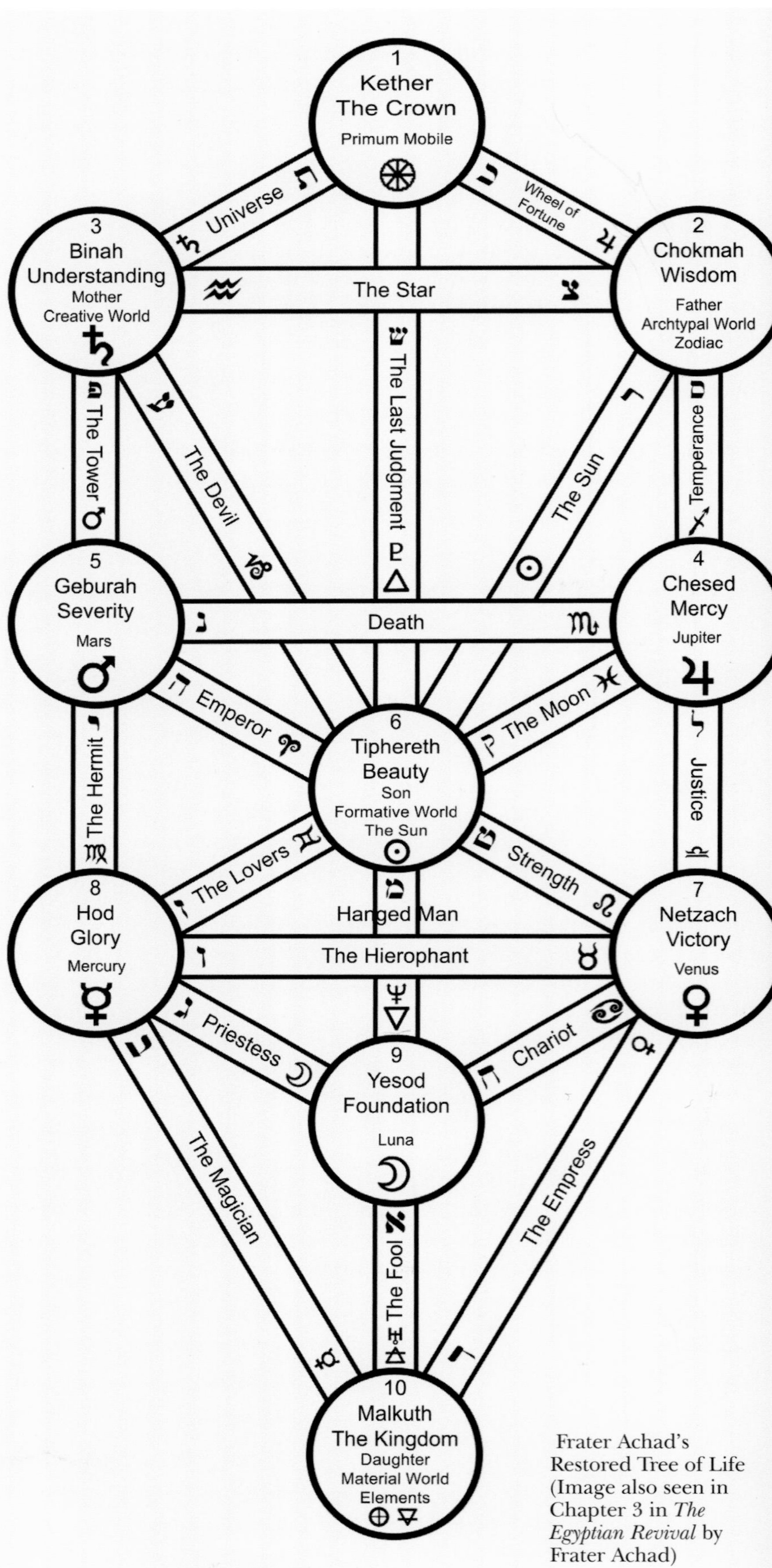

Frater Achad's Restored Tree of Life (Image also seen in Chapter 3 in *The Egyptian Revival* by Frater Achad)

Now became extended as the serpent of time (Saturn) tempted Eve (Matter) and caused the Fall. The illusion of Space made it difficult to imagine or find the center, for we could not comprehend how the center could be present everywhere at the same moment of Time. The World card reveals the result of the "marriage" of Hadit and Nuit.

Much of humanity believes that the Secret Father is the Sun and worships him as such; eventually each individual must draw out that Sun within his or her heart and look at things from His viewpoint. Only then does Hadit, the True Father of Now that is in each one of us but has been veiled by the light of the Sun of our own being, become the manifest Ever-Coming Son of Light.

As Frater Achad wrote, "Truly the Kingdom of Heaven is within us, it will never be found outside amid the illusions of space and time" (Achad 1997, *The Egyptian Revival*, Chapter 5). When Malkuth is united with the Son, she begins to view the world from His standpoint; the animal soul that perceives and feels the joys of the world, once despised as the fallen daughter, is in fact our greatest treasure. The truth of the greatest story ever told becomes revealed: how the woman clothed with the Sun became great with child, how the beast tried to devour the child and stop further progress in order that he might continue to be worshipped as the lord of the heaven, how the woman escaped into Egypt and expanded to the limits of time (Saturn) and beyond until the True Child was brought to light within her and the dual light of the Sun and Moon were no longer needed. The Ever-coming Crowned Child now reigns in the Holy City of Heaven: This is the purpose of the present Age of Humanity.

As you begin to read the following in-depth analyses of the Major Arcana, please note that the final section of each card's analysis, entitled *Qabalistic Symbology*, is my own interpretation and restatement of Achad's original texts. To further understand Tarot with regards to the Restored Tree of Life, please find Achad's *Q.B.L.* and *The Egyptian Revival* online or in print; both are excellent resources for the advanced student of Qabalah.

Finally, we will explore an additional card, called the Kingdom Within All that is unique to *The Kingdom Within All Tarot* deck. This card was created to embrace humanity's developments beyond the original standardization of the Tarot.

O The Fool

– Uranus –
Path 11: Malkuth to Yesod
Aleph – א : Ox / 1 / A

Astrological Meaning: The Unexpected

The Personality of Uranus:

If Uranus were a person, he would be a young, eccentric genius of the mad scientist persuasion. It is his goal to force us to broaden our vision; he is rebellious by nature and is willing to destroy everything, if necessary, to invent a new world. The problem with Uranus (from our human perspective) is that he seems to destroy indiscriminately; he has no qualms about destroying our marriages, our homes, or our countries. He obeys no rules, and therefore he scares us. He always endeavors to rise above the material; thus, his ideas are often too idealistic and unstable for planet Earth.

Element: Air, Androgynous
Rules: Aquarius

Minor Arcana Association: Swords Suit (Air)

Key Phrases:

- A force beyond your control—BE CAREFUL!
- Unexpected events for good or evil.
- Uranus shatters and destroys all boundaries—from disease, to divorce, to revolutions.
- Uncontrollable disasters such as tornadoes, lightning, earthquakes, or accidents.
- The pure, unadulterated wildness of children.
- Folly, eccentricity, even mania.
- Places that are far away and out of reach.
- Power and power plants; technology, electricity, and electronics; Uranium.
- The nervous system, circulation of the blood, and pineal gland. Sudden illnesses, growths, or spasms (like epilepsy or a paralyzing stroke), sudden falls; accidents due to electricity, explosions, lightning, or natural disasters.

Spheres: UL sphere is purple (Yesod) while LR sphere is divided into four equal colors of russet, navy, citrine, and olive (Malkuth).

Path 11 indicates: Incarnation of the Eternal into Matter; Divine Ecstasy that transcends time and space. The path of truth and harmony with oneself and All That Is; the power of now.

Qabalistic Symbology:

The Fool is a unique card. In some decks it is number zero, in others it is twenty-two, and in still others it has no number. It is both the beginning of existence, the end of existence, and exists outside and throughout all existences. The Path of the Pure Fool accomplishes All Things by doing No-thing, immersed in the Divine Madness of Ecstasy. He is Percival, who sought the Holy Grail and brought down the Swan of Ecstasy to Earth with his Bow of Promise and Arrow of Pure Aspiration, for he sees no past or future to cloud his visions; he overcomes his own obstacles and unmasks his own illusions. The Fool traverses The Path until he has become The Path itself. The Fool is the Path of Air; he is the All-Wandering Air, the reconciler in all things, the True Spirit of every being who is brought to birth in a physical body upon the Earth. This is the Path of those who follow neither the way of magic nor of mysticism, but the Way of the Tao. This Path transmits the universal Tradition of the central Pillar—the Pillar of Mildness and Peace. It is the Path of birth and death, for both are really different directions on the same Path—just as birth is the passage of the spirit into matter, so death is the release of spirit from matter. This is the Pathway of the light to be discovered amid the contending forces and darkness of matter. The Fool is a wild child, uncontrollable, pure deva outside of duality. However, he often foolishly plays the game of existence, far too frequently believing his own lies. This is the Path of the Here and Today, transcending Time and Space. This is the Path of Truth, the Power of Now.

1 The Magician

– Mercury –
Path 12: Malkuth to Hod
Beth – ב : House / 2 / B

Astrological Meaning: The Connector

The Personality of Mercury:

If the planet Mercury were a person, he would be the Sorcerer's Apprentice. He has a quick, brilliant mind and is a skillful student; his master chose him for these attributes as well as his sociable nature and his silver tongue, skills of connection that the sorcerer utilizes. Mercury loves solving problems and winning debates, and even though he finds most common people ignorant and slow, he can persuade them to do or believe anything he wants. One of Mercury's favorite perks to his job is all the traveling he gets to do as he delivers messages for his master. Although he has studied magic for many years, Mercury often lacks the fundamental discipline and consistency to truly master the sorcerer's arts; therefore, he can use his considerable knowledge to create elaborate illusions of magic that trick the uninitiated. At his best, he wisely makes the connections necessary to see and understand the truth, but at his worst, he is much more concerned with making connections and proving his postulates than with seeing things for what they truly are.

Element: Air, Androgynous

Rules: Gemini and Virgo (although some astrologers believe that the natural ruler of Virgo was the planet that was destroyed and is now the asteroid belt)

Minor Arcana Association: 8 Wands, 5 Pentacles, 10 Pentacles, 3 Cups, 6 Swords.

Key Phrases:

- Signifies an important message for the querent's life, for the Roman god Mercury is the great messenger of the gods.
- The intellect, learning, and the mind; therefore, Mercury's greatest strength is also his greatest weakness, for although he is clever and excels at categorizing, he tends to be harsh, cold, rationalizing, and calculating, with no emotions.
- Mercury makes moving connections: He moves information from one place to another, like oral speech, telephone conversations, mailed letters, translations, messengers, and email.
- Mercury works well with numbers, such as in math, computers, and statistics.
- Paperwork, credentials, words, and perjury (transgressions resulting from words).
- Moving modes of transportation that make connections between one place and another: cars, bikes, planes, etc. Also, traveling short distances.
- The left hemisphere (the logical, analytical portion) of the brain, along with arms, legs, shoulders, the lungs, the eyes, and the tongue.
- If adversely aspected, signifies illnesses associated with thinking and communication: brain tumor, headaches, stammering tongue, delusions, memory problems, insanity, dumbness, etc.
- Adaptable, mercurial, changeable, wishy-washy, bi-sexual, and confusing.
- Strongly influenced by the other planets and easily swayed by outside events or on a whim.
- Skill, wisdom, adaptation, subtlety, craft, cunning; sometimes occult wisdom because of the association with the Greek god Hermes and the Egyptian god Thoth.
- Trickster, juggler, sexual difficulties.
- Places of communication and thinking, such as schools, telephone companies, Internet providers, newspapers, etc.
- Small animals and veterinarians.
- Alchemically, Mercury rules the metal mercury.

Spheres: UL sphere is orange (Hod) while LR sphere is divided into four equal colors of russet, navy, citrine, and olive (Malkuth).

Path 12 indicates: The Magic of Light and Occultism. Messenger of Wisdom and Will. Hadit, the center of self-awareness and the kingdom of heaven.

Qabalistic Symbology:

The Magician is the Wisdom and Will of the Father in Heaven (Chokmah) brought down to the Kingdom of Earth (Malkuth). The Magician controls the four elements through his Higher Will; for whether he chooses to manipulate entities with his commanding authority or applies his arts to climbing the Tree of Life, his is the Path of the Magic of Light and of Occultism. He transmutes the energy of Mercury into the physical universe, and is the representative of the Great Father upon the Earth; his influence is within every man who realizes that he is a Star.

2 The High Priestess

– Moon –
Path 13: Yesod to Hod
Gimel – ג : Camel, Rope / 3 / G

Astrological Meaning: The Initiatrix

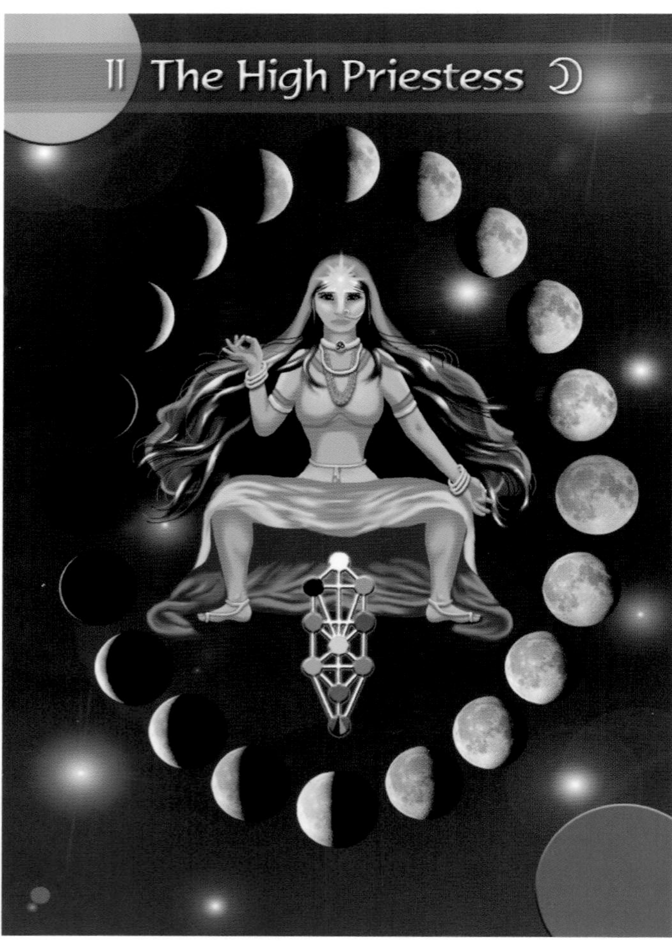

The Personality of the Moon:

If the Moon were a person, she would be a young woman experiencing the entire cycle of conception, pregnancy, birth, and motherhood for the first time. Her emotions change with the tides of her body; she seems to be different everyday—one moment elated about the life growing within her, and the next weeping over another load of dirty laundry. She is both passionate and scared about her new responsibilities, yet it amazes everyone how quickly she accomplishes the new tasks set before her. Her husband, her child, and her home are the center of this phase of her life, and she has an instinctive knack for providing what is needed to birth, grow, and sustain; she is regeneration incarnate. She has discarded the flashy spotlight of the young ingénue to become the foundation for growth.

Element: Water, Feminine
Rules: Cancer
Minor Arcana Association: 9 Wands, 6 Pentacles, 4 Cups, 2 Swords, 7 Swords

Key Phrases:

- The Moon signifies the birth of all things; she is the initiator, the verb.
- She is cyclical in nature and represents the feminine cycles; she rules our emotions and our subconscious.
- She is protective and nurturing, governing home, pregnancy, and children.
- She heralds change, alteration, increase or decrease, and fluctuation. (Whether it is desirable or undesirable depends upon the surrounding cards.)
- She regenerates and manifests; she reveals significance.
- Every woman is a moon; therefore, the High Priestess may represent a woman (especially a young woman).
- She is moody like the tides and reflects the light of those around her.
- If poorly aspected (void of course), there is nothing that can be done to alter the situation; now is not the time to act.
- The Moon suggests that you will either obtain something or that you will have an upcoming move or initiation.
- Any place or job connected with water or women—rivers, ponds, baths, bogs, sailors, gynecologists, etc.
- Stomach, womb, breasts, the left eye of men and right eye of women.
- Alchemically, the Moon rules silver.

Spheres: UL sphere is Orange (Hod) while LR sphere is purple (Yesod).
Path 13 indicates: Inspiration and mystery; the Pure influence of the True Self on the Subconscious Mind. Nuit, the Initiatrix who gives birth to all things.

Qabalistic Symbology:

The High Priestess is the "Priestess of the Silver Star," the Moon, the Path from Hod to Yesod. She is the Initiatrix, the birther, the manifester, who takes the secret powers of Mercury's dual knowledge of the Lovers (Gemini) and the Virgin (Virgo), and alchemically combines them with the light of the

Prince (Tiphereth)—the Son who shines his rays upon Yesod—giving birth to all material things. She is the Pure Influence of the True Self on the Subconscious Mind, who transmits the secret of the Star Universe and of the Silver Star. She is the Initiator into the Mysteries of Nuit, just as her counterpart, The Chariot, indicates those of Hadit; together they unite for the purpose of manifestation in the womb of Yesod. For most of humanity, the secrets of the High Priestess are still trapped in the subconscious, that elusive muse of emotion and inspiration that changes with the tides of the Moon. Many ancient mythologies teach that the Earth "gave birth" to the Moon, and recently scientists have discovered that this may actually be true, as it seems that at some point the Moon broke away from the Earth's surface. The Moon does not desire to remain mysteriously hidden within us—she longs to be openly free.

3 The Empress

– Venus –
Path 14: Malkuth to Netzach
Daleth – ד : Door / 4 / D

Astrological Meaning: The Lover

The Personality of Venus:

Venus might be a Courtesan from the golden age of Venice, the Geisha of Japan, a Priestess in the Temples of Aphrodite and Demeter, or the Temple Dancer of India; she has been thoroughly tutored in sensual pleasure and the arts, yet she is beholden to no man as she takes lovers from amongst the most wealthy and noble of her country, who pay her well for her services. She is disarmingly good looking with an hourglass figure, full lips, eyes of amorous enticement, and an adorable dimple when she smiles. She believes that pleasure is essential to life, and enjoys music, jewelry, food, wine, lovemaking; she is not at all interested in hard work. She loves the games of sex and romance and is a master of temptation; she naturally beautifies everything she touches. For some reason, things just seem to work out for her, and most love and desire her. The rest judge her out of their envy and puritanical values.

Element: Earth, Feminine
Rules: Taurus, Libra (although some astrologers speculate that when we discover a tenth planet, it will actually be the natural ruler of Libra)
Minor Arcana Association: 4 Wands, 9 Pentacles, 2 Cups, 7 Cups, 5 Swords

Key Phrases:

- Venus is the Lesser Benefic; everything tends to get better when Venus appears in a reading.
- Increases happiness, success, pleasure, luxury, prosperity, artistic value, and monetary situation. Rules affection, love, amusement, and enjoyment.
- Venus is womanhood at its best; sometimes she represents pregnancy, but the emphasis is upon fertility rather than regeneration (as with the Moon). Also wives and mothers.
- Venus is female sexuality and tantalizing temptation.
- Anything beautiful and alluring—lovely young women, flowers, jewelry, perfume, art, musical instruments, etc.
- Any work associated with beauty or aesthetics—jewelers, musicians, songs, decorators, female adornment, and beauty items (including purses and cash).
- Any location that is beautiful and alluring—gardens, outdoors, meadows, fountains, bedrooms, beds, wardrobes, cushions,

- dancing schools, places connected with beauty and art.
- If poorly aspected, Venus is extravagant, careless, lazy, without credit or repute, as well as inclined to inappropriate bedfellows and dissipation.
- Back, belly, veins, hernias, female reproductive organs, and the skin (as it beautifies us).
- Alchemically, Venus rules copper.

Spheres: UL sphere is green (Netzach) while LR sphere is divided into four equal colors of russet, navy, citrine, and olive (Malkuth).

Path 14 indicates: Mysticism, Devotion, and Understanding; the Great Mother, center of love and absorption into the Absolute.

Qabalistic Symbology:

The Empress represents the Love that regenerates the Kingdom (Malkuth); she transmits the Understanding of the Great Mother (Binah), and combines the influences of Justice, Strength, and the Hierophant. Hers' is the Path of Mysticism and Devotion, and of those who would be absorbed into the Absolute. She demonstrates the double-edged adage that "Love Conquers All," for she represents the Great Mother on the material plane and is the influence within every woman who knows herself to be a Star.

4 The Emperor

– Aries –
Path 21: Tiphereth to Geburah
Heh – ה : Window / 5 / H

Astrological Meaning: The Ram

Characteristics of People with a Strong Aries in their Astrological Charts:

Lean, with large bones, and a strong face and chin. Loves competition, red cars, and the fast lane. Daring, active, impulsive, direct, courageous, and forceful. Enjoys the rush of danger and the unknown; life's a challenging adventure for an Aries. Has a "me first" attitude and generally pushes to the front of the line; one of the most admirable traits of a developed Aries—with his strong sense of self—is his willingness to sacrifice himself to rescue a damsel from the dragon or else a child that runs out in front of a moving bus. An Aries begins with great energy, but struggles to finish. At his best, he may be an independent pioneer, a record-breaking athlete, or a successful leader. At his worst, Aries is power-hungry, angry, intemperate, and violent.

Element: Fire, Masculine, Transmissive, Cardinal sign
Ruled by: Mars
Minor Arcana Association: 2, 3, 4 of Wands

Key Phrases:

- The Sun is in Aries from March 20th to April 19th.
- First sign of the zodiac; has a natural affinity with the First House.
- New starts or beginnings (sunrise); immediate past or future.
- Aries is powerful, aggressive, and authoritative; therefore, it is associated with war, conquest, victory, strife and ambition.
- Shows the length of life of the querent.
- Aries brings you back to yourself, so it is excellent for Pathworking.
- The father and fatherhood.
- Rules engineering, architecture, athletics,

mechanics, the military, and construction.

- Rules sharp peaks or mountains, pastures, hiding places, isolated places, angry animals, any competitions or sports, and iron.
- Rules the head and face, and any related maladies (i.e., pimples, disfigurements, headaches, baldness, etc). Also the blood and muscles.

Spheres: UL sphere is red (Geburah) while LR sphere is yellow (Tiphereth).

Path 21 indicates: Fiery Light of Retribution and Substitution; the Personal Will.

Qabalistic Symbology:

The influence of Mars as it passes through Geburah (the sphere of Severity) is transmitted to Tiphereth by the Path of Aries, the Emperor. Mars and the Sun combine to create the Fiery Light of Retribution on this Path. The Ram (or Lamb) was sacrificed as a substitute for man, so this Path represents Retribution and Substitution as that of Pisces, on the opposite side, represents Restriction and Reflection. Both are partial truths. This Path also transmits the Personal Will of Geburah to Tiphereth, the Heart, wherein both the Personal and True wills are harmonized. The Sun (Tiphereth) is the Reconciler between the Paths of the Emperor and the Moon, temporarily harmonizing the Tradition of Darkness with the Tradition of Light.

5 The Hierophant

– Taurus –
Path 16: Hod to Netzach
Vav – ו : Nail / 6 / V, O, U

Astrological Meaning: The Bull

Characteristics of People with a Strong Taurus in their Astrological Charts:

Because permanence and security are important to this sign, Taurus's are concerned with having or possessing money, valuable objects, land, and relationships. Males tend to be short and strong, with muscular necks, chests and shoulders; females are more graceful and Junoesque, with a stately bearing and imposing loveliness. They are known for their sensuous, melodious voices. They adore beauty, sumptuous food and music, and the finer things in life; they fall apart at the first sign of financial troubles. Gentle and practical by nature, they are often conservative and obstinate, yet when they make up their minds you can trust them to keep their promises. At her best, Taurus builds and develops things, strengthens family and societal bonds, and shares her bounty; at her worst, on the other hand, Taurus hordes her wealth, refuses to change or even budge, and is consumed with acquiring beauty, treasures, and pleasure.

Element: Earth, Feminine, Receptive, Fixed sign

Ruled by: Venus

Minor Arcana Association: 5, 6, 7 of Pentacles

Key Phrases:

- The Sun is in Taurus from April 19th to May 20th.
- Second sign of the Zodiac; has a natural affinity with the Second House.
- Resources on all levels to accomplish the querent's goals. (Why associate the Bull with resources and money? Ancient man used cattle as the first recorded medium of exchange; the Greeks valued items for trade by heads of cattle, and the Romans placed

the image of an Ox upon their coins. Even our English words for coin and capital are based upon the Latin words for cattle and property.)

- The querent's money, finances, and investments; natural talents or gifts.
- Represents a professional or expert in his/her field; this card either indicates that the querent is a professional, or else it suggests that the querent needs to consult a professional, such as a doctor or lawyer.
- Rules lawsuits initiated by the querent, the querent's resources in a lawsuit, and the lawyer hired by the querent.
- Slow to change.
- Because of its connection with Venus, Taurus rules fashion and beauty experts, landscapers, artist, musicians, and designers. Also banking, investing, and landowners.
- Rules hidden places of the Earth, like forests, caves, and mines, also farm buildings, pasture, countryside, and cellars.
- The neck and throat and any maladies affecting the throat; a fine singing voice.

Spheres: UL sphere is green (Netzach) while LR sphere is orange (Hod).

Path 16 indicates: Guardian of the Ancient Mysteries; relying upon systems of belief and structures outside oneself for salvation.

Qabalistic Symbology:

Uniting Netzach and Hod is the Path of the Hierophant, the Initiator into the Mysteries of Eleusis and Osiris the Bull. The Hierophant from ages past has served as Guardian of the Ancient Mysteries; it is only through his wisdom that we may continue our ascent up the Tree of Life. He proffers the resources necessary to unite the wisdom of Mercury and the Initiated Love of Venus with reciprocity, guiding us to discover our own Guardian Angel, our True Self.

The Hierophant pictured in *The Kingdom Within Tarot* deck, unlike other interpretations of this card, grasps the staff of the three ages (Isis, Osiris, and Horus) in his right hand. In Crowley and Achad's understanding of Egyptian cosmology, the first age is of Isis, wherein mankind worshipped Mother Earth in all her bounty; the second age is that of Osiris, when humanity believed that the heavens revolved around the Earth and worshiped the Dying and Rising Sun; however, this current age is that of Horus, for with the discovery that the Earth revolves around the Sun, we have begun to realize that every man and woman is a star and that the Kingdom is Within. The Christian view of these ages are perhaps best summed up by the 12th Century monk, Joachim de Fiore: the first was the Age of the Father, the creation of the world, the establishment of Law, and the Old Testament; the second was the age of the Son, with Christ's sacrifice, the New Testament, and the beginning of the Church; the present age is that of the Holy Spirit, in which the Church is dissolved as Love becomes the Law and the individual communes directly with the Divine. The Hierophant points the way of the Third Age.

Perhaps Will Durant, in his monumentous work The Story of Civilization, expresses the gift of the Hierophant the best:

> "Hence a certain tension between religion and society marks the higher stages of every civilization. Religion begins by offering magical aid to harassed and bewildered men; it culminates by giving to a people that unity of morals and belief which seems so favorable to statesmanship and art; it ends by fighting suicidally in the lost cause of the past. For as knowledge grows or alters continually, it clashes with mythology and theology...The movement of liberation rises to an exuberant worship of every idea. Conduct, deprived of its religious supports, deteriorates in epicurean chaos; and life itself, shorn of consoling faith, becomes a burden alike to conscious poverty and to weary wealth. In the end a society and its religion tend to fall together, like body and soul, in a harmonious death. Meanwhile among the oppressed another myth arises, gives new form to human hope, new courage to human effort, and after centuries of chaos builds another civilization" (Durant 1935, 71).

I Love Cats

Bookmark

6 The Lovers

– Gemini –
Path 17: Hod to Tiphereth
Zain ז – Sword / 7 / Z

Astrological Meaning: The Twins

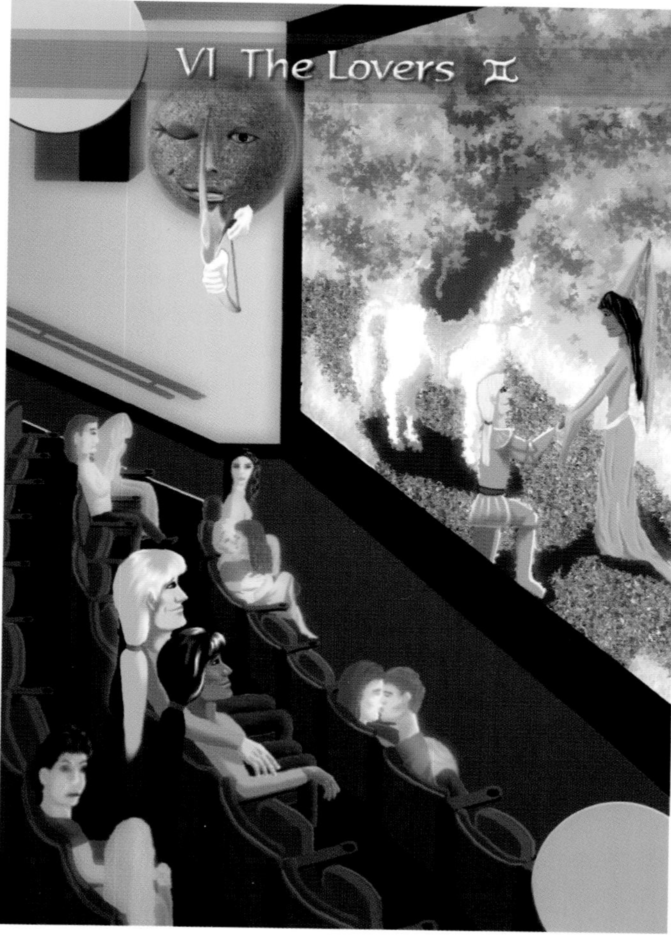

Characteristics of People with a Strong Gemini in their Astrological Charts:

Geminis can talk other people into or out of anything. They are typically tall, with excellent posture, high foreheads, and superior eyes that actually twinkle; they are known for being astute, clever, witty, adaptable, and quick. They usually have an uncanny understanding of the relationships between things, and tend to have many interests, becoming a sort of jack-of-all-trades; however, they constantly change their minds and it is practically impossible to pin them down about anything. They long to be as free as the air they breathe. Geminis love to talk, and they gesticulate frequently while they're doing it. They're full of contradictions yet act as though life is simple, mentally sensitive yet emotionally tough as nails, and generally consider Life to be their greatest teacher. At his best Gemini is an inspiring teacher, a brilliant writer, or the quintessential Renaissance man (or woman). At his worst, he is two-faced, inconsistent, superficial, and all talk...no action.

Element: Air, Masculine, Transmissive, Mutable sign
Ruled by: Mercury
Minor Arcana Association: 8, 9, 10 of Swords

Key Phrases:

- The Sun is in Gemini from May 20th to June 20th.
- Third sign of the Zodiac; has a natural affinity with the Third House.
- Gemini represents our reflection in the mirror—not what we really are, but what we seem to be; therefore it rules the querent's image, the surface, and the superficial. Also the skin.
- Rules infatuation and puppy love—the love of the reflection of oneself in the other.
- Because if its connection with twins, it rules twins and many parts of the body that come in pairs—arms, eyes, hands, lungs, shoulders. Also brothers and sisters.
- Because of its emphasis upon image, Gemini rules image-conscious professions like acting, fashion, stage, television, and movies.
- Because of its bond with Mercury it rules students, writers, public speakers, teachers, and secondary schools, as well as data, information, computers, and the Internet.
- Any written or verbal contract or communication.
- Rules veins, arteries, and nerves...since they connect all the systems of the body.
- Rules high, airy places, like hilltops, mountaintops, upstairs rooms, and skyscrapers.
- Rules places of connection like hallways and windows; places of communication like rooms for debating, reading, or writing. Also storage places, like chests, boxes, or computer memory.
- Smaller living spaces, like apartments and condominiums; traveling or moving a short distance.
- Never long term, maximum 12-18 months.

Spheres: UL sphere is yellow (Tiphereth) while LR sphere is orange (Hod).

Path 17 indicates: Confront duality and pairs of opposites; overcome restrictive illusions.

Qabalistic Symbology:

The Moon emerges from its Solar Bath in Tiphereth as the Path of The Lovers, or Gemini, which unites Tiphereth with Hod. We trace the Wisdom from Chokmah, through the Paths of Light, as it flows into this reservoir of pure Reason, carrying with it the idea of the Pairs of Opposites from Temperance, the Moon, and the Lovers. Here the Twins must overcome the illusions of the Moon with its restrictions, and confront the oppositions of duality. This is a necessary lesson for the followers of the Tradition of Light to learn, for the twilight can make their view narrow and restricted, therefore the elements of Sin (the Moon) enter, and the earlier Wisdom can become muddled and lost.

7 The Chariot

– Cancer –
Path 15: Yesod to Netzach
Cheth – ח : Fence / 8 / C, Ch

Astrological Meaning: The Crab

Characteristics of People with a Strong Cancer in their Astrological Charts:

Cancers are driven by a need for security and a home base. Emotional and changeable by nature, they are protective, romantic, maternal, and sentimental. They have large, round faces with small eyes, high-bridged noses, and sensitive skin; their chests are normally much bigger than their hips. Saturn in Cancer changes their appearance, making them bonier. They love eating and cooking, and tend to be either domestic homebodies or gourmet dining buffs. They prize antiques, tradition, and family; most adore their mothers. Their feelings seem to shift with the phases of the Moon; as a consequence their moodiness sometimes causes them to miss timely opportunities. At their best, they make wonderful parents, passionate historians, or innovative chefs. At their worst, they are oversensitive, controlling, manipulative, and unable to deal with criticism.

Element: Water, Feminine, Receptive, Cardinal sign

Ruled by: Moon

Minor Arcana Association: 2, 3, 4 of Cups

Key Phrases:

- The Sun is in Cancer from June 20th to July 22nd.
- Fourth sign of the Zodiac; has a natural affinity with the Fourth House.
- The end of the matter—this will happen. The end of a cycle.
- A matter of control and/or containment: either someone secretly wants control, the querent needs to get control or get things contained, or else it's under control, depending upon dignity. Anything conservative or controlling.
- Represents querent's foundation—home, mother, family, children, genetics, or ancestry. Also moving one's home or traveling close to home; often a car because many people live in their car as much as they live in their home. Things close to home, like neighbors or yard.
- Any profession having to do with food, comfort, or home—like restaurants, cooking, hotel work, real estate, or homemaking.
- Watery places—lakes, harbors, moving water, beaches, seaside, springs, wells, marshes.

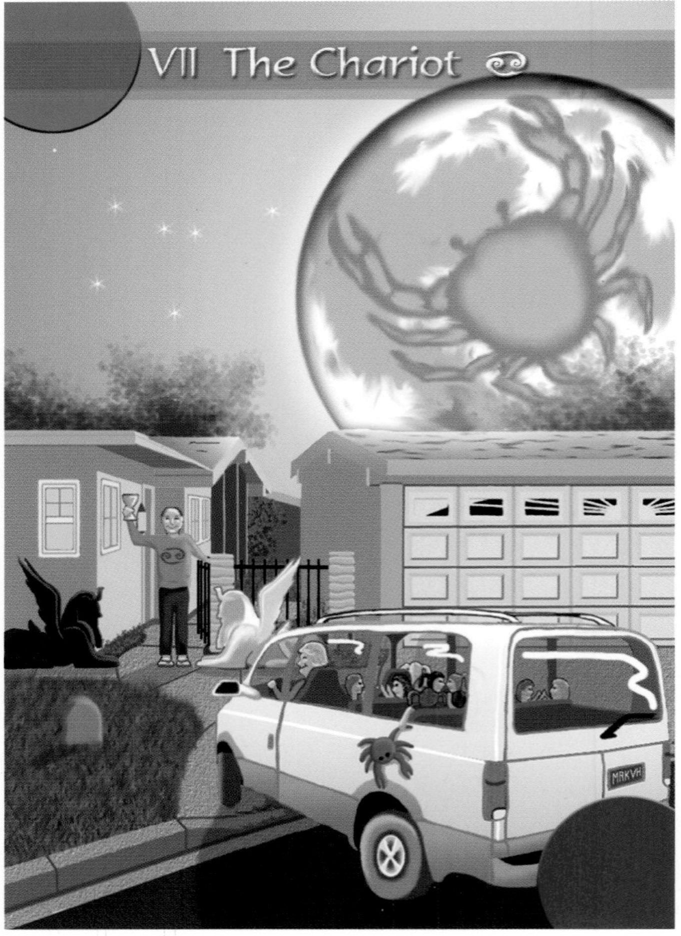

- Problems with water, from edema to flooding.
- Rules the stomach, mouth, womb, breasts, and women.

Spheres: UL sphere is green (Netzach) while LR sphere is purple (Yesod).

Path 15 indicates: Harness the traditions of Light and Darkness, the choice to become both One and Many. Uniting strength and balance through the power of love, to attain the foundation of control.

Qabalistic Symbology:

The tradition of the Chariot (or "Merkavah," MRKVH, in Hebrew) comes from Ezekiel's prophetically symbolic account of a chariot that bears us to the Divine. The Chariot card unites within itself the influences from the Paths of Strength (Leo) with that of Justice (Libra), having both the Strength of the "Lion" and the balance of "Justice" combined with Netzach's Power of Love, as it makes its way to Yesod, the Foundation. Just as the Moon, the Initiatrix, rules Cancer, so the Chariot has harnessed the black and white sphinxes, the Traditions of Light and Darkness, in order to initiate us into the mysteries of Hadit, the All manifesting as a Single Point of Light and the focus of matter, the choice to become simultaneously both One and Many.

8 Strength

– Leo –
Path 19: Netzach to Tiphereth
Teth – ט : Serpent / 9 / T

Astrological Meaning: The Lion

Characteristics of People with a Strong Leo in their Astrological Charts:

You can't help but notice a Leo because of his dignified carriage, presence, and dramatic flair. Look for prominent eyes, upturning curly hair, and a well-proportioned face and body with excellent posture. Leos are courageous, creative, proud, and love to be the center of attention. They are generally lavish, forgiving, generous, and authoritative, although there is sometimes a paradoxical coldness in their most intimate relationships. Leos are always known for their personal panache and their love of entertainment. At their best, they make charismatic leaders, popular entertainers, and benevolent bosses; at their worst they are dominating, live out their self-worth issues through their children, and are attention whores.

Element: Fire, Masculine, Transmissive, Fixed sign

Ruled by: Sun

Minor Arcana Association: 5, 6, 7 of Wands

Key Phrases:

- The Sun is in Leo from July 22nd to August 22nd.
- Fifth sign of the Zodiac; has a natural affinity with the Fifth House.
- Leo is the Lord of Life; therefore, he rules our general health and physical vitality as well as the things that make life worth living for most of us—happiness, fun, and amusement.
- The querent's self esteem and luck.
- The heart, back, ribs, spine, sides, and any related illnesses, also fevers.
- Sex, lust, and desire at its most basic level, love affairs.
- Leo is primal, animalistic; it's Nature's Law.
- Any place or work that deals in fun, entertainment, or amusement—any kind of performer, the stage, bars, theatres, etc.; in

the 11th house, Leo shows fame and a large public following.

- Any places that are wild, rocky, barren, or generally accessible to animals but inaccessible to humans.
- Eminent structures, like castles, national monuments, and palaces.

Spheres: UL sphere is yellow (Tiphereth) while LR sphere is green (Netzach).

Path 19 indicates: Animal nature subdued by pure love; merging of masculine and feminine.

Qabalistic Symbology:

In Strength, the Woman of Venus, or Netzach, is united with the Masculine Lion of the Sun, or Tiphereth. The Ram, or Lamb, of Aries has been sacrificed as a substitute as it passed through the Solar Fire at the "Passover" point, Tiphereth. In the City of the Sun it may truly be said that the "Lion lies down with the Lamb"; both are aspects of Horus, their Paths are seen united in Tiphereth. We find the symbolism of the Twin Lions (horizons) of Horus: here the animal nature is subdued by the pure love of the woman of Netzach, the process that purifies the Dark Tradition.

9 The Hermit

– Virgo –
Path 20: Hod to Geburah
Yod – י : Hand/ 10/ Y, I, J

Astrological Meaning: The Virgin

Characteristics of People with a Strong Virgo in their Astrological Charts:

Virgos usually have very sensitive constitutions their entire lives, requiring more attention to health than other signs. They have oddly proportioned bodies that are generally slim, and as they quickly walk by they have a tendency to look downwards, so that they are always finding lost articles on the ground; in fact, these types seem to notice everything. They are studious, astute, meticulous, critical, and practical by nature. The most notable characteristic of any Virgo is his or her innate desire and ability to analyze and classify details; they also have a strong instinct to prove their worth through service and hard work. At their best, they make assiduous accountants, detailed lawyers, and versatile technicians, but at their worst they are critical, materialistic, and miss the larger picture in their over-emphasis of minutiae.

Element: Earth, Feminine, Receptive, Mutable sign

Ruled by: Mercury (although some astrologers believe that the natural ruler of Virgo was the planet that was destroyed and is now the asteroid belt)

Minor Arcana Association: 8, 9, 10 of Pentacles

Key Phrases:

- The Sun is in Virgo from August 22nd to September 22nd.
- Sixth sign of the Zodiac; has a natural affinity with the Sixth House.
- Rules acute illnesses, as well as doctors, nurses, hospitals, and clinics.
- Rules institutions and bureaucracies.
- Rules the power of assimilation, and therefore the intestines and the lower stomach.
- Rules employees and service organizations.
- Service occupations, like secretaries, accountants, lawyers, health practitioners; any work that requires considerable attention to detail.

- Rules hidden fetishes, fixations, and compulsions, from masturbation to compulsive organizers.
- Rules both virgins and kinky sex (like bondage and S&M, wherein there is an element of punishment, atonement, or self-flagellation).
- Any place wherein work is carried out, such as offices and studies; anywhere books or merchandise are kept, such as cupboards and storerooms; any place at floor level or low down.

Spheres: UL sphere is red (Geburah) while LR sphere is orange (Hod).

Path 20 indicates: Virginity as severity rather than innocence; excessive control begets semblance and secrecy.

Qabalistic Symbology:

The Path of the Virgin transmits the Severity of Geburah to Hod. One must be reasonable in regard to one's Virginity, but the apparent Power of the Virgin is great. Here we find the Dark Tradition transformed into Detailed Reserve and Secrecy. The Hermit tempers the excesses of the Path of the Tower, perhaps controlling and obscuring the Light too much. The enforced innocence of the Virgin is a semblance, hiding the secrets of the Tradition of the Widow's Son, the Substitute, and the Lost Word.

10 The Wheel of Fortune

– Jupiter –
Path 31: Chokmah to Kether
Kaph – כ : Palm of hand / 20 / K

Astrological Meaning: The Expander

The Personality of Jupiter:

Jupiter is most like the current secular conception of Santa Claus: He is larger than life as he magically swoops down into our lives to bestow upon us everything we ever wanted. However, Jupiter is also a bit grander, a bit more distinguished than the cartoonish caricature of Santa; in this way he is more like Britain's Father Christmas. Jovial, magnanimous, and wise, he was called by the ancients the Greater Benefic for he desires to bring us more and more and more...more wealth, more merriment, more luck, more success, more spiritual wisdom, more material happiness. He is known for his excellent judgment, and he broadens our horizons, whether through achievement or traveling or learning. He loves to give; therefore, everything grows, expands, and multiplies under his golden touch. But just like King Midas, Jupiter can provide us with too much of a good thing. Too much money may make us greedy and wasteful; too much festivity will make us inebriated, fat, and unhealthy. Too much success can make us lazy, hypocritical, and arrogant. At his best Jupiter is generous, judicious, and expands our blessings, but at his worst his excesses just might destroy us.

Element: Air, Masculine

Rules: Sagittarius, Pisces (classical astrologers consider Jupiter to share rulership of Pisces with Neptune)

Minor Arcana Association: 6 Wands, 2 Pentacles, 9 Cups, 4 Swords, 8 Swords

Key Phrases:

- Jupiter is the Greater Benefic; it enlarges all that it touches (from your money to your waistline).

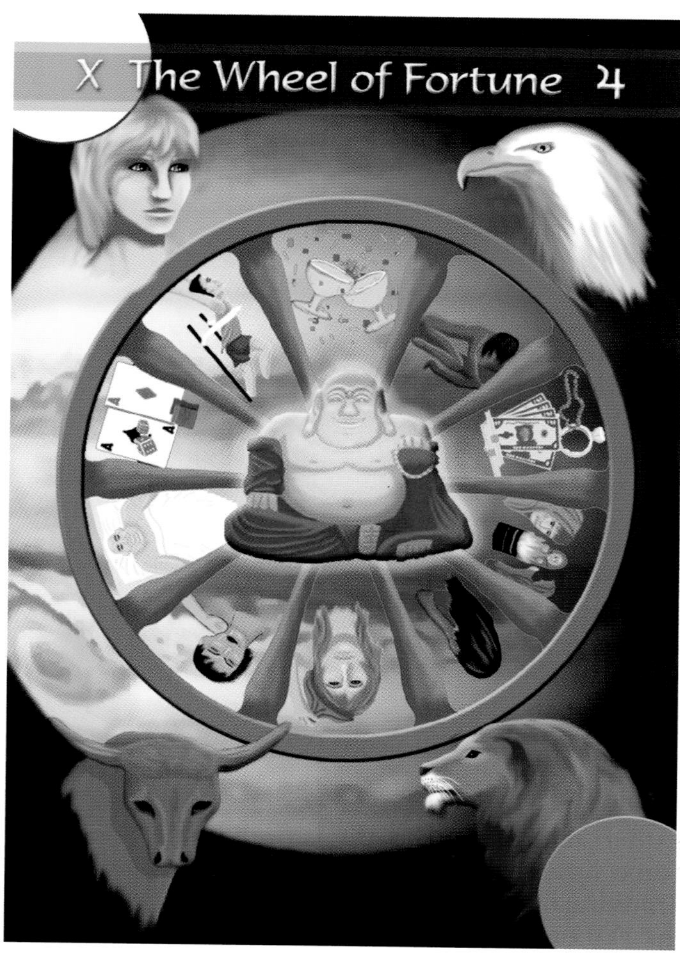

- Brings good fortune, luck, prosperity, grandeur, and growth.
- Rules divine power, blessings, spirituality; your destiny as opposed to your future.
- Rules the liver, hips, thighs, sciatic nerve, the pituitary gland, and any illness resulting from too much good living.
- If poorly aspected, Jupiter can bring intoxication and excess—whether from celebration, riches, comfort, success, or eminence.
- Rules jobs requiring just judgment—judges, senators, councilors, clergy, lawyers; also foreigners and middle-aged men.
- Rules sweet scents and large gentle animals, such as horses and whales.
- Rules grand, large places, such as courts, important public places, and foreign places.
- Also rules spiritual places, like altars, churches, and cathedrals.
- Rules gambling, horse race jockeys, and the winner in any matter.
- Alchemically, Jupiter rules tin.

Spheres: UL sphere is white (Kether) while LR sphere is gray (Chokmah).

Path 31 indicates: The Ray of Light—the essence of Wisdom—that begets existence, and thus the illusion of Space and Duality; the Purpose or Destiny of All That Is, via Chance.

Qabalistic Symbology:

The Wheel of Fortune is the Key of Destiny that is one with the True Will of the Father, and also (some say) with Chance. This is the Card of Jupiter, and symbolizes the Great Wheel of Life; the Whirling Forces of the Primum Mobile (Kether), which resulted in a System of Revolving Orbs—the Star Universe and the sphere of the zodiac—that resides in Chokmah. The Life Force is active in the One Substance, which becomes differentiated into the four elements as symbolized by the Four Cherubic Beasts at the cardinal corners of the wheel.

This is the birth of Existence; this Ray of Light is the essence of Wisdom, the Higher Will or Purpose of the World, and as the Star Universe this becomes apparent in Chokmah, the Sphere of the Zodiac, the Second Sephirah. Thus originates the illusion of Space, the other great limitation of the mind of man, the Path of Light. It is the root of the Tradition of the Fatherhood of God as the supreme and concealed Force, little comprehended by those who accepted the Tradition of a Mother and Son, with the Son preceding the Father. This Ray is the Essence of Light, but it is represented in Chokmah as Grey, a mixture of colors that partially conceals the Supreme Essence, thus causing the root of Duality. From this Path comes the Tradition of the Light as the Word or Logos, who was in the Beginning with God and who was God.

11 Justice

– Libra –
Path 22: Netzach to Chesed
Lamed – ל : Ox Goad or Whip / 30 / L

Astrological Meaning: The Scales

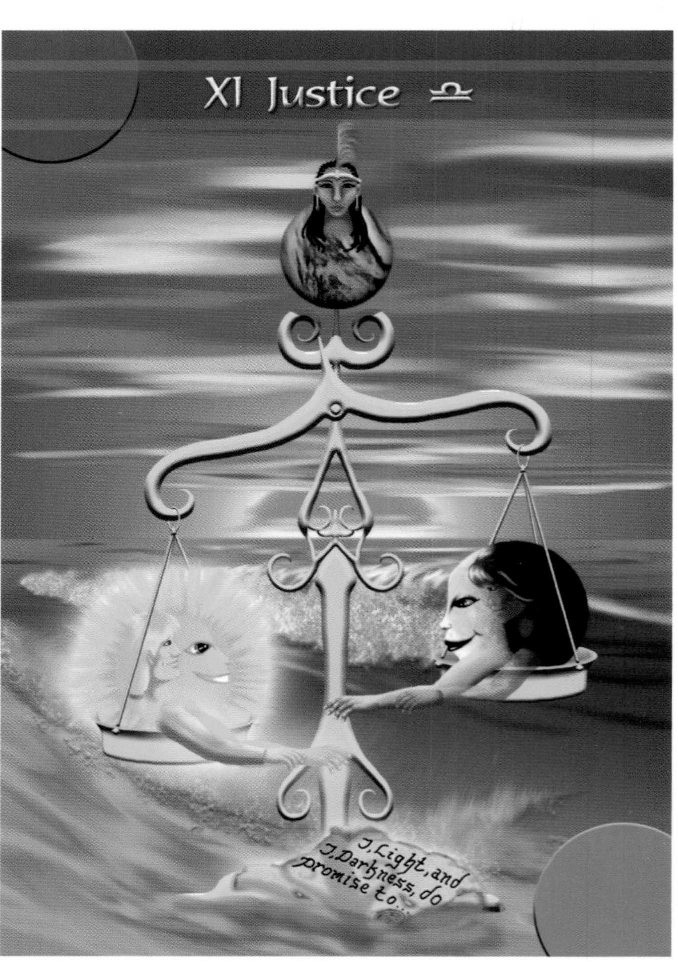

Characteristics of People with a Strong Libra in their Astrological Charts:

Libras are the most social of the signs, and their primary motivation in life is harmonious human relationships. Unlike Cancers, whose relationships are controlled by their emotions, a Libra's thought predominates over his or her emotion in relationships; thus, the over-riding goal of Harmony must be achieved at all costs. Although this talent makes them amazing diplomats, party hostesses, and referees, it can also breed the weaknesses that Libra's are known for: manipulation, little white lies, and superficiality. Charming, attractive, and having a friendliness that often becomes flirtatiousness, Libras are beauty-conscious, stylish dressers, sensitive to Harmony and balance, and require a peaceful environment to thrive. They struggle with decision-making because of their uncanny ability to look at all sides of a situation as it is easier for them to take another's point of view than to form or stick to their own.

Element: Air, Masculine, Transmissive, Cardinal sign
Ruled by: Venus (although some astrologers speculate that when we discover a tenth planet, it will actually be the natural ruler of Libra)
Minor Arcana Association: 2, 3, 4 of Swords

Key Phrases:

- The Sun is in Libra from September 22nd to October 22nd.
- Seventh sign of the Zodiac; has a natural affinity with the Seventh House.
- Rules marriage, equal partnerships (both business and personal), and significant others.
- Rules lawsuits, legal proceedings, and open enemies.
- Rules contracts being made or broken.
- The balance of opposing forces, as in war and places of war.
- Airplanes, airports, and anything with two wings.
- Rules the area of the body encompassing the lower back and buttocks; also the kidneys.
- Libra is called the Portal of Death, for its natural placement in the zodiac is at sunset.
- Rules high places, windy places, hillsides, mountains, upstairs, and attics, as well as one room within or joined to another.

Spheres: UL sphere is blue (Chesed) while LR sphere is green (Netzach).
Path 22 indicates: The Will balances the Law of Love; Universal Harmony.

Qabalistic Symbology:

Ma'at, the daughter of Ra and the wife of Thoth, is the Egyptian goddess of Truth, Justice, Righteousness, Measurement, and Balance, who shows us the journey to Universal Harmony. Justice is Ruled by Venus and brings down the Mercy of Chesed to Netzach, the Sphere of Venus; here we see the Law of Love coming into operation under the Will of Chokmah, as it is written in Crowley's Book of the Law, "Love is the law, love under will" (or under wish, as some have recommended). Love needs to be balanced in Netzach, thus avoiding extremes.

12 The Hanged Man

– Neptune –
Path 18: Yesod to Tiphereth
Mem – מ : Seas or Water / 40 / M

Astrological Meaning: The Visionary

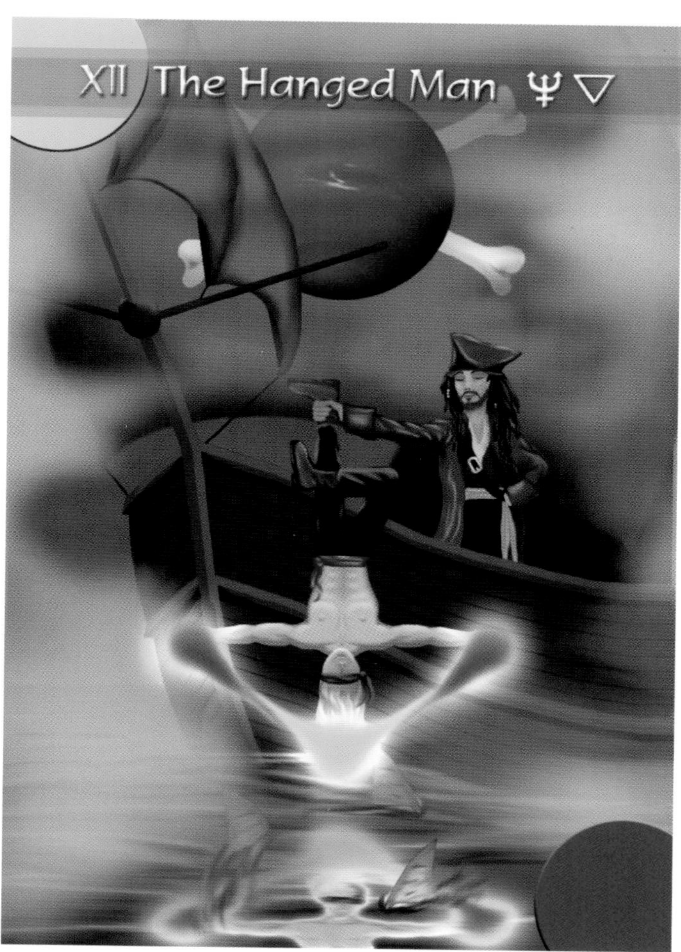

The Personality of Neptune:

Neptune can be a Saint who uses hallucinogens to induce his ecstatic utterances, a Poet who renounces society to wander the world as a recluse, or a Pirate who breaks all of civilization's rules to live on his own terms as he steals what he needs from people who, in his opinion, have too much anyway. No matter which of these alter egos that Neptune wears today, however, the only thing you can count on for this Chameleon is that it will be a different one tomorrow. Change and inconstancy, like the nature of water, are Neptune's middle name. For Neptune, distinctions do not exist. It is the Great Dissolver; vague, nebulous and ungrounded, it confuses and disperses all it touches. Actions, words, and ideas influenced by Neptune are like smoke—although they can begin with great fervor, they rapidly diffuse into the air and come to naught, unless it receives assistance from a more stable planet through a strong, positive aspect. Nothing is solid or permanent in Neptune's world; everything blends, morphs, and flows. Neptune acts at all costs; it doesn't perceive anything outside its own purposes and thus takes what the individual is feeling and exaggerates it to the exclusion of other considerations. Everything is equally significant for Neptune; hence, right and wrong are based entirely upon the individual's significances of the moment. All lines, rules, and limitations blur in this planet's watery depths.

Element: Water, Androgynous
Rules: Pisces (astrologers consider Neptune to share rulership with Jupiter)
Minor Arcana Association: Cups Suit (Water)

Key Phrases:

- Positively speaking, Neptune rules imagination, poetry, otherworldly artists, psychics, fantasy, science fiction, visions, and visionaries.
- Negatively speaking, Neptune is known for its lack of earthly reality, illusion, inconstancy, impracticality, delusion, swindling, and deception.
- Neptune signifies fog, drugs, gasses, and drug addicts.
- Neptune, like Uranus, moves us towards the future; however, it operates through the water element, thus using emotion, intuition, and psychic force to shake things up. Where Uranus dissipates (like air) all boundaries in order to make a new world, Neptune dissolves (like water) all distinctions that prevent us from being whole.
- When Neptune is very well placed, the person is probably psychic, tending to lose him or herself in another person or in an ideal; they are also willing to sacrifice anything, including themselves, to bring their visions into reality,
- When Neptune is poorly placed, people cannot be trusted. They behave like pirates: they ignore social mores, make their own rules, and live for their own profit. Neptune tends to make us devious, unfaithful, spacey, and uncivilized.
- Rules insanity, hypnosis, sleepwalking, and fraud.
- Rules feet, weakening and debilitating illnesses, illnesses that are difficult to diagnose and treat, the thalamus, and the lymphatic system. The right hemisphere of the brain (the seat of creativity and imagination).
- Rules occupations of the sea, such as sailing, fishing, and piracy.
- Neptune turns our world upside down. Just as the Hanged Man looks at the world from an upside down position, Neptune encourages us to be imaginative and consider new vantage points (perhaps even those that we deem to be "fiction").

Spheres: UL sphere is yellow (Tiphereth) while LR sphere is purple (Yesod).
Path 18 indicates: The Power of Redeeming Love; Light's descent into self-destruction to en-light-en the darkness.

Qabalistic Symbology:

Depicted on *The Kingdom Within Tarot* card we see a man who is suspended by one foot, his head and arms forming a triangle as his legs form a cross above him. He is the son of the Sun, bringing down the Light as far as Yesod, the Subconscious Mind of Humanity. Just as the subconscious is best represented by the element of water, so the Hebrew letter Mem is attributed to The Hanged Man, and he hangs above the ocean. His body is reversed, as if reflected in the waters; his head is surrounded by Glory, the reflection of Tiphereth and Kether. His hands are in Yesod, the Sphere of the Moon that reflects the Sun upon the Earth, Malkuth. His is the power of the Redeeming Love, usually considered as self-sacrifice, but more truly representing the Justified One, who says: "This is my body which I destroy, in order that it may be renewed." The Hanged Man symbolizes Light's descent into darkness, in order to redeem or enlighten it; this initiation is presided over by The Hierophant.

13 Death

– Scorpio –
Path 24: Geburah to Chesed
Nun – נ : Fish; eagle, snake, scorpion; to sprout, to grow/ 50/ N

Astrological Meaning: The Scorpion

Characteristics of People with a Strong Scorpio in their Astrological Charts:

Scorpio is the only sign that in fact has three symbols—the scorpion, the serpent, and the eagle; each is a progressively higher representation of resurrecting change. It was probably a highly advanced Scorpio of the eagle type who coined the phrase, "Die Daily!" A Scorpio wants to be private, but is noticed by everyone. With a square jaw, an intense stare, and a strong body that simply exudes sexuality, the depths of a Scorpio are bottomless—especially to themselves. Willful, passionate, probing, and secretive by nature, they have a tendency to repress their strong feelings until they explode. Having a preference for one-on-one relating, they make intense lovers as well as probing psychologists, and since they adore "digging beneath the surface" they are also formidable detectives. Don't ever lie to or cheat on these jealous types, for, not only will they ferret out your secret, but their primal vengeance will be a thousand times worse than your paltry crime. A developed Scorpio is in complete control of every situation; in fact, their creative domination is so subtle that we only call the ones who fail at their art "manipulative control freaks."

Element: Water, Feminine, Receptive, Fixed sign
Ruled by: Pluto (classical astrologers consider Mars to share rulership with Pluto)
Minor Arcana Association: 5, 6, 7 of Cups

Key Phrases:

- The Sun is in Scorpio from October 22nd to November 21st.
- Eighth sign of the Zodiac; has a natural affinity with the Eighth House.
- Scorpio rules transformation, change, and growth. It moreover rules death and destruction, as they are the ultimate catalysts for transformation, change, and growth. Likewise transitions, endings, and beginnings.
- Signifies the resources of the other, whether your spouse, your business partner, or your opponent in a lawsuit; also other people's money (bills, taxes, bankruptcies, or inheritances).
- Rules anything extreme, dark, dangerous, violent, or poisonous. Places with lots of insects or reptiles as well as poisonous and stinking places. Also deep, watery, dark locations like lakes, bogs, moors, and muddy places. Rules kitchens, bathrooms, and any room that contains water; also damp places.
- Professions concerned with birthing and dying, deep and penetrating professions like psychologists and detectives, along with surgery and sanitation.
- Rules our survival issues, our reproductive urge, our desire for power and control, and our will to both destroy and create.
- Rules the groin area and organs of elimination (organs of creation and destruction) as well as the illnesses thereof.

Spheres: UL sphere is blue (Chesed) while LR sphere is red (Geburah).
Path 24 indicates: Change is the Resurrection, Regeneration, and Re-creation that restores the equilibrium of Life and Death, Light and Darkness.

Qabalistic Symbology:

The reciprocal Path from Chesed, Mercy, to Geburah, Severity, is that of Death—the Great Transformer. Death is both enemy and friend, for in truth there is no "death," but only a "change of life." Although the Grim Reaper cuts the deceased's silver cord, she in fact rises again as soon as her True Self is separated from her material form. The influences of the Paths of Resurrection, Regeneration, and Re-creation all play upon this one Path. The Path of Shin restores equilibrium to the Light and Darkness and rules over all, for this Path is the influence of the Ever-coming Son, the true Horus who appeared in Aries as the Lamb, in Pisces as the Fish, or in the earlier signs as the Lion, the Beetle, the Twins, and the Bull. Thus the Tradition of Light flows down into Tiphereth through two channels: the Wheel of Fortune, Chokmah, and the Sun, as well as the Wheel of Fortune, Chokmah, Temperance, Chesed, and the Moon.

14 Temperance

– Sagittarius –
Path 25: Chesed to Chokmah
Samekh – ס : Prop/ Tent peg/ Tent pole / 60 / S

Astrological Meaning: The Archer

Characteristics of People with a Strong Sagittarius in their Astrological Charts:

Everything about a Sagittarius is long and open—their faces, their eyes, their teeth, their noses, their height, and their vision, often with an endearing messiness and clumsiness, as though their bodies just can't seem to keep up with their spirit's goals. They love anything that is far away, from the great outdoors to foreign, exotic places; they walk quickly, with long strides, and drive fast. Happy-go-lucky, playful, and confident, they trust, take risks, and dream big dreams with a wide-eyed optimism that confounds the rest of the Zodiac, because things generally seem to work out for them. Their basic goal is to broaden and stretch themselves; therefore, they are generally attracted to new experiences, travel, sports, education, and philosophy. Many a college professor, travel writer, or wartime broadcaster had Sagittarius play a prominent role in his or her natal chart. Of course, they tend to take on more than they can handle—as well as having a problem with keeping track of the little things in life like their keys, their credit cards, their bank balances, and their appointments—but a developed Sagittarius has a disarmingly free spirit that seems to use the flesh only to accomplish, instead of imprison, him or her.

Element: Fire, Masculine, Transmissive, Mutable sign
Ruled by: Jupiter
Minor Arcana Association: 8, 9, 10 of Wands

Key Phrases:

- The Sun is in Sagittarius from November 21st to December 21st.
- Ninth sign of the Zodiac; has a natural affinity with the Ninth House.
- Sagittarius rules aims, long-term goals, destinies, spirituality, and quests; it conquers.
- Rules anything far, such as exotic or foreign lands, long journeys, immigration, or diplomacy; it can also suggest something that's gone too far.
- Signifies anything high, such as philosophies, universities, or mountains.

- Governs anything hot, fast, and intense, like races, fast cars, swift horses, and jets.
- Rules the hips and thighs; also falls from horses and sports injuries.
- Rules locations that are open and high, where one can see in the distance, like the open sea; also wherever large animals live, like hills and fields. Upstairs and near fireplaces.

Spheres: UL sphere is gray (Chokmah) while LR sphere is blue (Chesed).

Path 25 indicates: Balance of Preservation with Destruction, Order with Chaos, Light with Darkness, Fire with Water, Will with Love.

Qabalistic Symbology:

The key to the Path between Chokmah and Chesed is called "Temperance." In the foreground of *The Kingdom Within Tarot* card we see a female centaur pouring light from one cup into the other (many Tarot decks instead depict an angel or human woman pouring water); this represents Preservation, as opposed to the Destruction of the Path of The Tower on the opposite side, while the equilibrated Path in the center is that of Creation and Regeneration. In this Temperance card we find the symbol of the centaur archer, half man and half horse. In mythology, the horse was the Goddess of Wisdom's gift to man, and so the legendary centaur was known as the wisest of all Earth's creatures. Sagittarius is ruled by Jupiter, and thus receives the influence of the Path of Jupiter through Chokmah. It is also connected directly with the sphere of Jupiter, Chesed. This gives us a hint of the dual-symbolism of the Forces of Life in the two cups held by the female centaur on the card. Just as Percival wrought the miracle of redemption, when the spear and the grail were re-united, so the male centaur represents the arrow of Chokmah, the Root of Fire, while the female represents the cup of Chesed, the Sphere of Water.

15 The Devil

– Capricorn –
Path 28: Tiphereth to Binah
Ayin – ע : Eye / 70 / O

Astrological Meaning: The Goat

Characteristics of People with a Strong Capricorn in their Astrological Charts:

These people are hardworking, ambitious, materialistic, and efficient. Men are frequently bearded, while women's hair is often thin; they tend to have terrible posture, unless they apply themselves to conquering it. Capricorns have a bittersweet loveliness in their tragic eyes, for usually their life starts in childhood traumas that they must rise above. As children, Capricorns act like serious, miniature adults who bear the world upon their tiny shoulders; however, they seem to grow more youthful and attractive as they age. No matter where a Capricorn starts from, she/he labors with great discipline to climb higher and higher in career and social status. They dress in formal clothes and dark colors professionally, but don't seem to care about their physical appearance when they're not working. Tending to be distant and restrained, attaining power through social position and authority matters most to this sign. They are generally successful in the corporate world. Guilt often plagues them. At their weakest, they feel inferior, melancholy, and have difficult bouts with depression. At their best, they are structured, self-disciplined, and goal-driven, with an innate business sense.

Element: Earth, Feminine, Receptive, Cardinal sign

Ruled by: Saturn

Minor Arcana Association: 2, 3, 4 of Pentacles

Key Phrases:

- The Sun is in Capricorn from December 21st to January 20th.
- Tenth sign of the Zodiac; has a natural affinity with the Tenth House.
- Under the influence of Capricorn, each person shall reap what they've sown and pay the dues for what they've done (whether the consequences are positive or negative depends upon the individual's original deeds.)
- Capricorn rules authority figures as well as career or professional calling (as opposed to Virgo's service and servants).
- Rules one's professional reputation or standing in the world.
- Capricorn judges and controls things; therefore it rules judges, the parent who is the authority figure in the home, CEOs, bosses, administrations, government agencies, and police.
- Capricorn, sometimes called the Great Earth Mother, is the darkest, earthiest, and most material of all the signs; its influences weigh us down, cementing us to the material plane.
- Thus, it rules earthy, dark locations, such as mines and other places that are deep underground. Also rules mining.
- Rules bones, teeth, and knees.
- Rules farming; therefore rules anywhere animals are kept (especially goats), farm implements or places where wood is stored, barren fields, dung heaps, bushy or thorny land, and mountain paths; also places near a floor or threshold.

Spheres: UL sphere is black (Binah) while LR sphere is yellow (Tiphereth).

Path 28 indicates: Confrontation of our Darkness and Duality; adoration of the material universe, no matter how marvelous or base.

Qabalistic Symbology:

It is no accident that the symbol for Capricorn is the goat, for "The Devil" has become the "scapegoat" for all the evils and temptations that have led humanity towards self-destruction. Capricorn occupies the Midheaven or Zenith in the Zodiac, and in *The Book of Thoth*, Aleister Crowley asserts that Capricorn is therefore the most exalted of all the signs in the kingdom of Malkuth as "it is the goat leaping with lust upon the summits of Earth" (Crowley 1974, *The Book of Thoth*, 52). This Path exemplifies ecstatic love and adoration of all things existing in the physical world, no matter how marvelous or base.

In some earlier decks this card is called Typhon, after the monster that almost destroyed the ancient gods of yore. The Devil is called "The Lord of the Gates of Matter" and "The Child of the Forces of Time." It represents the Birth of Matter from the Great Mother Sea, the One Substance. This is the way of the children enslaved to the Lord of Time, called Saturn or Cronos. It is the Path of the Tradition of Darkness, the twin of Light, of Lucifer, the Satanic Savior who fell from Heaven (remember the Sut-Typhonian tradition, the dark twin of Osiris, who was named Set in Egyptian cosmology, and later called Satan). The twins are chained by Time and Darkness, for each of us must confront our duality, the darkness and shame of our own fall, or else it becomes our chain to matter. This card portrays the illusion of incarnation as a prison rather than as the game it's meant to be. The Path opposite to the Devil is the Sun, which represents the tradition of the Jupiter-Ammonians with Horus as its ruler. Horus of the Star is the reconciler between Light and Darkness, Osiris and Set, the Sun and the Devil. The traditions of light and darkness are progressively more and more opposed to each other as we progress down the Tree of Life, but in the Primal Idea of the Pure Spiritual Light of The Ever Coming Son, the Holy Child of Kether, they are not two—but One.

16 The Tower

– Mars –
Path 27: Geburah to Binah
Peh – פ : Mouth / 80 / P

Astrological Meaning: The Destroyer

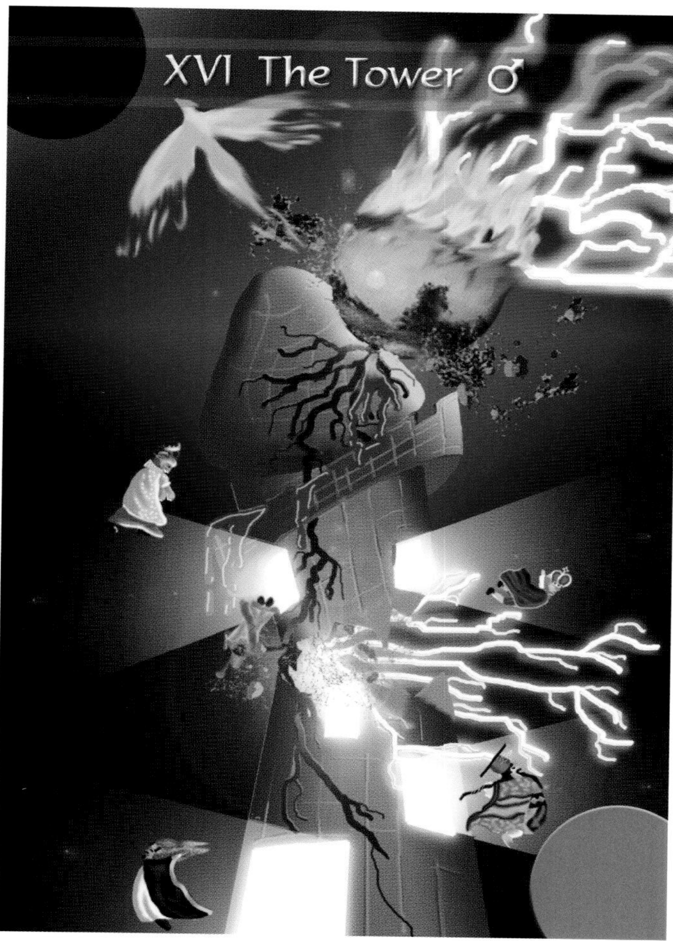

The Personality of Mars:

Mars is the Warrior Hunter, the Archetypal Male, the Pure Action, the Eternal "ING." He is strong, with big bones, a lean, ruddy face, sandy red hair, and sharp eyes; he is covered with battle scars. Courageous, war-like, bold, dominant, confident, immovable, territorial, contentious, and challenging, he enjoys the thrill of conquest and peril. He knows that only in facing, knowing, and conquering Death do we comprehend Life and thus truly live. Mars is not interested in reason and submits to no one! He glories in stimulation, lust, slaughter, quarrels, triumph, fights, and riots, and seems far too obscene, rash, ungrateful, furious, violent, and boastful to the tender sensibilities of the rest of the planets. Of course, what the other planets miss in their judgment of the Roman god of war is the fact that Mars embodies the energy of tooth-and-nail survival...all the niceties and pleasantries, all the civil pursuits and political correctness doesn't matter when you're facing the Beast and it remains to be seen just who will be the hunter and who will be the prey. Soldiers are known to behave very differently on the battlefield than when in their comfortable homes, as do people in situations of life and death survival. All the things that society and civilization teach us seem to melt away when we are brought face to face with our own survival. Mars burns through all appearances, all imperfections, all expectations, all justifications... and brings us back to What Is.

Element: Fire, Masculine
Rules: Aries, Scorpio (classical astrologers consider Mars to share rulership of Scorpio with Pluto)
Minor Arcana Association: 2 Wands, 7 Wands, 5 Cups, 10 Cups, 9 Swords

Key Phrases:

- Mars is the Lesser Malefic; it attacks anything with the appearance of perfection. Mars cuts, kills, and ends all persistence.
- Mars rules accidents (often involving bloodshed), sharp objects, and violent threats.
- Rules the muscles and muscle control, blood and arteries, the male sex organs, infectious diseases and epidemics, wounds and cuts, bruises and burns; also the adrenal gland (activated when one's survival is threatened). Signifies high fevers, migraines, shingles, and frenzies.
- Mars rules activity, construction, competition, and conflict. It is the planet of anger, burning passion and ambition, war, strife, and struggle. Mars is the initiator of action; it starts things. Therefore, it starts quarrels, conflict, rage, struggles, and destruction.
- Rules anything or anyone who cuts, like surgeons; anything or anyone involved in fighting or war, like soldiers, boxers, and guns; anything or anyone who works with fire, like firemen. Mars also rules locations associated with these attributes, such as places of war, bloodshed, and destruction, as well as hot, arid places like deserts.
- When poorly aspected, Mars signifies destruction, danger, fall, and ruin.
- Often signifies an older woman in the post-menopausal or "crone" stage of life, wherein

the softer, feminine energies (estrogen) of her youth have lessened as her more forceful, masculine energies (testosterone) now rise to dominance.

- Alchemically, Mars rules iron or anything with high levels of iron (like nettles and spinach); any hot or spicy food, like chili peppers and radishes; anything that grows in hot and dry places, like cactus and desert plants.

Spheres: UL sphere is black (Binah) while LR sphere is red (Geburah).

Path 27 indicates: Destroy the lies to reveal the true; to become perfected, all must be annihilated.

Qabalistic Symbology:

Destroy the fortress of your ego that your true self may spring forth free from the ruins! The Tower is the Path from Binah, the Primal Mother, to Geburah, the sphere of Mars; here we see Horus as the god of war, vengeance, and perfection. It is the image of the biblical Tower of Babel, with the power of the Supernal Triad (Kether, Chokmah, and Binah) rushing down and destroying the Column of Darkness (the Pillar of Severity, also called the Tradition of Darkness.) In this Path, just as in the story of the Tower of Babel, this is the power that strikes down all of our man-made illusions on our journey towards enlightenment. Too often, however, this power becomes the tradition of over-indulgence and destruction through waste of life.

The fall of the Tower of Babel resulted in the loss of the Universal Language, and since then confusion has prevailed in the physical universe, preventing us being like one of the gods. The Sons of Darkness for a time retrogressed, as the followers of the Tradition of Light continued to advance. The Tower is the result of the positive and negative currents from the Path of Saturn (the World card) through Binah. Its message is that the Absolute is Nothingness; thus all that is created, all that manifests is only a shoddy reflection or blemish of Truth. To become perfected, *all* must be annihilated.

17 The Star

– Aquarius –
Path 29: Binah to Chokmah
Tzaddi – צ : Fish hook / 90 / Tz, X

Astrological Meaning: The Water Bearer

Characteristics of people with a strong Aquarius in their astrological charts:

You can spot this person a mile away because they are so different from everyone else. They often have a lighter complexion, but it is their unconventional, eccentric choice in hairstyle and attire that distinguishes them so notably. Both intellectual and artistic, Aquarians are the epitome of individuality. Experimental, rational, and idealistic by nature, they are the quintessential humanitarians who are passionately dedicated to the progress of society, all the while having trouble relating to normal people on an interpersonal level. They are drawn to waves of all types (from the sea, to sound, to new trends, to statistics). At their best, they are the reformers, the inventors, and the artists of society. At their worst, they are extremists, fixated on their own ideals to the point of inflexibility, and just plain weird.

Element: Air, Masculine, Transmissive, Fixed sign

Ruled by: Uranus (classical astrologers consider Saturn to share rulership with Uranus)

Minor Arcana Association: 5, 6, 7 of Swords

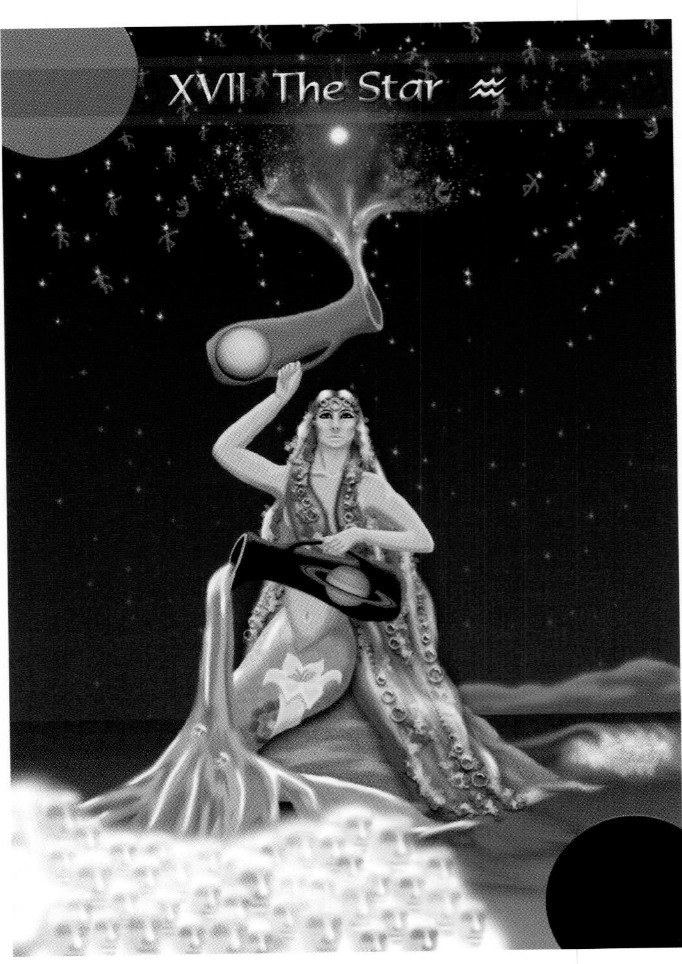

Key Phrases:

- The Sun is in Aquarius from January 20th to February 18th.
- Eleventh sign of the Zodiac; has a natural affinity with the Eleventh House.
- Aquarius rules the future; it encompasses our dreams, hopes, ideals, and wishes.
- Rules anything that frees us from our bounds and restriction (i.e., democracies, revolutions, philosophies, unity, friendship, communistic brotherhood, etc.)
- Friendship, as well as the dream of love and the perfect mate.
- Open, large, pleasant places; any place that is hilly, uneven, off the floor, or near a window.
- Things have tendency to fall in Aquarius (from the lofty heights of dreams and ideals).
- Rules large people groups, such as the public, juries, and congress. Also public service, populations, the Internet, and film.
- Rules legs, ankles, and defects of blood circulation.

Spheres: UL sphere is gray (Chokmah) while LR sphere is black (Binah).

Path 29 indicates: The Dream of the Restored World; fallen humanity and the physical universe redeemed to sovereignty of the spirit and eternal life.

Qabalistic Symbology:

Aquarius, the Water Bearer, is the sign ruled by Saturn, the Sephirah of Binah, the Great Sea, pouring the Waters of Creation upon the Earth. Her two pitchers are Binah, the Mother, and Chokmah, the Father. In Chokmah we find the mystery of the star universe. Everything in existence came from and returns to the stars. Every one of us is a Star in his or her own right. In *The Kingdom Within Tarot* deck, the black pitcher pours the Tree of the Knowledge of Good and Evil, which leads to incarnation into the physical world (the fall of man); the grey pitcher pours the Tree of Life, which leads to sovereignty of the spirit (eternal life). In the Egyptian sense, Sirius (the Dog Star) is the Star of Isis, used by the ancients to calculate time. The mermaid in *The Kingdom Within Tarot* symbolizes the elements of earth and water, just as the star symbolizes the elements of fire and air. The Water Bearer is the symbol of Isis and Nuit, and this card represents the Dream of the Restored World.

[Additional Note: For those acquainted with Crowley's changes in the Tarot attributions based upon his assertion that "Tzaddi is not the Star" (Crowley 1976, *The Book of the Law*, 26), I shall quote Achad's explanation for not making this change:

> "I think this means that Tzaddi is NOT (=LA=31) the Star, for she is combined with the Origin-AL Shin (Hadit) of the 31st path, and is herself the 29th Path which =11. This was the 4th path of the Old System and 31=3+1=4. I shall therefore leave all the attributions of Letters and Cards as they were, all that one has to do is arrange them in their proper order and BEHOLD. This is the Mystery of the THIRD ORDER of the QABALAH... (The decision between the SUN and JUPITER.) THE FIRST ORDER is for those who must PASS THROUGH FIRE, the SECOND ORDER is to try the INTELLECT, and THE THIRD ORDER for those who have COORDINATED their UNDERSTANDING" (Achad 1997, *Q.B.L.*, Appendix).

For those not familiar with The Book of the Law, it states that its "key" is the Gematric equation that the number 31 = the letters AL = God and All; while the letters LA = Not.

[Achad also suspected it possible that the Star and the Sun should share the same letter, Resh, for the Sun is the Star of our solar system. In this configuration, the Supernal Triad in the Restored Tree of Life is Kaph, Tau, Resh = KThR = Kether.]

18 The Moon

– Pisces –
Path 23: Tiphereth to Chesed
Qoph – ק : Back of the head / 100 / Q

Astrological Meaning: The Fish

Characteristics of People with a Strong Pisces in their Astrological Charts:

It was with regards to a Pisces that someone coined the phrase, "Still waters run deep." If anyone seems dreamily mysterious, indecisively impressionable, incredibly receptive, and eerily intuitive, odds are you're looking at someone with an unimpeded Pisces in their natal chart. These people generally have fine hair, which the women like to wear long like mermaids, enticing "bedroom" eyes, and tend to be shorter in stature. They love the watery world, from the sea to the rain to their bathtubs, and relish eating seafood. Anything mystical or irrational is appealing to this sign, for they are always moving beyond ordinary reality in all their pursuits. They are adaptable and particularly sensitive to their environments, which they soak up like a sponge, making them empathetic and often psychic; however, this tendency necessitates the need for regular intervals of privacy or else they lose their sense of self and find it difficult to act. At their best, they are devoted, imaginative, and display a deep understanding of the subtleties of life; at their weakest, they are sneaky and covert, confused and chaotic, as well as restless and escapist.

Element: Water, Feminine, Receptive, Mutable sign

Ruled by: Neptune (classical astrologers consider Jupiter to share rulership with Neptune)

Minor Arcana Association: 8, 9, 10 of Cups

Key Phrases:

- The Sun is in Pisces from February 19th to March 20th.
- Twelfth sign of the Zodiac; has a natural affinity with the Twelfth House.
- Pisces is the gateway to our unconscious mind, those horrors that we imagine things to be, rather than their reality. It is our desire to avoid that which scares us, those things that we don't wish to be aware of or to see fully; therefore, its influence makes things invisible to us.
- Trying to see the truth when under the sway of Pisces is like trying to see the bottom of the ocean.
- Rules anything that is hidden, like unknown enemies, the "other" woman, your past, unidentified resources, concealed identities or motives, and family scandals; also obscured places, such as oceans, thick forests, and jungles.
- Rules the subconscious activities of the mind, like sleep, dreaming, paranoia, madness, and psychic ability.
- Rules anything that restricts or binds us—prisons, blackmail, closed systems of belief.
- Rules dark, unseen forces, such as black magic, psychic attack, and spiritual manipulation.
- Governs the feet and lymphatic system of the body. Also anything having to do with feet, such as shoes, shoe salesmen, podiatrists, wherever shoes are stored, and dancing.
- Strong affinity with the ocean and any place full of water or fish, like springs, wells, pools, pumps, rivers, and even bathtubs.
- Also rules places in which we seclude or hide our selves from the world, such as cloisters, chapels, and retreats. Rules anything with the

purpose of hiding or restraining something else, like floor coverings, clouds, handcuffs, and safes.

- Rules religions, large institutions, or any group wherein the individuals become less important than "the mission." Also martyrdom or self-sacrifice for a "cause" or another person.
- Rules professions that work with liquids such as paint, alcohol, or water.
- Pisces signifies a crisis of faith or the poet's "dark night of the soul;" it is the last stage of a cold and dark winter before the light of the Sun reappears to bring warmth and illumination to our world.

Spheres: UL sphere is blue (Chesed) while LR sphere is yellow (Tiphereth).

Path 23 indicates: The rebirth of Darkness into Light; the light created by darkness. Awakening of the repressed unconscious.

Qabalistic Symbology:

Although the scarab beetle of the Egyptians is traditionally a solar deity, it really symbolizes the story of the journey from realm of the Moon (darkness) into the realm of the Sun (light). After laying its eggs in a ball of dung and leaving them encased in its darkness for one cycle of the Moon, or twenty-eight days, on the twenty-ninth day the beetle pushes the dung into water so that it may soften and dissolve until the eggs hatch when exposed to the warming rays of the Sun. Like the scarab beetle, this Path carries the Sun out of the dark, poisoned waters of the winter of the nightmares, the prejudices, the insanities, and the dead superstitions of our unconscious, and into the rebirth of the light. Fish, as they navigate the realms where we humans cannot easily follow, represent the unconscious. Most of humanity is spiritually asleep, lost in its sins and restrictions and unable to see the truth.

Just as the Earth's Moon reflects the light of the Sun, so the Path of the Moon is the light created by darkness. The Moon transmits some light, albeit internal and intuitional, even if it is a reflection of the Sun. This Path is attributed to Pisces, and through this Path came the Piscean Tradition of the Fish-God, another aspect of Horus as the Sun (or Son). This Path is that of the Sun hidden in the bowels of the Earth, just before its resurrection; in ancient Mesopotamian mythology, the moon god was known as "Sin," the word of restriction, and this has been characteristic of the Piscean Age that has just finished. The true tradition of the Sun became clouded during that age. Through the Restriction of Sin, the influence of Temperance's Preservation became that of Repression, only a partial understanding of the original idea. By the placement of the Emperor (Aries) meeting Tiphereth (the Sun) as the 21st path and the Moon (Pisces) meeting Tiphereth as the 23rd Path, we have the representation of the Sun's yearly procession from Aries through Pisces around the zodiac.

19 The Sun

– Sun –
Path 26: Tiphereth to Chokmah
Resh – ר : Head or face / 200 / R

Astrological Meaning: The Center

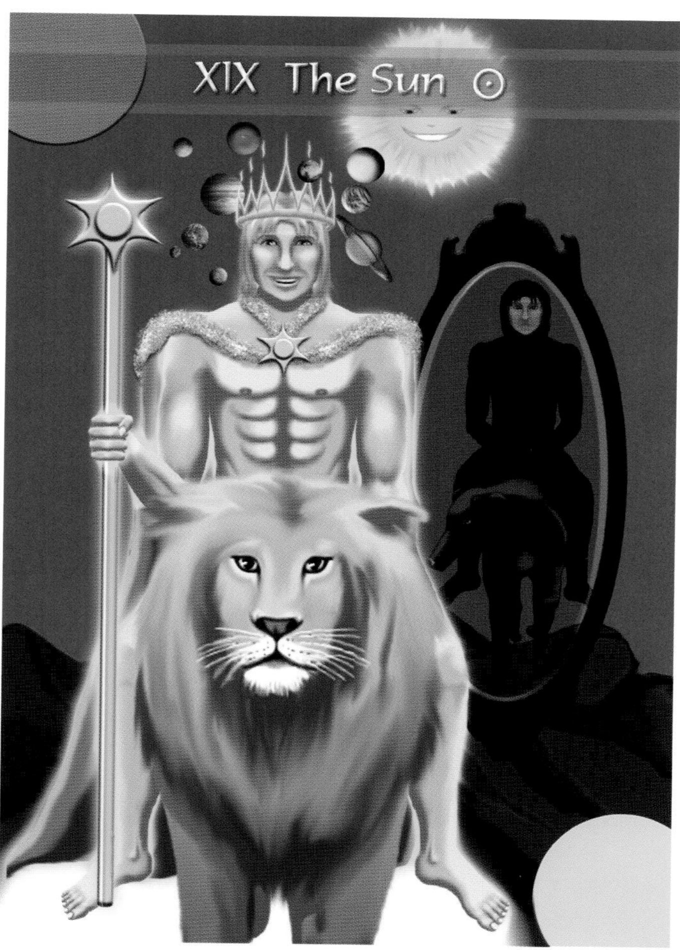

The Personality of the Sun:

The Sun is best characterized as a powerful, benevolent sovereign whose greatest strength is also his greatest weakness: He is the supreme center of his kingdom and his subjects' lives, as well as his own estimation. If there was ever a person in history who epitomized the personality of the Sun, it was the king of France who was christened Louis Dieudonne, which means "Gift of God." Born in 1648, at just four years old he was crowned King Louis XIV, and he ruled France during its Golden Age until his death in 1715. He adopted Apollo, the Greek god of the Sun, as his personal emblem, and is remembered even today as the "Sun King." Under his leadership, France became a dominant world power and a leader in the arts. He was an absolute monarch, as expressed in the famous quote attributed to him, "*L'etat c'est moi*" (I am the state.) He is perhaps most famous as the king who built the magnificent palace of Versailles; ten thousand people lived at the chateau of Versailles, and the court revolved around Louis like planets around the Sun. Although tender towards his Queen, Maria Theresa, he was a rampant womanizer and was known for his endless list of mistresses and conquests.

At his best, Louis demonstrated all the greatest strengths of the Sun: He was adored by his subjects and governed humanely; was ardently devoted to his kingdom, his beliefs, the arts, entertainment, and luxury; was passionate, sexual, and sensual; ruled with limitless authority and was known for his extravagant kindnesses. However, Louis also demonstrated the greatest weaknesses of the Sun: He refused to alter or admit his poor judgment when he revoked the Edict of Nantes, even when it seriously weakened France's economy and culminated in war with Protestant Europe; he demonstrated an arrogance and decadence during his reign which many historians believe began the ultimate bankruptcy of France; he behaved as though the world existed purely for his own pleasure, often letting his passions and his love affairs dictate his national decisions. Also, he had a single younger sibling, a brother named Philippe, who grew up in his shadow and was never allowed to shine, lest he diminish his older brother's brilliance. The Sun's brightness disperses the darkness, but the darkness does not comprehend it.

Element: Fire, Masculine
Rules: Leo
Minor Arcana Association: 3 Wands, 4 Pentacles, 8 Pentacles, 6 Cups, 10 Swords

Key Phrases:

- Just as the Sun of our solar system is the central life-giving force around which everything else revolves, so the Sun rules the integrity of the entire human being's system. It governs our vitality, the amount of energy available to us, and our will to live, as well as our heart and spine. Also the right eye of men and the left eye of women.
- Wherever the Sun shines its light, it disperses the darkness.
- Rules our happiness, fun, joy, and integrity, as well as the individual's ego strength, self-worth, and self-esteem.
- Signifies royal, benevolent leadership, such as kings, heroes, and fathers.
- Sexuality of a masculine nature as well as masculinity in general.
- The Sun reveals an individual's innate talents and abilities, the direction of his or her natural development and growth, along with personal flair and style.
- Rules plants that smell pleasantly, grow majestically, and love Sunlight.
- Rules grand buildings like theatres and palaces.
- Alchemically, the Sun rules gold.

Spheres: UL sphere is gray (Chokmah) while LR sphere is yellow (Tiphereth).

Path 26 indicates: Order victorious over Chaos in the realm of duality. The Son as the reflection of the Father; the Absolute in a form that can be comprehended by Humanity.

Qabalistic Symbology:

Throughout all the ancient civilizations—from Greece and Rome, to the Aztecs and the Olmecs, to Egypt and Israel, to India and Babylon—there is a consistent cosmology that seems to have been passed down through the ages in the written records and mythologies. (Some authorities even theorize that this consistency continues into the legendary lost lands of Atlantis and Lemuria, or even off of our planet entirely and into outer space.) While the Golden Dawn and Aleister Crowley often focused upon the Egyptian version of this cosmology, modern academia prefers the golden age of Greece and Rome; even the Bible focuses upon the Mesopotamian version. But archeologists and anthropologists have considerable proof that all these nations owe their civilization, writing system, architecture, astronomical knowledge, and mythology to the land of ancient Sumer, which predates each and every one of them in circa 3500 BCE.

What do these ancients all have in common? Although the names and some particulars may vary, the stories are very much the same. After universal order was created out of chaos or nothingness, a group of celestial bodies or "mighty gods" of the heavens governed who never appeared on Earth, but then the God of Thunder and Lightning (Zeus, Jupiter, Osiris, Enlil) deposed his father, the God of the Sky (Uranus for both the Greeks and the Romans, Ra, Anu), and came down from heaven to Earth to set up a new world order with eleven other "olden gods," making a grand total of twelve. The Storm God struggled to preserve his right to rule against a rival twin brother and/or a dark mother deity (turned monster) whom he only succeeded in defeating with the assistance of a goddess who "resurrected" him and/or the son who succeeded him. Although through intermarriage with each other and the "daughters of men" there were eventually many more gods and lesser deities than the primary twelve (and the actual twelve divinities often changed), at any one time this group—whether called the "Devas," the "Elohim," the "Watchers," or the "Olympians,"—generally numbered twelve, and were responsible for the creation of civilization on Earth. Thus we have the roots of the ancient struggle between the Father/Son tradition of light and the Mother/Son tradition of darkness.

The Path of the Sun card represents the influence of Chokmah (the Father of the Star Universe) upon Tiphereth (the Son); now, he descends to take up his office in Tiphereth, as the Son of the Father. Historically, there was a split between the followers of the Father/Son (the Tradition of Light) and the followers of the Shadow Brother/Dark Mother (the Tradition of Darkness) in how to configure the division of time; the Tradition of Light calculated 365 ¼ days in a year by the procession of the equinoxes, while the Tradition of Dark based their (shorter) year upon the Dog-Star. In this card, we have the royal twins, the Two Traditions; the true king at the center of the card represents the correct theory, as the shadow of the reflected king represents the flawed theory. (Historically, although the Mother/Son tradition has continued underground and in the shadows, it only gained precedence for a time. The Father/Son tradition has been the central focus throughout the ages.) Chokmah is the Root of Fire and this card is called "The Lord of the Fire of The World," showing the Sun as representative of the star universe while ruling the Kingdom of Malkuth. This is the Path of the Tradition of Light; the Crowned King, the Son of the Sun, who has overcome Death and is the ruler of this age. The Sun opposes the Path of the Devil…but only in this realm of duality.

20 The Judgment

– Pluto –
Path 30: Tiphereth to Kether
Shin – ש : Tooth / 300 / Sh

Astrological Meaning: The Transformer

The Personality of Pluto:

Here we have the Sorcerer to whom Mercury (The Magician) plays apprentice. Pluto understands the secret forces of the world and how to manipulate them; he commands total power and knowledge of the nature of existence, and his amoral lack of concern for the dualities of black and white, evil and good, or wrong and right horrifies us. He eliminates that which is no longer useful with a daunting singleness of purpose, and has no time for emotional relationships or idle chitchat. It is fitting that this planet was named after the Roman god of the Underworld, for he rains down Hell upon us in order to restore us to Heaven. He is not unlike the two-faced Janus, Roman god of gates and doorways, with one face evil and the other face good. It seems appropriate that, in Greek mythology, Persephone is his queen: She who lives with her husband, Hades, for six months in the Underworld as life is destroyed on Earth by her absence, so that she may return to the surface for six months bringing springtime, life, and renewal. Why, even as Pluto orbits around the Sun, from Earth's vantage point the planet appears to travel forward six months and then travel backwards for six months. Pluto understands the glory of power for power's sake; whether that power creates, preserves, or destroys matters little in his greater context. Nothing repulses him as he digs deeply into the bowels of the Earth and the filth of our secrets to uncover the truth, the legendary philosopher's stone, eliminating everything blocking his intentions. His ways are beyond us, for they do not acknowledge our small illusions of how life is supposed to be.

Element: Fire, Androgynous
Rules: Scorpio (classical astrologers consider Pluto to share rulership with Mars)
Minor Arcana Association: Wands Suit (Fire)

Key Phrases:

- Pluto is the purifying fire that burns away all the refuse in order to bring the truth to light; it exerts tremendous pressure on the coal of our lives (and on humanity as a whole) to transform us into the diamond we're meant to be. Rules the need for change, purification, elimination, regeneration, crisis, and renewal.
- Pluto rules the Underworld, and therefore governs anything deliberately hidden, such as criminality, pornography, psychological warfare, or espionage.
- Pluto behaves amorally and unethically, thus it influences us to act without concern for rules, authority, or consequences; hence, it rules our darker urges and compulsions.
- Rules toilets, garbage, and waste. Also rules radiation—in that it burns through the cancer to bring forth new life—as well as plutonium, nuclear power, live bombs, and radiation poisoning.
- Rules the final decision, judgment, sentence, or determination of a matter without appeal in the material plane.
- Rules plutocracies, taxes, and exorbitant amounts of money (since excessive riches are rarely obtained through principled means). Rules the depravity of the mob, networks, the corporate world, insurance, and banking.
- Pluto is not so much a personal planet, as a planet of generations, mass society, and large populations. For Pluto, the progression of humanity as a whole outweighs the concerns of the individual.
- Rules the power of survival, of inevitable transformations, of beginnings and endings, of births and deaths. Rules sexual reproduction, in the sense that it is the process by which life regenerates itself and survives beyond death. Rules the sex glands, the organs of elimination, and the DNA found in cells. Also, the essential but unconscious bodily functions.

Spheres: UL sphere is white (Kether) while LR sphere is yellow (Tiphereth).
Path 30 indicates: The cleansing powers of fire and transformation. The Resurrection of Spirit and the Regeneration of Matter; the Everlasting One entering Manifestation.

Qabalistic Symbology:

Judgment is the Path from Kether to Tiphereth, that of the influence of the Supreme and Concealed Father of All becoming manifested in the Son in who Glory and Suffering are an identical and integral part of transformation. This card is attributed to the Hebrew letter Shin, the true fire of the Spirit, and the progenitor of the Sun behind the Sun; it is the cleansing powers of fire.

The influence of this Path scours the world, causes the Dead to rise in the Resurrection of pure Spirit and the Regeneration of Matter. It passes through the Path of the Star as the Child of Chokmah and Binah overcomes Death. It is the Path of the everlasting One entering Manifestation, and it represents the Absolute and Universal Tradition of the golden age. The old spiritual points of view of the previous ages are now burned away and purified on this Path. The Paths of the Sun and the Devil are man's attempts to discover the true motions and order of the world, and to translate them into time; this Path actually regulates these motions, the true calculation of the course of the whole solar system round the invisible Center of All. This represents the roots of the elements—the essences of Kether, Chokmah, and Binah—concentrated in Tiphereth.

21 The World

– Saturn –
Path 32: Binah to Kether
Tau – ת : Mark, Signature, Cross / 400 / Th

Astrological Meaning: The Limiter

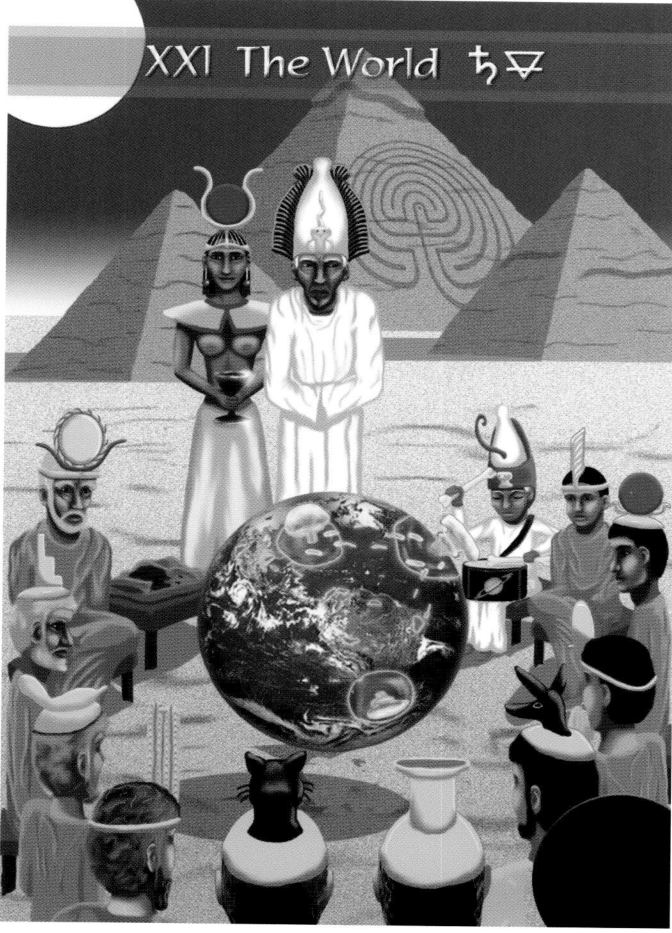

The Personality of Saturn:

Saturn is the ultimate caricature of how the average U.S. citizen imagines the Director of the Internal Revenue Service. He is the antiquated keeper of all accounts, who is cold, meticulous, pessimistic, and solitary by virtue of his unpopular duty. Severe and austere, he speaks little but notices and tallies everything; nevertheless, he communicates quite competently when it is time for a citizen to face his financial consequences and "pay up." He patiently acquires his own earthly goods by carefully following the rules in steady stages, and enforces the regulations without exception. He is of nondescript height and build, a pallid complexion, a melancholy disposition, with black pits for eyes. Most of us grumble and complain about what he takes from us and how he limits our enjoyment of our lives, but we forget that without him there would be no public services, no law to protect us, and no defense against foreign interests.

Element: Earth, Masculine
Rules: Capricorn, Aquarius (classical astrologers consider Saturn to share rulership of Aquarius with Uranus)
Minor Arcana Association: 5 Wands, 10 Wands, 7 Pentacles, 8 Cups, 3 Swords, Pentacles Suit (Earth)

Key Phrases:

- According to classical astrologers, Saturn is called the Greater Infortune or Malefic; for thousands of years this planet presided over the outermost limits of the solar system as man knew it (until the comparatively recent discovery of the three outer planets) and thus it ruled boundaries and limits (as Time is the great limiter of the human condition). The World card however, represents Saturn at his best. Saturn teaches us the cosmic lesson that as you limit yourself or are limited by outside circumstances, so will you grow.
- Saturn rules responsibility, duty, order, honor, work, discipline, and tradition.
- Rules the loss of flexibility, hardening, and weighing down of any issue; therefore, it rules old age and persistence, for as the body ages, we place the purpose of endurance as paramount and begin to fear new change and growth.
- Saturn rules governments and their resources, rules, laws, and regulations.
- Governs older men, fathers, solitary religious people, and beggars. Relates to those who work with the earth, such as farm laborers, miners, and plumbers who work with lead; also lead and lead poisoning.
- Represents world events, the Kingdom of Earth, and the physical universe; moreover, the matter under consideration and the synthesis of all the elements.
- Rules the skeleton, knees, teeth, deafness, and any illnesses caused by cold, melancholy, fears, or old age. Also the skin (as it protects us).
- Rules any location that is earthy, dirty, harsh, cold, or dark, such as deserts, deep pine forests, obscure valleys, church yards, holes, ruins, and graves; also rules places that set

boundaries, like eaves, doors, fences, and thresholds.

- Alchemically, Saturn rules lead.

Spheres: UL sphere is white (Kether), while LR sphere is black (Binah).

Path 32 indicates: The synthesis of the life force (Father) with the substance of all things (Mother) to produce the Living Substance (Son) from which all patterns of existence (Daughter) proceed; the Whole Self returns to the suffering world with the Elixir of Life.

Qabalistic Symbology:

The World corresponds to Saturn, Cronos, or Time. It represents the early Egyptian tradition of Sut, who later became identified with Set or Satan. Here we have the beginning of the Tradition of the Fatherless Child and the Mother, the Sut-Typhonian Mystery. This card introduces the dual son, Sut-Horus, as Darkness and Light and the Two Horizons. The Pharaoh in *The Kingdom Within Tarot* card represents the beginning of the time cycle, for Saturn was the Devourer of his children, the Hours. This card is called "The Great One of the Night of Time." In this Path "The Light shines in the Darkness, but the Darkness can not comprehend it," for the children of time know not the mystery of the Here and Now.

Within the World card is the synthesis of the elemental forces, both positive and negative. It manifests the influences from the Crown (Kether) that resulted in the formation of the Sphere of Saturn (the Limiter) or the Sephirah Binah (the Great Mother, also called the Great Sea). All is said to have been produced from the Water brooded over by Spirit. Binah is the Sphere of the substance of all things, and it balances that of Chokmah wherein is concentrated the Life Force. Together they represent Living Substance, the Father-Mother from which all proceeds. Everything manifested in the physical universe is the crystallized pattern of a pattern of a pattern: The world of Action (Assiah) is based upon the patterns of the Formative World (Yetzirah) which emanate from the Creative World (Briah) from the pattern of the Archetypal World (Atziluth). Sacred Geometry reveals these patterns that form the foundation of the oneness of existence amid diversity.

The Kingdom Within Tarot card depicts the union of Osiris (the Pharaoh and Father) with Isis (his Queen and Purified Bride) as well as the fruit of their union, Horus (the True Sun/Son who has mastered the drum of Saturn and reigns supreme outside the prisons of the physical universe). However, with enlightenment and salvation one becomes a Savior, and so it is time for the Whole Self to return to the World with the Elixir of Life (contained in the image of the Holy Grail in the hands of Isis).

Remember the conclusion of Herman Hesse's *Siddhartha*: Once Siddhartha achieves enlightenment by the side of the river, he himself becomes the ferryman who carries others from the bank of suffering within the illusion of time and separateness, across the river of life, to the far shore of freedom and oneness with all.

This is the final Path on the Tree of Life, for now the Transformed Spirit has crossed the Abyss, integrating all the disparate parts and remembering the True Self that was once shattered throughout this lifetime and eternity, and discovered Ecstasy beyond both the darkness of understanding and the light of wisdom. For the few who discover the Kingdom Within, the Center of All, the Ever-coming Crowned Child, the World is neither an illusion nor a prison, but truly becomes the Kingdom of Heaven. This is the final Path of Integration, Return, and Redemption of The World.

Restored Tree of Life with the Major Arcana

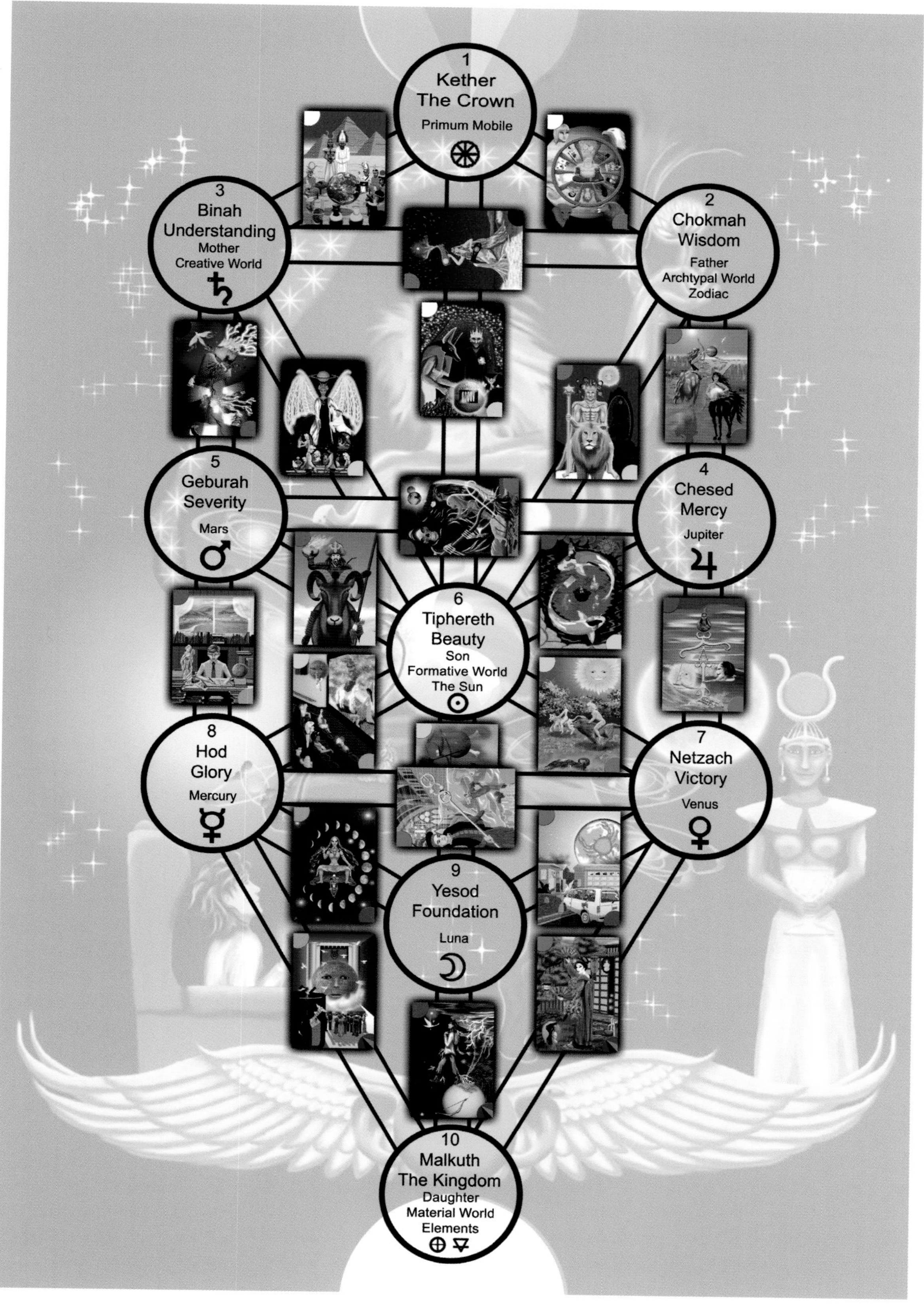

Finally, let us consider one addition to the traditional Tarot deck—a card of my own making, and included here for your contemplation.

Kingdom Within All

No Path or Planetary Attribution
No Hebrew Letter

Beyond the Confines of Astrology:

It might seem odd to find this unique, unnumbered Major Arcana card within an otherwise conventionally structured Tarot deck like *The Kingdom Within Tarot*; perhaps its image even vaguely reminds the reader of the traditional World (or Universe) card because of the bi-gender nature of the central figure. However, here any similarities cease.

While immersing myself in the energies of the Tarot, I eventually recognized the need for an additional card to thoroughly explore the Kingdom Within. Our modern conception of existence has expanded exponentially since the arrangement of the Tarot deck was, for the most part, standardized, and although some Tarot creators have attempted to reinterpret the cards to allow for the vast distances traveled by the human race in past years, something always seems lost to me in attempting to merge too many factors into the established twenty-two Major Arcana cards.

The traditional World card initially depicted the Renaissance vision of the restored Soul of the World; as our conception of the solar system progressed past the belief that Saturn marked the outer limits with the Earth as its center, to an emphasis upon the Vast Universe (literally one verse) with its solar systems and galaxies as an infinite whole, the World card was reinterpreted as the Universe card. Now, with the advent of quantum physics, our conception of One Grand Universe has been shattered into the model of the Mulitverse, wherein simultaneous possibilities, from the infinitely immense to the illimitably microscopic, abound.

On the other hand, some might suggest that the Kingdom Within All card can be subsumed within the energy of Trump 0, The Fool. After all, the Fool represents Zero, the Qabalistic triple veil of the negative (see the introduction to Chapter Three for more information), and represents each one of us, for the Pure Fool is everything, but doesn't know it—already has everything needed, but doesn't see it. However, the Fool brings us back to the Kingdom Within the Here and Now, or Hadit, while the Kingdom Within All shows us what happens AFTER Nuit and Hadit are reunited. (The central figure in this card—Ardhnarishwara, the Hindu hermaphroditic deity who is half Shiva and half Shakti—is surrounded by both the Fool from Trump 0 and Isis from Trump 21, but they are simply elements of the Kingdom Within All.)

From both an Astrological and Qabalistic point of view, there IS existence outside of the confines of the Zodiac and the Tree of Life, respectively. While the World (or Universe) card represents ultimate ascension both Astrologically and Qabalistically, there are still those whom we have called Master…Bodhisattva… Buddha…Christos....those watchers (or referees) who have expanded upwards…downwards…inwards… outwards; who are beyond playing even the game of enlightenment itself, for they ARE the Symphony of the Spheres and the Tree of Life…the Kingdom Within All.

Key Phrases:

- Worlds upon worlds (universes within universes) of infinite possibility.
- Change—creation, preservation, destruction—expansion and contraction—is the only constant of the physical universe. As creator, releases all creations from obligation, giving each the freedom to be what it is. As preserver, allows life to grow and transform as it will. As destroyer, terminates without regret or malice.
- Plays whichever roles or archetypes are required to achieve a particular goal; is able to be pan-deterministic (acting to satisfy the dynamics of each and all) as well as self-deterministic (acting to satisfy one's own dynamics) as opposed to being other-determined (being determined by another's self-determinism).
- Perspicacity Incarnate: perspicacity in usually defined as insight, wisdom, and sagacity, its antonym being dense. Literally, per-space-ity is the state of perceiving spaces within spaces, the opposite of being quagmired within the density of matter and the limitations of space (and therefore time). One is insightful, wise, and sagacious to the degree that one can perceive infinite spaces; one is slow, stupid, and dense to the degree that one is limited in perception of space. To quote author Geoffrey Filbert, "Time and its perception remain a substitute for space" (Filbert 1982, 792).
- Holographic Universe: every part contains the whole in its entirety. The larger the part, the clearer the image of the whole. Microcosm of the macrocosm—as above, so below. Synchronicity.
- Vibration, Frequency, and Resonance: all things in this physical universe vibrate. The rate of this vibration is called frequency. The slower the vibration, the denser the thing will appear. All things are composed of wave/particles, and may appear as either one or the other, either a wave or a particle, depending upon the subjective perspective from which the thing is viewed. The observer is just as important in determining the outcome of phenomena as the thing which is observed. When two things are vibrating at the same frequency, energy is shared between them—each affecting the other by resonance. Higher frequencies eradicate lower frequencies, and lower frequencies disorganize higher ones.
- The Actual, the Idea, the Virtue, the Purity, or the Essence—in contrast to the unending Mobius of duality (right/wrong, good/bad, beautiful/ugly, etc).
- Freedom from humanity's attempts to first grasp a-hold of a pleasant sensation, thought, or idea; then re-create it and make it last; eventually altering it beyond recognition until all that is left is an empty, evil imitation that allows no escape.
- Seeing the web of all the intersecting points of actuality—matter, energy, space, time, thought, idea—and acting (or plucking a particular string) in agreement with each (Hadit) and All That Is (Nuit), for the benefit of each and All That Is, from the will of each and All That Is, from a place of preference, rather than impulsion.
- Existence is a game made up of barriers, freedoms, and goals; all the games of the physical universe can be summed up in three verbs: being, doing, and having, with the physical universe itself serving as the fundamental barrier through matter, energy, space, and time.
- Serene and spacious, silent and still, clear without distortion.
- Recognizing that the source of all illusion, pain, and suffering is denial of what is. To the degree that an individual resents, denies, or avoids the failure to achieve one's goals, he or she will experience suffering, trauma, and *avidyā*.
- Acknowledging Ego and the Analytical Mind as the ultimate tricksters.
- The "teacher who does not teach"; it is within the static of the teacher that learners discover their own truths reflected. Pure energy provoking energy.
- Seeing that truth vanishes, while lies persist; rather than an all-or-nothing phenomenon, truth is measured in percentages and by its applicability to circumstance. Truth is not found by holding on to anything, whether beliefs or social conditioning; witnessing with both detached clarity and internal intuition, untainted by emotionalism or fixation upon achieving or attaining a particular goal.
- Symbolically, the lemniscate, the mathematical symbol for infinity, representing the balance of opposing forces; the Mobius strip, a strip of paper which is twisted and attached at both ends, forming a two dimensional surface without beginning or end; ouroboros, the circular infinity snake (or dragon) which bites its own tale, a widespread symbol among the

ancients—from the Egyptians to the Mayans to the Tibetans—of both the entire Zodiac as well as the continual cyclical renewal of life.

Beyond Qabalistic Symbology:

The Kingdom Within All has no place on the Tree of Life, for the Tree of Life simply contains the symbolic story of the fall of individuated spirit into the limitation of matter and its redemption from this fallen state. The Kingdom Within All is the static of pure being, the birth of existence, existence itself, and beyond the story of salvation and enlightenment. Purely stated, the Kingdom Within All is the essence of Divinity and Eternity inspiring the spark of all religions, philosophies, sciences, and artists. IT IS.

Chapter Two
The Court Cards

The Lords and Ladies of the Tarot

The remaining fifty-six cards in any standard Tarot deck are divided into four suits: Pentacles (also called Coins, Disks, or Diamonds), Wands (sometimes named Staves, Staffs, Rods, or Clubs), Cups (occasionally Hearts), and Swords (infrequently Spades).

Firstly, "suit" is defined as a set of matching outer garments or a costume intended for a special activity, and all the cards within a particular suit definitely share similarities in their outward appearance and purpose.

Secondly, it is a group of things used together, a set or collection, as each suit most certainly is a collection of cards to be used together.

Thirdly, it is defined as the attendance required of a vassal at his feudal lord's court or manor, which illuminates not only the medieval stereotypes of the four characters of the Court Cards, but also their place within the Tarot, for they are simultaneously subservient to the Major Arcana while being the ruling Nobles of the Minor Arcana.

There are four Court Cards in each suit of *The Kingdom Within Tarot* and most other Tarot decks: King, Queen, Prince (many standard Tarot decks prefer Knight), and Page (other common names are Princess or Knave). Some Tarot decks even call their Court by quite unique monikers; to consider Kings, for example, Crowley's *Thoth* deck changes Kings to Knights, and I've seen sundry other titles such as Father, Master, or Lord. Just as the Major Arcana represent the twenty-two powers (plus the Kingdom Within All card) that are generally *beyond* the world of men, so the Court Cards represent the powers that *rule* the world of men:

Kings, just like their medieval counterparts, have substantial power and complete support.

Queens, while they have access to the same power as their husbands the Kings, resort to more hidden, indirect methods in their wielding of it.

Princes, as the heirs apparent, have the far greater passion and virility of youth that is lacked by their elders, without the earned wisdom of experience and the resources of their parents.

Pages in medieval society were generally the younger children of a noblemen who either served as a knights' attendants as the first stage of chivalric training, or else were royal messengers and ceremonial attendants at court; thus, although Pages have little or no power in the present, there is hope for their future prospects.

The Four Core Sephiroth

More importantly, each of these four characters symbolizes the four core Sephiroth of the Tree of Life. In each of the four corners of the Court Cards you will notice a colored sphere:

> The Kings have four grey spheres (for their correlation with Chokmah, the Father) in each corner,
>
> The Queens have four black spheres (for Binah, the Mother),
>
> The Princes have four golden spheres (for Tiphereth, the Son), and
>
> The Pages have four spheres divided into equal colors of russet, navy, citrine, and olive (for Malkuth, the Daughter).

For further insight into the Qabalistic symbolism of the Court Cards, review the introduction to the Major Arcana in the previous chapter; however, to spark your memory, allow me to repeat a few sentences from that introduction:

Restored Tree of Life with the Court Cards

Chokmah (the Father) is its formal cause and Binah (the Mother) is its material cause. Malkuth (the Fallen Daughter) must unite with Tiphereth (the Son) and be raised to the throne of Binah (the Mother) to re-awaken Chokmah (the Father), so that all things are re-absorbed into Kether (the Crown) and yet continue in their evolving individual state. Rather than the retrogression of Father and the Mother simply reuniting into perfect union and thus returning to a zero state, their consummation gives birth to evolution as they go forth into matter and produce a Son and a Daughter, beginning the progressive cycle of the cosmos (and of mankind) once again.

Three Basic Interpretations

Using these four personas, there are three basic methods of interpreting the Court Cards in the querent's life:

Level of Power
Sign Correspondence
Actual People

It is crucial in an accurate reading to interpret the Court Cards *in order* of the methods as listed above. Always implement the first method of interpretation at the initial stages of a reading, *Level of Power*, and then add the second, *Sign Correspondence*, if further information is needed with regards to the Court Card. The final method, *Actual People*, should only be utilized when the first two methods have been completely exhausted, and the entire spread has been laid out for consideration.

Method One: Level of Power

The Level of Power addresses the amount of energy that is available to accomplish the matter at hand:

You may notice in the court cards of *The Kingdom Within Tarot* that the Pages in the deck are seated (Page of Swords), reclining (Page of Pentacles), kneeling (Page of Wands) or crouching low to the ground (Page of Cups); this is to visually depict the relative powerlessness of a Page: there's not enough behind the issue to carry it to fruition in its current stage of development.

The Princes in the deck, on the other hand, are in the act of jumping or leaping; they have a much greater level of power than the Pages, but any ventures must be completed quickly because Princes accomplish their tasks alone, with little support from others: their power does not endure.

Because Queens represent latent, passive, concealed power, they are all standing, yet partially concealed by something: the Queen of Pentacles by a hooded cloak; the Queen of Wands by a rainbow; the Queen of Cups by the hands of her husband, Uranus; the Queen of Swords by the veil that separates this world from the afterlife. A Queen's power is formidable, but for some reason her energy is trapped, bubbling beneath the surface, waiting to give birth or manifest an undertaking. Queens often communicate a need to remain dormant in a given situation: it is prudent to wait instead of act.

Each of the Kings, in contrast, is active and riding a mighty steed that displays the characteristics akin to his Suit; Kings portend enduring strength that is wholly supported to accomplish all goals. A King usually predicts great success in the endeavor under discussion.

Method Two: Sign Correspondence

The next enlightening method of interpreting the Court Cards is their Sign Correspondence. Each Tarot suit has three corresponding astrological signs:

Pentacles are the **earth** signs Taurus, Virgo, and Capricorn;

Wands are the **fire** signs Aries, Leo, and Sagittarius;

Swords are the **air** signs Gemini, Libra, and Aquarius;

Cups are the **water** signs Cancer, Scorpio, and Pisces.

The twelve astrological signs of the zodiac are really the four elements (or states of matter) of the universe:

Fire (plasma)
Air (gas)
Water (liquid)
Earth (solid)

—combined with the three expressions of energy—

START (a scattering, dispersal, or release of energy in all directions)

CHANGE (directed flow of movement or action)

STOP (friction, opposition, or blockage)

— and the three categories of astrological signs (**Cardinal**, **Mutable**, or **Fixed**)—

The **Cardinal Signs** of the Zodiac (Aries, Cancer, Libra, and Capricorn) are goal-oriented and focused upon accomplishing a specific task through direct action or *doing*, *changing* energy from one point in space to another point along a straight line.

The **Mutable Signs** (Gemini, Virgo, Sagittarius, Pisces), in contrast, demonstrate a general all-directions *start* of energy either from or to a point in space; they have a rapid, constantly fluctuating viewpoint that is primarily concerned with *being*.

The final four signs, the **Fixed Signs** (Taurus, Leo, Scorpio, Aquarius), display a stubborn holding position of *having* as their energy movements conflict directly with themselves or others, forming a standing wave or mass, a *stop*.

To integrate all this information:

Pages STOP action.
Pages signify the Fixed Sign in a particular suit; thus, the Page of Pentacles is Taurus, the Page of Wands would be Leo, the Page of Swords would be Aquarius, and the Page of Cups is Scorpio: the Pages express the energy of their equivalent element by causing some sort of stop.

Princes START action.
Princes share characteristics with the Mutable Sign in their elemental suit, combining their matching element with the energy expression of starting.

Queens and Kings CHANGE action.
Sharing the traits of the Cardinal sign in their elemental suit, they combine the energy of changing with the corresponding element of their suit. The difference between the action of a Queen and a King of the same suit is the DIRECTION of the change: Queens are passive, representing the *other* in the energy transaction, while Kings are active in their manifestation of the suit's energy, the *originator* of the outflow of energy.

Thus, we discover the method in which energy is manifesting in our lives through the Court Cards.

On each of the Kingdom Within All Court Cards, to the left of the character's name you will see the astrological symbol for the astrological sign associated with that character, and to the right you will find one of the following three symbols:

A symbol of a *solitary arrow* pointing to the *right*→ for a **change outwards** (or outchange) and pointing to the *left*← for a **change inwards** (or inchange),
A *circle of lines* (for **start**) ✲

An *arrow pointing towards a line* (for **stop**) ⇥

Method Three: Actual People

The final, and by far the most widespread, interpretation of the Court Cards are as Actual People in the querent's life:

A Page is generally a child or maiden.

Princes are young men (or occasionally young women), usually single, under the age of forty—a person who is actively seeking, but hasn't yet attained, a complete sense of self.

An older woman—or any woman, at any age, who has given birth—is represented by a **Queen**.

Any older man, or highly successful man, is signified by a **King**.

Each person displays the characteristics of the corresponding Tarot suit:

Wands talk about matters of creativity, desire, and power.

Pentacles discuss the resources (usually career and money) to attain one's goals.

Cups deal with the inner realms of emotion, intuition, love, and mysticism.

Swords focus on the demesnes of the mind, communication, and conflict.

For instance, the Queen of Swords might be an older, intelligent divorcee. The Page of Wands could be a precocious, creative child. If the querent has a wealthy, successful father, he would appear in the reading as the King of Pentacles, while a charming suitor who's pursuing the querent could appear as the Prince of Cups.

If the querent knows the sun sign or ascendant from the natal chart of the important people in his or her life, this can reveal further insight. The King of Cups would be a successful older man who is emotionally mature and spiritually grounded, but if the querent knows two men who fit this description, then the one with a water sign (Cancer, Scorpio, or Pisces) for his sun sign or ascendant would be the correct individual. However, knowledge of sun signs and ascendants are not necessary, and should only be referred to when there are multiple people who seem to fit the personality of the particular Court Card.

Reversed Court Cards

If a Court Card is reversed, it does not represent an actual person in the querent's life, but instead either characterizes the energy that emanates from the querent, or else suggests that the querent is thinking of or concerned about a person whom the Court Card characterizes.

Card Analysis Classification

For each Court Card you will find the following information:

Name of Court Card: Character
Archetype and its Significance
Dynamic of Existence
Method One: Level of Power
Method Two: Astrological Association
Type of Sign
Energy of Sign
Personality of Sign (Similar to the **Major Arcana description of the characteristics** of a strengthened sign in an astrological chart)
Method Three: Actual People

Archetypes

The characters associated with each of the Court Cards are symbolic archetypes drawn from the rich, fertile history of our own western myths, religions, and literature. As archetypes, each reveals an *image, ideal, or pattern that has come to be considered a universal model of humanity*. Initially, Jungian psychology introduced the concept that there are seven major archetypes, each based upon a Greek god or goddesses, which arise from the reoccurring images of the collective unconscious of humanity as a whole (Jung 1971). Caroline Myss, author of *Sacred Contracts*, has built upon Jung's ideas and considerably expanded the scope of archetypes. If you shuffle through the Court Cards of any random sampling of Tarot decks, you will find quite a spectrum of archetypes portrayed; to minimize confusion, I have used the images from the *The Kingdom Within Tarot* deck, as they have been deliberately crafted to reveal the basic archetypes upon which each Court Card is based. (For more information on archetypes, please read both Jung and Myss; the corresponding archetypes of the sixteen characters of the Court Cards were created from their rich material.) Although archetypes saturate the entire Tarot deck, we can use the sixteen archetypes of the Court Cards to help recognize *the basic patterns and roles that we naturally enact when incarnated into a physical body.*

The danger of any archetype is mistakenly over-identifying with it, falsely believing that we are actually the "face" of any given archetype, rather than seeing that it is simply a role played by our spirit in order to accomplish some desired result in the material realm.

Pentacles:

King of Pentacles: Father Time
Archetype: Capitalist, Authority, Destroyer

Queen of Pentacles: Mary, the Virgin Mother
Archetype: Channel, Queen, Pilgrim

Prince of Pentacles: The Oak King (Holly King)
Archetype: Critic, Martyr, Rival

Page of Pentacles: The Newborn King
Archetype: Eternal Child, The Rock, Epicure

Wands:

King of Wands: Jesus Christ
Archetype: Hero, Wounded Healer, God

Queen of Wands: Eostre
Archetype: Goddess, Creator, Artist

Prince of Wands: Dionysus
Archetype: Philosopher, Rebel, Player

Page of Wands: Mary Magdalene
Archetype: Prostitute, Seductive Muse, Seeker

Cups:

King of Cups: The Green Man
Archetype: Counselor, Father, Protector

Queen of Cups: Gaia
Archetype: Mother, Healer, Avenger

Prince of Cups: Sir Galahad
Archetype: Mystic, Innocent, Romantic

Page of Cups: Faerie Puck
Archetype: Trickster, Shape-Shifter, Spy

Swords:

King of Swords: Mictlantecutli
Archetype: Mentor, Sage, Advocate

Queen of Swords: Hecate
Archetype: Witch, Crone, Scapegoat

Prince of Swords: The Lord of Misrule
Archetype: Storyteller, Clown, Thinker

Page of Swords: Persephone
Archetype: Victim, Damsel, Ingénue

Minor Arcana Connection

When you begin your study of the Minor Arcana, you may notice that the characters from the Court Cards of *The Kingdom Within Tarot* pictorially play a major role in the Minor Arcana cards that correspond to his or her suit. (For example, Father Time, the King of Pentacles, is the central figure in the illustration of the Two of Pentacles.) While their involvement in the Minor Arcana often mirrors each character's actual myth, there are some Minor Arcana cards in which a character is used to portray the *meaning* of the card, rather than relate a moment from the character's own story. (For example, Hecate, the Queen of Swords, portrays the Goddess mourning the deceased God in the 3 of Swords—not a chapter from her own mythology, but vital to understanding the energy of this card and the mythological cycle story of the suit.)

Seasons and Celebrations

Also, you will probably notice while you study the Court Cards and the Minor Arcana that each Tarot suit corresponds to a particular season in the year's cycle:

Pentacles are set in Winter
Wands are set in Spring
Cups are set in Summer
Swords are set in Autumn

On the wheel of the zodiac, the Sun enters the constellation of Aries (the cardinal fire sign) at the start of Spring, travels through Cancer (the cardinal water sign) during Midsummer, journeys through Libra (the cardinal air sign) during the season of Autumn, and enters Capricorn (the cardinal earth sign) in Winter; thus, each suit is set in its corresponding astrological season of the year:

Wands are fiery, a time of resurrection and rebirth as the sleeping Earth awakens and bursts forth with new life and promise;

Cups are watery, a time for the fecund Earth to present us with her bounty as we vacation, relax, and celebrate all the riches that the year has produced, heavy with our treasures;

Swords are airy, for with the coming of Autumn we face shorter days, beautiful endings in both gorgeous sunsets and multi-colored falling leaves, and the destruction of the Earth's excesses;

Pentacles are earthy, as the Sun is little with us and the Earth withdraws into herself for her winter hibernation as she awaits the returning strength of the Sun in springtime.

Within the illustrations of *The Kingdom Within Tarot* deck, the characters' mythological traditions correlate to the time-honored events and significances that represent the seasonal celebrations and customs attributed to their suit; for instance, just as Springtime focuses upon the renewal of the Sun and the Earth, so the King of Wands (Jesus Christ) and the Page of Wands (Mary Magdalene) represent central figures in the Christian celebration of Easter; meanwhile, Eostre (the Queen of Wands) is the Anglo-Saxon goddess of Springtime, and Dionysus (the Prince of Wands) represents the ancient Greek mystery cycle of resurrection and transformation.

Please Note: Since I live north of the Earth's equator, the seasons of the four suits of this deck correlate to the seasons as I have experienced them during my lifetime. If you live south of the equator (such as in Australia), your seasons are opposite to those above.

The 16 Dynamics of Existence

Just as the second level of interpreting the Court Cards reveals the method in which energy is manifesting in our lives, so the Court Cards also indicate the sixteen essential motivations that drive an individual to act, called the *Dynamics* by Geoffrey Filbert in his pioneering book, *Excalibur Revisited* (Filbert 1982). Because these basic motivations are progressive, each dynamic can be seen at its most rudimentary form in one of the Court Cards. Each dynamic with its corresponding Court Card, in order of its evolution, is as follows:

The Sixteen Dynamics of Existence:

Dynamic:	Court Card:
1. Self	Page of Cups
2. Sex, family	Page of Wands
3. Groups	Page of Pentacles
4. Mankind	Page of Swords
5. All Life Forms	Queen of Cups
6. The Physical Universe	Queen of Pentacles
7. Thought	Queen of Swords
8. God, Infinity, All That Is	Queen of Wands
9. Aesthetics	King of Cups
10. Ethics (Rationality)	King of Swords
11. Decency	King of Pentacles
12. Truth	King of Wands
13. Awareness	Prince of Pentacles
14. Individuality	Prince of Wands
15. Coexistence	Prince of Swords
16. Spirit that is non-being	Prince of Cups

It might surprise the reader to discover that Princes represent higher dynamics than Queens and Kings, but the further one travels beyond the urges and concerns of the physical universe, the less stable (less persisting, less material) one becomes. As one moves from the sixteenth to the first dynamic, the tendency is to become more solid, and thus START—an action that may be created out of nothingness—is followed by CHANGE—an action that requires something substantial to exist in the first place that can thereby be changed—which is followed by STOP; each step is progressively more solidified. As you have the trend of getting smaller and more dense, one moves from Being (Princes/ Start) to Doing (Kings and Queens/ Active and Receptive Change) to Having (Pages / Stop).

The Myers-Briggs® Connection

It has also been suggested by popular writers on the Tarot that the sixteen Court Cards match up nicely to the sixteen personality types of the Myers-Briggs Type Indicator® (MBTI®) personality test. Simply put, the MBTI® (based upon the work of psychologist Carl Jung) introduces four main criteria for classifying people—

Introvert (I) vs. Extrovert (E):
The source and direction of a person's energy.

Intuition (N) vs. Sensing (S):
The method of information perception.

Thinking (T) vs. Feeling (F):
How a person processes information.

Perceiving (P) vs. Judging (J):
How a person implements the processed information.

These criteria in turn produce four basic human temperaments and sixteen personality or character types. Each of the four temperament may be assigned to a Court suit, based upon the core temperaments: *SJ, SP, NF,* and *NT*. For those who are interested in utilizing this additional aspect of the Court Cards, the correlations are as follows:

Pentacles

The Guardians of Society (SJs), Who Primarily Use Their Experiences and Senses…

King of Pentacles: ESTJ
Extraversion/ Sensing/ Thinking/ Judging

ESTJs enforce and supervise by nature; focusing their energies outwards, they are most comfortable dealing with facts, logical structures, and common sense as they build and establish reality.

Queen of Pentacles: ISFJ
Introversion/ Sensing/ Feeling/ Judging

ISFJs nurture and protect; focusing their energies inwards, out of their quiet, conscientious observations of those around them they are able to offer clarity and remain grounded in the most extreme situations.

Prince of Pentacles: ISTJ
Introversion/ Sensing/ Thinking/ Judging

ISTJs inspect and discriminate; focusing their energies inwards, they stress clear knowledge and trust their previous experiences to supply them with the basis for reliable progress.

Page of Pentacles: ESFJ
Extraversion/ Sensing/ Feeling/ Judging

ESFJs help and provide; focusing their energies outwards, they are encouraging and work to build security and personal Harmony.

Wands

The Artisans of Society (SPs), Who Primarily Use Their Creativity and Initiative...

King of Wands: ESTP
Extraversion/ Sensing/ Thinking/ Perceiving

ESTPs are adventurous entrepreneurs who make things happen; directing their energies outwards, they courageously take on challenges, solve problems, and actualize their ideas.

Queen of Wands: ISFP
Introversion/ Sensing/ Feeling/ Perceiving

ISFPs have finely tuned, aesthetic sensibilities; focused on their inner world, they excel in the fine arts and are dedicated to expressing their opinions and ideals.

Prince of Wands: ISTP
Extraversion/ Sensing/ Thinking/ Perceiving

ISTPs are adaptable gamblers who can analyze and manipulate anything; they are action oriented and cannot stand to be "tied down."

Page of Wands: ESFP
Introversion/ Sensing/ Feeling/ Perceiving

ESFPs are performers and entertainers; playful and fun-loving, they enjoy pleasureful experiences, luxuriate in arousal, and live life to the fullest.

Cups

The Idealists of Society (NFs) Who Primarily Use Their Intuition and Emotions:

King of Cups: ENFJ
Extraversion/ Intuition / Feeling/ Judging

ENFJs are teachers and counselors; they are most concerned with harmonious human relationships and make charismatic and successful group facilitators.

Queen of Cups: INFJ
Introversion/ Intuition / Feeling/ Judging

INFJs are inspirational and insightful; with an uncanny understanding of the complexities within and between people, they are the poets, the mystics, and the martyrs of this world.

Prince of Cups: INFP
Introversion/ Intuition/ Feeling/ Perceiving

INFPs are the dreamers and healers of this world; their ideals and beliefs are paramount to them and their work must have meaning or they escape into fantasy to compensate.

Page of Cups: ENFP
Extraversion/ Intuition/ Feeling/ Perceiving

ENFPs are the champions and experimenters; their lives are dedicated to the new as they constantly initiate change and focus on possibilities.

Swords

The Thinkers of Society (NTs), Who Primarily Use Their Intelligence and Reason:

King of Swords: ENTP
Extraversion/ Intuition / Thinking/ Perceiving

ENTPs are the innovators and inventors; striving for a balanced and just world, they are able to both successfully mediate change as well as challenge and improve the status quo.

Queen of Swords: INTP
Introversion/ Intuition / Thinking/ Perceiving

INTPs are both architects and magicians; they love intellectual problems and seek to understand and manipulate the people and phenomena around them.

Prince of Swords: INTJ
Introversion/ Intuition / Thinking/ Judging

INTJs are free-thinkers and masterminds; ingenious by nature, they stretch and play with ideas and conventions like taffy.

Page of Swords: ENTJ
Extraversion/ Intuition / Thinking/ Judging

ENTJs are best at motivating others to grow to new heights; they logically apply their ideals to improve and create their conceptions of a "brave new world."

Obviously, if the MBTI® method of interpreting the Court Cards is employed, then each of the sixteen Court Cards may represent either a male or female in a reading, rather than Kings and Princes representing males, Queens being females, and the Pages appearing as either. The gender of the MBTI® is spiritual, as opposed to physical. (For further information on the sixteen personality types and the Myers-Briggs Type Indicator in general, I suggest reading *Please Understand Me: Character and Temperament Types* by David Keirsey and Marilyn Bates.)

Growth in Relationships

One final aspect of the Tarot court is its ability to pinpoint our growth with regards to our human relationships. We all begin as Pages, with much promise but little power. The Page phase of life is full of wonder as we explore the world around us and (hopefully) build a solid foundation. As teenagers and young adults, when we begin to expand our horizons and discover our selves, all men and most women go through the Prince phase (some spending considerably longer in this phase than others.) As Princes we freely disperse in all directions with no particular focus or accomplishment, but we experientially learn important lessons and have tremendous fun! (Some women go directly from the Page phase to the Queen phase, but with our changing society we see this less and less.) Most men and women, however, eventually become Kings and Queens, respectively. This phase of life can be accomplished in one of two ways—generally through a committed partnership with another, but some choose the road of singleness, instead going within and uniting the masculine and feminine within oneself. Generally, a man becomes a King by uniting with a Queen (and a woman becomes a Queen by uniting with a King, but this may also happen within single-sex relationships or within oneself as well). This union brings wholeness to the individual's life, the King supplying the dynamic force and the Queen supplying the creative substance so that the Prince may stop wildly dispersing in all directions and now begin to accomplish his or her goals, and the Page can leave the life of being nurtured by others and instead discover self empowerment in the role of nurturer. It is always interesting to consider how you are conducting yourself in a given relationship—as a Page, a Prince, a King, or a Queen—and whether or not this is the best place to be for all involved. From a Qabalistic perspective, this progressive union needs not only to be experienced in our relationships with others, but most importantly in our relationship with our self.

The Pentacles Court

King of Pentacles

– Father Time –

Archetype: Capitalist, Authority, Destroyer

Significance of the Archetype:

In our contemporary New Year's celebration, Father Time is the ancient watcher of the passing hours of the old year who is replaced at midnight by the Baby New Year. This tradition, of course, is easily traceable back to the Greek god Cronos, as the Lord of Time who slowly cuts away (or kills) the hours of humanity. Old Father Time rules the material realm as he determines the lifespan of everything in it—our jobs, our possessions, our relationships, our lives, and even our world.

Dynamic: Decency

Level of Power:

The power, the support, and the resources are available for success in any financial, career, or material endeavor.

Astrological Association: Capricorn

Type of Sign: Cardinal

Energy of Sign: The King of Pentacles actively reaches outwards to the relationships, workplace, or society around him and causes others to compel him to do his duty. (Outchange of doing combined with earth element)

Personality of Sign: Hardworking, ambitious, materialistic, and efficient. Demonstrates great discipline to climb ever higher in career and social status to gain power, wealth, and authority. Controls and dominates others, or conversely uses authority to help.

Actual People: ESTJ

ESTJs enforce and supervise by nature; focusing their energies outwards, they are most comfortable dealing with facts, logical structures, and common sense as they build and establish reality.

An older man (probably married) who is successful in the areas of finances, career, and standing in society—perhaps a banker, government official, or any professional man. May have an earth sign (Taurus, Virgo, Capricorn) for his sun sign or ascendant.

Queen of Pentacles

– Mary, the Virgin Mother –

Archetype: Channel, Queen, Pilgrim

Significance of the Archetype:

Mary, the "Madonna" (from the Italian *mi donna*, "my lady"), represents the mortal (or earthly) half of Jesus Christ, who was called both the "Son of Man" and the "Son of God." In this scene she is riding towards the cave (many scholars suggest that Jesus was actually born in a cave, as was the common place to stable animals at that time) wherein she will give birth to the baby Jesus, a blessed event that Christians celebrate as "Christ-Mass" every December 25th. ("Mass" is the Christian celebration of the Eucharist, partaking in the bread and wine as the body and blood of Christ.)

The word "virgin" in ancient Greek—the language in which the New Testament was written—was most commonly used to denote an unmarried young girl. The critical misinterpretation of the word "virgin" in Isaiah 7:14 by the Septuagint was a translator's error; the Hebrew word *almah*, denoting the social and legal status of an unmarried girl, was read as the Greek *parthenos*, which actually refers to a physiological and psychological fact. (The Hebrew word for a physical virgin is *bethulah*, not *almah*.) Parthenogenesis is the conception of a child by a female without the fertilization of mortal male seed, and was most commonly used in the Greek myths to describe the many half-god, half-human children fathered by Zeus.

In Latin, the language of Rome (wherein all the events of the Gospels take place) the word for "virgin" is *virgo*, which is best translated *young girl*; if a girl was

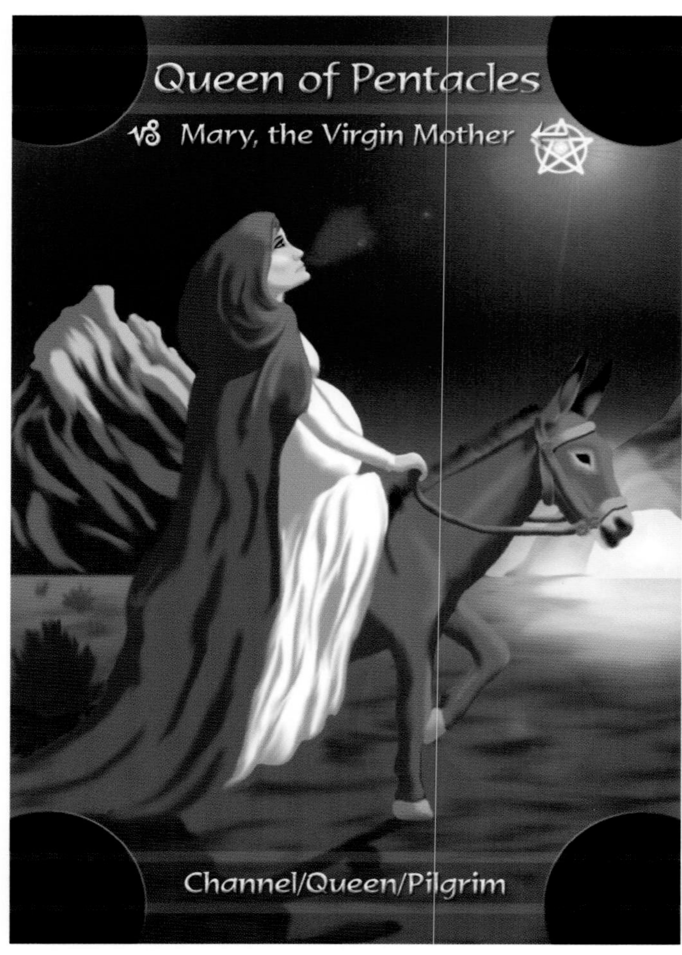

physically a virgin she was a *virgo intacta*. The singular word *virgo* was also often used as a label of power and independence that classified those goddesses who were neither owned nor beholden to any male. Often a *virgo* was a priestess to the goddess of the harvest, Demeter, in the Mediterranean temples during the golden age of Rome.

The Virgin Mother Goddess giving birth to the Newborn God King also plays a crucial part in the winter rites of the Pagan Mystery Traditions.

Dynamic: The Physical Universe

Level of Power:

The querent has the potential for financial, career, or material success, but for some reason it is not ready to manifest. It is not yet time to give birth to the matter under consideration. Remain passive.

Astrological Association: Capricorn

Type of Sign: Cardinal

Energy of Sign: The Queen of Pentacles allows others to use her as a device to force themselves to do their duty. (Outchange of doing combined with earth element)

Personality of Sign: Hardworking, ambitious, materialistic, and efficient. Demonstrates great discipline to climb ever higher in career and social status to gain power, wealth, and authority. Uses her authority and standing in the world to force others to do their duty.

Actual People: ISFJ

ISFJs nurture and protect; focusing their energies inwards, out of their quiet, conscientious observations of those around them they are able to offer clarity and remain grounded in the most extreme situations.

An older woman (or any mother) who is successful in the areas of finances, career, and standing in society. May have an earth sign (Taurus, Virgo, Capricorn) for her sun sign or ascendant.

Prince of Pentacles

– The Oak King (Holly King) –

Archetype: Critic, Martyr, Rival

Significance of the Archetype:

In Norse and Celtic mythology, the changing of the seasons is explained as a perpetual conflict between the Oak King (lord of light and the waxing year) and the Holly King (lord of darkness and the waning year). At Winter Solstice, the Oak King kills the Holly King and reigns supreme until Midsummer. The Holly King, on the other hand, is the Lord of the Winterwood who rules from Midsummer—when he kills his brother the Oak King—to Midwinter.

In the Oak King we see the image of the Green Man, Lord of the Greenwood, who represents growth and expansion, while in the Holly King we find the first Santa Claus, with his furred cloak and team of deer. The oak and the holly trees were sacred to the Druids; holly (in honor of the Holly King) and mistletoe (in honor of the Oak King) came into our modern Christmas celebrations as remembrance of this battle. Traditionally, the two kings battle for the favor of the Goddess, and although they fight as adversaries, they are really two sides of the One God.

Each king's reign represents the Earth's cycle of fertility, death, and rebirth: At Lammas, the height of the Holly King's reign, he sacrificially mates with the Great Mother, dies in her embrace, and is

resurrected, while the Oak King mates, dies, and is resurrected at Beltane. This theme of the dying and resurrecting god is found in many mythological traditions, such Osiris, Tammuz, Dionysus, Balder, and even Jesus. Vestiges of this duel can still be found in the myth of Gawain and the Green Knight from Arthurian Legend. An even older version of this myth is the battle of the Wren (associated with the Holly King) and the Robin (associated with the Oak King), who also battled twice a year—the Robin winning at Winter Solstice and the Wren winning at Midsummer.

Dynamic: Awareness

Level of Power:

There is substantial power available to the querent, but the support and resources are not there. The querent must act quickly with regards to the matter at hand, for the current potential for success in financial, career, or material endeavors will be brief. Odds are that anything undertaken at this time will not last.

Astrological Association: Virgo

Type of Sign: Mutable

Energy of Sign: The Prince of Pentacles differentiates details, discerning the differences between things from all perspectives; he considers all viewpoints as he observes every aspect of something. (Start of being combined with earth element)

Personality of Sign: Studious, astute, meticulous, critical, and practical by nature. Talented in analyzing and classifying details, with a strong instinct to prove their worth through service, sacrifice, and hard work.

Actual People: ISTJ

ISTJs inspect and discriminate; focusing their energies inwards, they stress clear knowledge and trust their previous experiences to supply them with the basis for reliable progress.

A younger, single male (probably in his twenties or thirties) who is still in the process of building his finances, career, and standing in society. May have an earth sign (Taurus, Virgo, Capricorn) for his sun sign or ascendant. Because the Prince of Pentacles is Virgo, and Virgo rules servants, this card may also represent an employee or a pet or animal in the querent's life (for our pets and animals serve us).

Page of Pentacles

– The Newborn King –

Archetype: Eternal Child, The Rock, Epicure

Significance of the Archetype:

All of creation praises the Eternal King! The Newborn King is an important archetype in midwinter: not only were many dying and resurrecting gods purportedly born on December 25th—such as Horus of Egypt, Mithra of Persia, and Jesus of Christianity—but the Sun which "died" at Winter Solstice, the shortest day of the year, is afterwards "born" as the days begin to grow longer once again. The Sun, which was "dead" in the underworld during winter, must now be reborn to return or "resurrect" in the Spring. The old has died, now the new is come.

Dynamic: Groups

Level of Power:

There is little power, support, or resources available to the querent. The financial, career, or material matter under consideration will not materialize at this time.

Astrological Association: Taurus

Type of Sign: Fixed

Energy of Sign: The Page of Pentacles attempts to pull something towards itself out of the stops of matter. (Stop of having combined with the earth element.)

Personality of Sign: Concerned with having or possessing money, valuable objects, land, and relationships. Adores beauty, sumptuous food and music, and the finer things in life, falling apart at the first sign of financial troubles.

Actual People: ESFJ

ESFJs help and provide; focusing their energies outwards, they are encouraging and work to build security and personal harmony.

A child or young woman who is struggling to establish himself or herself in the material world; often has security issues. May have an earth sign (Taurus, Virgo, Capricorn) for his sun sign or ascendant.

The Wands Court

King of Wands

– Jesus Christ –

Archetype: Hero, Wounded Healer, God

Significance of the Archetype:

The Lord Jesus Christ—the Son of Man and of God, who lived a mortal life, died on the cross (one of the oldest symbols of the intersection of the elements as well as of spiritual progression and degeneration), and defeated death as he resurrected to Eternal Life—is the perfect image for the King of Wands. Here we have the modern archetype of the resurrected Sun King, the Light of the World, who was separated from us for a time as he defeated death in the Underworld, only to return to us to light the Way.

Dynamic: Truth

Level of Power:

The querent will be victorious in any matter regarding creativity, desire, or power.

Astrological Association: Aries

Type of Sign: Cardinal

Energy of Sign: The King of Wands directly outflows energy from himself or his own viewpoint to another or a different viewpoint, simple and straight. (Outchange of doing combined with fire element)

Personality of Sign: Daring, active, impulsive, direct, courageous, and forceful. Enjoys the rush of danger, adventure, and the unknown; loves conquering anything new.

Actual People: ESTP

ESTPs are adventurous entrepreneurs who make things happen; directing their energies outwards, they courageously take on challenges, solve problems, and actualize their ideas.

An older man (probably married) who is powerful, creative, and goal-oriented; perhaps he is an artist, entrepreneur, or philosopher. May have a fire sign (Aries, Leo, Sagittarius) for his sun sign or ascendant.

Queen of Wands
– Eostre –

Archetype: Goddess, Creator, Artist

Significance of the Archetype:

Eostre is the Teutonic goddess of spring, fertility, and the East; her sacred month is April (once called "Eostremonth") and her coming is celebrated around the Vernal (Spring) Equinox with the ritual lighting of bonfires. She represents the creation and rebirth of life after the harsh winter months. She "paints" the Earth with new life every spring. Her symbols are the egg that represents rebirth, and the hare that represents fertility—the age-old ancestor of today's Easter bunny. In fact, most of the customs that we still celebrate every Easter—the theme of resurrection and new life, newborn chicks, decorated eggs, white bunnies, giving sweets and candies—are a result of the appropriation of the festival of Eostre by the Christian Church, which adopted the traditional celebrations and created "Easter," a celebration of the resurrected Christ. (Many authorities also connect the world "Easter" to Ishtar, the Sumerian goddess of love and war, whose celebration also took place at the Spring Equinox.)

Dynamic: God/Goddess, Infinity, All That Is

Level of Power:

More time is necessary before the querent pursues any areas of creativity, desire, or power; the energy is considerable, but lies dormant within the querent in some crucial way. Remain passive at this time.

Astrological Association: Aries

Type of Sign: Cardinal
Energy of Sign: The Queen of Wands receives the direct energy flow from another person or viewpoint, simple and straight. (Inchange of doing combined with fire element)
Personality of Sign: Daring, active, impulsive, direct, courageous, and forceful. Enjoys the rush of danger, adventure, and the unknown; loves being conquered.

Actual People: ISFP

ISFPs have finely tuned, aesthetic sensibilities; focused on their inner world, they excel in the fine arts and are dedicated to expressing their opinions and ideals.

An older woman (or any mother) who is powerful, creative, and goal-oriented. May have a fire sign (Aries, Leo, Sagittarius) for her sun sign or ascendant.

Prince of Wands
– Dionysus –

Archetype: Philosopher, Rebel, Player

Significance of the Archetype:

Dionysus, the bull-horned god, is known as the Greek god of dance, poetry, song, and drama, as well as wine and intoxication; but most importantly, he is the god of sacred mysticism and the cycle of death and resurrection. He purportedly traveled the world with his intoxicated female worshippers, the maenads, whom he stimulated to ecstatic frenzies of sexuality and slaughter. The most represented god in ancient art, even Homer spoke of Dionysus as one of the "olden gods." Although Dionysus was originally a Minoan god of rebirth who emphasized the sacred feminine, the Greeks eventually adopted him as the central god of their sacred rites of Eleusis. There was constant conflict between the followers of Dionysus and the followers of Apollo—the Greek god of the Sun, prophecy, healing, and music—who tried to characterize Dionysus as a god for the young and intemperate. Nietzsche in *The Birth of Tragedy* even pointed out that Dionysus' dynamic of destruction and creation greatly contrasts with Apollo, the god of light and established forms.

Dionysus is known as the "twice-born" god, for he actually had two births. His first birth was a divine one to the goddess Persephone (or Demeter in some accounts) and the god Zeus, in a cave. Jealous Hera bid her uncles, the Titans, to attack the young Dionysus, and even though he attempted to escape by turning himself into a bull, they tore him into seven pieces and cooked him in a cauldron. After the Titans devoured six of the seven pieces, Zeus discovered them and razed them with his mighty thunderbolt. Only Dionysus' heart remained unharmed.

Dionysus was "born again," however, to the mortal woman Semele when Zeus appeared to her as a mortal and impregnated her with a potion made from the heart of Dionysus. Semele asked Zeus to reveal himself to her in his true, godly form, and she was reduced to ashes by his divine fire. Zeus saved the unborn Dionysus from his mother's ashes, and stitched the fetus into his own thigh, from which Dionysus was later born. His aunt, Ino, raised him in secret, but Dionysus had the tendency to drive ordinary mortals insane; Ino eventually went mad and ran into the ocean to kill herself, but instead she was transformed into a sea goddess. As an adult, Dionysus journeyed to the Underworld and saved his mortal mother, Semele, taking her to Mount Olympus where she, just like her sister Io, became a goddess.

Because of his own resurrection, Dionysus became the god of both death and rebirth, the symbol of the divine spark in every human; his followers called him Lysios, "Redeemer." His sacred orgias (the Greek word for "divine rites") included dancing, singing, and prophesying through divine inspiration; ritual feasts wherein his followers symbolically ate of his flesh and drank of his blood; and ritual baths for the purpose of becoming a new creation, with the ultimate goal of each member awakening to his or her divine consciousness. Dionysus was the ever-coming god, and he was said to resurrect from the dead every year at his sacred rite at Delphi. The first Greek dramas were held in honor of Dionysus.

Dynamic: Individuality

Level of Power:

The querent has the passion and power to achieve his or her goals, but the resources and support are lacking. Even if immediate action is taken, it will be a struggle for any success to endure.

Astrological Association: Sagittarius

Type of Sign: Mutable

Energy of Sign: The Prince of Wands is the purest expression of a spirit incarnated in matter; he creatively outbursts his energy in all directions from himself without consideration, order, or worry. (Start of being combined with the fire element)

Personality of Sign: Carefree, playful, confident, trusting, risk-takers, and eternal optimists. Attracted to new experiences, travel, higher education, and philosophy, as well as amazingly lucky.

Actual People: ISTP

ISTPs are adaptable gamblers who can analyze and manipulate anything; they are action oriented and cannot stand to be "tied down."

A younger, single male (probably in his twenties or thirties) who is actively pursuing his goals in the areas of creation and power. May have a fire sign (Aries, Leo, Sagittarius) for his sun sign or ascendant.

Page of Wands

– Mary Magdalene –

Archetype: Prostitute, Seductive Muse, Seeker

Significance of the Archetype:

Mary Magdalene is one of the most disputed characters in the New Testament. According to the Gospels, we are told that she was from a town called Magdala, near Tiberias. Jesus exorcised her of seven demons (Luke 8:2) and, after she remained with him during his death on the cross and burial in his tomb (Mark 15:40-47), she was the first to whom he appeared after his resurrection (Mark 16:9; Matthew 28:1-9).

This, however, is where the controversy of her story begins. Pope Gregory I was the first church official to equate Mary Magdalene with the "sinner" who anointed Jesus' feet with perfume in Luke 7:37-38, as well as with Mary the sister of Martha who also anoints Jesus in John 12:3. The Eastern Orthodox Church, however, insists that these are three distinct women. Most Protestants today think that Mary Magdalene was simply a prostitute who became one of Jesus' key female followers and financial supporters.

Two Gnostic gospels discovered in 1945 amongst a collection of thirteen ancient codices and over fifty texts at Nag Hammadi in Egypt, made some startling new assertions that raise the importance of Mary Magdalene considerably. In the first, the Gospel of Mary, Jesus reveals important secret truths to Mary Magdalene, but not to Peter and the rest of the apostles; even more controversially, the Gospel of Philip suggests a more intimate view of Mary's relationship with Jesus when it records that Christ "loved Mary more" than the other disciples and kissed her often on the mouth. This—along with much speculative research concerning the myth of the Holy Grail, the Black Madonna, the French tradition of Mary Magdalene's ministry, and the Priory of Scion—has lead many to believe that Mary Magdalene was actually Jesus' wife.

Many biblical scholars have departed even further from the Christian Church's standard view by suggesting that Mary Magdalene and Mary the mother of Jesus probably served as priestesses in a Temple, either in the service of the Hebrew goddess of wisdom, *Sophia*, or in one of the many Pagan temples that proliferated in Rome at the time of Christ. Ancient pagan temples of both Old and New Testament times were populated with sacred temple "prostitutes" or *hetaerae*, who, amongst their other

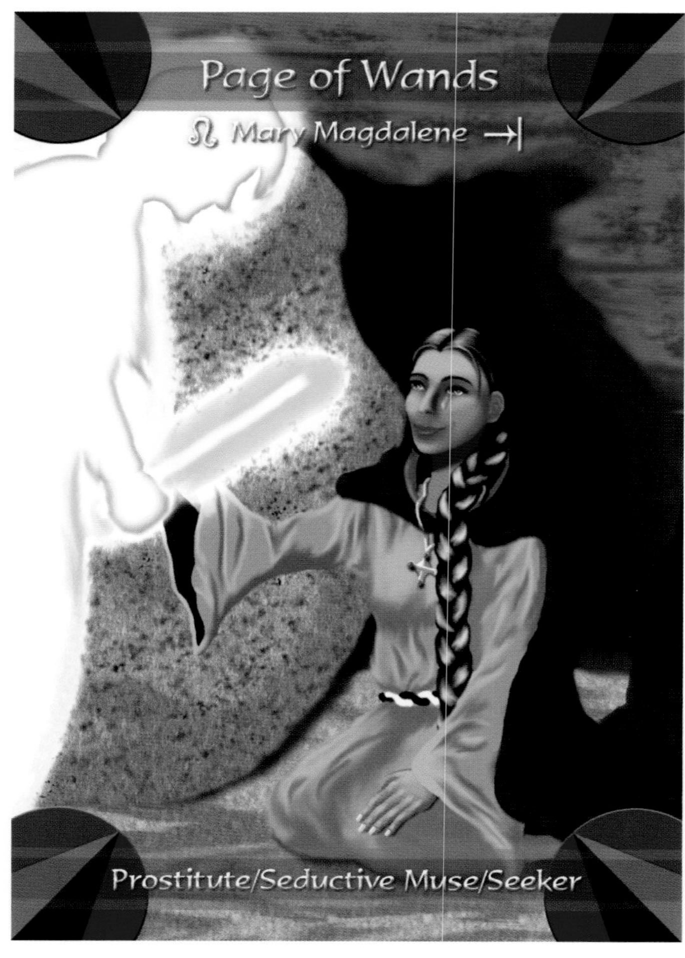

temple duties, used sexual intercourse as a rite of healing and spiritual transcendence, much like the Tantra of the Hindus. These scholars suggest that when Mary Magdalene was called a *hetaerae* back in the early centuries of Christianity, it was understood that she was a Temple Priestess, serving the Goddess. These same scholars assert that the term "Magdala" meant "high place" or "temple;" thus "the Magdalene" was actually the high priestess of the temple. When Mary anoints Jesus in the Gospels, it might have been a reenactment of the fertility rites of the ancient Middle East. In pouring the expensive perfume over the head of Jesus, "the Magdalene" would be performing the *heiros gamos*: the ceremonial anointing of the God King for the rite of "sacred marriage" between the representatives of the God and the Goddess. Even Mary's experiences at the tomb of Jesus reflect the pagan rituals surrounding the ancient myths, when the Goddess goes to the tomb in the garden to lament the death of her Bridegroom, but instead rejoices when she finds that he has resurrected.

No matter how the individual understands Mary Magdalene's role in the life of Jesus, she is a central character in the Gospel story of his ministry and resurrection.

Dynamic: Sex-Family

Level of Power:

Any matter involving creativity, passion, or power will fail at this time; the querent currently lacks what it takes to succeed. It is not yet the querent's time.

Astrological Association: Leo

Type of Sign: Fixed

Energy of Sign: The Page of Wands strongly outflows energy from himself or herself, only to be met with an equally strong outflow from the other or others; whether this stop manifests as attention or opposition, this makes the Page more solid. (Stop of having combined with the fire element.)

Personality of Sign: Charismatic, creative, proud, and craving to be the center of attention; also known for their personal panache and their love of entertainment.

Actual People: ESFP

ESFPs are performers and entertainers; playful and fun-loving, they enjoy pleasureful experiences, luxuriate in arousal, and live life to the fullest.

A young person who is struggling to express himself or herself in the areas of creativity, passion, or power; often this person is fixated upon seeking pleasure. May have a fire sign (Aries, Leo, or Sagittarius) for his or her sun sign or ascendant.

The Cups Court

King of Cups

– The Green Man –

Archetype: Counselor, Father, Protector

Significance of the Archetype:

Decorating the churches and cathedrals of Europe, as well as many pre-Christian pagan temples and graves, is the unusual carving of a human head within a mass of leaves: the "Green Man." In medieval times he was called "Jack in the Green," "Green Jack," or "Green George," and was associated with the original myths of Robin Goodfellow, Puck, and

Robin Hood, an ancient Lord of Misrule known as the "Lord of the Merry Greenwood." The Green Man danced ahead of the medieval May Queen in May Day pageants, a yearly celebration based upon the Christianization of ancient pagan spring fertility rites, still replete with hidden sexual images such as the phallic "maypole."

To the ancient Celts, he was the god of fertility, nature, and the underworld; they called him "Cernunnos," "Herne," or "The Horned One," and depicted him with the antlers of a stag. An ancient Sun god, he ruled the changing of the seasons. He was born at the winter solstice, married the goddess at Beltane (May 1st), and died at the summer solstice, wherein he ruled the underworld until his rebirth at the winter solstice; many scholars believe that his horned image was later merged with that of the Greek god Pan to create the common visual representation of the Devil for the Christian religion. The English epic poem *Gawain and The Green Knight* is a literary retelling of the Green Man, who yearly dies and is reborn.

Dynamic: Aesthetics

Level of Power:

Success is imminent in the areas of emotion, intuition, love, and spirituality.

Astrological Association: Cancer

Type of Sign: Cardinal

Energy of Sign: The King of Cups has the unique skill of pulling the whole universe towards himself, affording him remarkable emotive and intuitive abilities when dealing with others. (Outchange of doing combined with water element)

Personality of Sign: Emotional and changeable by nature, protective, romantic, nurturing, and sentimental; a wonderful counselor or confidant.

Actual People: ENFJ

ENFJs are teachers and counselors; they are most concerned with harmonious human relationships and make charismatic and successful group facilitators.

An older man (probably married) who is successful in the areas of emotion, intuition, love, and spirituality; perhaps he is a psychologist, a minister, or a nurturing husband and father. May have a water sign (Cancer, Scorpio, Pisces) for his sun sign or ascendant.

Queen of Cups

– Gaia, Mother Earth –

Archetype: Mother, Healer, Avenger

Significance of the Archetype:

The Greek philosopher, Plato, wrote that the world is in fact one living organism that possesses a psyche, or soul, and that all the individual souls of humanity are but fragments of this One Soul. The Romans called this the Anima Mundi, or World Soul.

According to the ancient Greeks, out of Chaos arose Gaia (or Ge), our bountiful Mother Earth. In some accounts she was a mystical egg from which Eros (Love) hatched, while in others she divided the sea from the sky in order to find a place to dance. From herself she created Uranus, the Starry Heavens. She married Uranus and gave birth to a race of giants, called "Titans," as well as to all living creatures. Uranus was continuously unfaithful, so she helped her youngest son, the Titan Cronos, rebel against his father and banish him to the distant heavens where he has since had little effect upon the affairs of this world; thus, Cronos became supreme ruler. Gaia transferred most of her previous responsibilities to her daughter Rhea, the wife of Cronos, and the other goddesses.

Eventually Rhea, grieved that her husband Cronos had swallowed their first five children in order to prevent one of them from usurping his throne as he had usurped his father's, turned to her mother for help in deposing him. Gaia helped hide their sixth child, Zeus, who eventually grew up to overthrow his father and become the great Sky God of Mount Olympus. Gaia prophesied through the Pythia at the Oracle of Delphi, the navel of the world, until she finally turned this sacred space over into Apollo's keeping. An earlier account calls her Eurynome, the "Goddess of All Things."

Influence of Gaia still permeates our modern culture. Even today, we speak of "Mother Earth" or "Mother Nature." The prefix "ge" in the words "geology" and "geography" is taken from the Greek word for the Earth. In the 1960's, the scientist James Lovelock proposed The Gaia Hypothesis, which states that our planet actually functions as a single organism that maintains the conditions necessary for its own survival. Some may question calling the Queen of Cups (the Water element) after Mother Earth, but remember—scientists estimate that 70-80 percent of the Earth's surface is, in fact, water.

Dynamic: All life forms

Level of Power:

Growing within the querent are potent emotions, intuition, love, and spirituality, but it is not yet time to release them upon the matter at hand. Be passive.

Astrological Association: Cancer

Type of Sign: Cardinal

Energy of Sign: The Queen of Cups passively allows herself to be pulled towards another with the rest of the universe; this ability makes her incredibly reflective and empathetic (as well as often psychic) in response to the energies of others. (Inchange combined with water element)

Personality of Sign: Emotional and changeable by nature, protective, romantic, nurturing, and sentimental. Fiercely maternal and responsive to others.

Actual People: INFJ

INFJs are inspirational and insightful; with an uncanny understanding of the complexities within and between people, they are the poets, the mystics, and the martyrs of this world.

An older woman (or any mother) who is successful in the areas of emotion, intuition, love, and spirituality. Often the Queen of Cups signifies a born psychic. May have a water sign (Cancer, Scorpio, Pisces) for her sun sign or ascendant.

Prince of Cups
– Sir Galahad –

Archetype: Mystic, Innocent, Romantic

Significance of the Archetype:

The Quest for the Holy Grail is an archetypal hero's journey that we will explore in much greater detail in Chapter Three's explanation of the symbol of the Cups Suit; Sir Galahad is the true Prince of Cups who finds the Holy Grail and, without undergoing physical death, enters the "spiritual city" because of his willingness to die to himself, or "lose himself." In Luke 9:24 Jesus said, "For those who want to save their life will lose it, and those who lose their life for my sake will save it." Reminiscent of the biblical characters Enoch and Elijah who also ascended to heaven without dying, Galahad's story is that of the being who has never lost his state of perfection and wholeness by believing the lies of the World of Matter and his own ego.

Lord Alfred Tennyson's epic poem, *Idylls of the King*, recounts the Quest for the Holy Grail through the eyes of Sir Percival the Pure. Sir Galahad was the youngest Knight of the Round Table, whom —

> "...some
> Called him a son of Lancelot, and some said
> Begotten by enchantment."

According to Tennyson, when Galahad sat in Merlin's chair, there was—

> "A cracking and a riving of the roofs,
> And rending, and a blast, and overhead
> Thunder, and in the thunder was a cry.
> And in the blast there smote along the hall
> A beam of light seven times more clear than day:
> And down the long beam stole the Holy Grail
> All over covered with a luminous cloud,
> And none might see who bare it, and it past."

Only Galahad saw the vision of the Grail; the other knights glimpsed the glory without the substance. King Arthur explains this disparity by saying—

> "for such
> As thou art is the vision, not for these."

When the Knights swear to find this Holy Grail, Arthur warns them that—

> "ye follow wandering fires
> Lost in quagmire! Many of you, yea most,
> Return no more."

Percival, Lancelot, Galahad, and the rest individually depart upon the Quest. After undergoing many trials and tests, Percival finally encounters a hermit who explains to him the reasons for his continuing failure—

> "'Thou hast not lost thyself to save thyself
> As Galahad.' When the hermit made an end,
> In silver armour suddenly Galahad shone
> Before us..."

Galahad tells Percival that he has never ceased seeing the image of the Grail since it first appeared in Arthur's Hall, and that he has followed it to this same place that Percival found by instinct. Galahad finishes by saying—

> "'Come victor. But my time is hard at hand,
> And hence I go; and one will crown me king
> Far in the spiritual city; and come thou, too,
> For thou shalt see the vision when I go.'"

Percival follows Galahad to a mighty shore, and watches Galahad continue alone—

> "At once I saw him far on the great Sea,
> In silver-shining armour starry-clear;
> And o'er his head the Holy Vessel hung...
> And when the heavens opened and blazed again
> Roaring, I saw him like a silver star—
> And had he set the sail, or had the boat
> Become a living creature clad with wings?
> And o'er his head the Holy Vessel hung
> Redder than any rose, a joy to me,
> For now I knew the veil had been withdrawn.
> Then in a moment when they blazed again...
> I saw the spiritual city and all her spires
> And gateways in a glory like one pearl...."
>
> (Tennyson 1983, 220)

Most of Arthur's knights did not return from their Quest. Lancelot and Gawain returned, but had failed. Percivale (after beholding the Grail, Tennyson adds an "e" to the knight's name for the remainder of the poem, since he "pierced the veil") and Bors found the Grail, but did not return with it. Only Galahad succeeded in finding the Grail and entering the "spiritual city," never to be seen on the Kingdom of Earth again.

Dynamic: Spirit that is non-being

Level of Power:

The querent has the ability to succeed in the realms of emotions, intuition, love, and spirituality, but lacks the support or resources. Immediate, decisive action is needed, but if the matter is not conquered quickly then the possibility for success will dissipate.

Astrological Association: Pisces

Type of Sign: Mutable

Energy of Sign: The Prince of Cups receives energy into himself from all directions; he identifies with everyone and everything to the point of losing himself. (Start of being combined with water element)

Personality of Sign: Dreamily mysterious, indecisively impressionable, incredibly receptive, and eerily intuitive; adaptable and particularly sensitive to the environment, empathetic and often psychic.

Actual People: INFP

INFPs are the dreamers and healers of this world; their ideals and beliefs are paramount to them and their work must have meaning or they escape into fantasy to compensate.

A younger, single male (probably in his twenties or thirties) who is still in the process of pursuing and establishing his emotions, intuition, love relationships, and spirituality. If poorly aspected, the Prince of Cups may be a charmer who enchants the querent with empty praises and promises. May have a water sign (Cancer, Scorpio, Pisces) for his sun sign or ascendant.

Page of Cups
– Faerie Puck –

Archetype: Trickster, Shape-Shifter, Spy

Significance of the Archetype:

The mischievous troublemaker "Puck," or "Robin Goodfellow," was one of the most popular imps in English Folklore. He was the naughty shape-shifting hobgoblin who would assume the "innocent" shapes of animals and children in order to fool humans and was blamed for sundry nuisances, such as spoons missing and travelers losing their way. His name comes from the medieval Welsh word for the devil, "Pwca," commonly pronounced "Pooka." He's been pictured as everything from a hairy brownie, to the Greek god Pan, to an innocent, elf-like child. Immortalized in Shakespeare's *A Midsummer Night's Dream* as the madcap servant of Oberon, the Lord of the Faeries, Puck's well-intentioned mistake of giving the wrong young man a love potion provides the conflict of the comedy. Traces of his memory can be found in our culture today, from the invisible "pooka" in the classic play and film starring Jimmy Stewart, *Harvey*, to the tenth moon of Uranus being named "Puck."

Dynamic: Self

Level of Power:

Any plans or desires in the areas of emotions, intuition, love, or spirituality will not work out: the essential elements are lacking.

Astrological Association: Scorpio

Type of Sign: Fixed

Energy of Sign: The Page of Cups creates his or her own stop, for while trying to communicate, she/he simultaneously holds something back; the Page shields his or her thoughts, desires, and intentions from others. (Stop of having combined with water element)

Personality of Sign: Willful, passionate, probing, secretive, and sexual by nature, often repressing their strong feelings until they explode.

Actual People: ENFP

ENFPs are the champions and experimenters; they constantly initiate change and focus on possibilities, avoiding the past with its consequences.

A child or young woman who is struggling with his or her emotions, intuition, love relationships,

and spirituality; generally, the person is engrossed with avoiding pain. The individual may be spiritually immature, with fanatical tendencies, or conversely may be amassing too much debt. May have a water sign (Cancer, Scorpio, Pisces) for his or her sun sign or ascendant.

The Swords Court

King of Swords

– Mictlantecutli –

Archetype: Mentor, Sage, Advocate

Significance of the Archetype:

Before the coming of the Catholic Spaniards, the indigenous Mexicans considered death and life as an opposite yet complementary duality: In order to embrace life, you must also embrace death. (Even Coatlicue, the Aztec goddess of life and the Earth, was pictured wearing a death mask.) Mictlantecutli, the Aztec god of the dead, was the ruler of Mictlan, the lowest layer of the Aztec underworld, located in the desolate reaches of the far north. Also called Tlalxicco, the "Navel of the Earth," he ruled his realm with his dreaded queen, Mictecacihuatl; his symbolic animals were the bat, the owl, and the spider. He was generally pictured as a huge skeleton with hands and feet made of flesh, or else wearing a huge skull with a gaping maw that ate the spirits of those who were unfit to enter the paradise of Tlaloc because they had not died honorably in battle, by drowning, or in childbirth. Since humans were ritually sacrificed to Mictlantecutli, he was also often portrayed with a bloodied sacrificial knife or sword. Mictlantecutli's message to the Aztecs and their descendants was an important one: The significance of a life is not determined by how one lives, but by how one dies.

Uniting pre-Columbian practices with the syncretism of the Dominican missionaries, an entirely new form of Catholicism emerged in Mexico. In numerous cultures, October 31st is considered to be the day that the veil between the world of the living and the world of the dead is at its thinnest, but Mexico celebrates this event distinctively. October 31st through November 2nd is the holiday of Dias de Muertos, the perfect example of the blending of Aztec and Catholic belief systems. The week prior is spent in busy preparations, as each family builds a fragrant altar made of sugarcane and marigolds, called an ofrenda, covering it with various foods, offerings, and mementos for their deceased. During the actual event, they travel to the village cemetery and decorate the graves of their dearly departed, sitting and communing with them as they share their bounty with their ancestors, celebrating and remembering those who have come before.

The image of Mictlantecutli is everywhere during Dias de Muertos: From the decorated shop windows to the folk art and children's costumes, you find hordes of skeletons celebrating gleefully. With the help of the satirical illustrators Manilla and Posada, the danse macabre or "dance of death" (artistically depicted skeletons dancing and playing musical instruments) of a plague-riddled medieval Europe made its way into the Mexican customs and folk art of this holiday in the form of las calaveras, literally "skulls;" these calaveras are either sugar skulls with the name of a deceased stamped on its forehead, sculptured or drawn cartoonish scenes of merrymaking skeletons, or satirical poems that all have one purpose: to celebrate the Mexican's view of the reciprocity of death and life. Whether venerated or feared, Death walks by our side—so why not be amigos? In present day Mexican folk art, the personified Death is sometimes called Santa Muerte, "Saint Death" and is depicted as a white-robed skeleton. Other times personified as a female—La Calaca or La Muerte—death incarnate stands robed like a saint and holds a scythe, an owl, and an hourglass; even a cartoonish version of death dressed as an elegant lady, the famous Catrina, is an artistic image that was popularized by the artists Posada and Rivera.

Mictlantecutli, the Skeleton King himself, reminds us of the important truth that Dias de Muertos celebrates: To be born is only to begin to die.

Dynamic: Ethics-Rationality

Level of Power:

The querent will win in matters pertaining to the mind, communication, or conflict.

Astrological Association: Libra

Type of Sign: Cardinal

Energy of Sign: The King of Swords mentally reaches out to perceive both sides of any directly opposing issue; his agile mind perceives far more because of his awareness of multiple viewpoints. (Outchange of doing combined with the air element)

Personality of Sign: Social and seeks harmonious human relationships above all else. Uncanny ability to look at all sides of a situation, easily accepting other's points of view over own.

Actual People: ENTP

ENTPs are the innovators and inventors; striving for a balanced and just world, they are able to both successfully mediate change as well as challenge and improve the status quo.

An older man (probably married or recently divorced) who excels at mental activities, communication, and winning conflicts; perhaps he is a lawyer, a journalist, or a teacher. May have an air sign (Gemini, Libra, Aquarius) for his sun sign or ascendant.

Queen of Swords

– Hecate –

Archetype: Witch, Crone, Scapegoat

Significance of the Archetype:

Hecate is a multifaceted goddess. Known as the Greek goddess of the dark moon, the night, midwifery, the crossroads, and the underworld, she was called the "far-seeing" goddess, for she had the ability to see in all directions, even the past, present, and future. Because of this unique ability, she was usually depicted with some version of three heads: either a beautiful woman with three human heads (one a maiden, one a mother, and one an old woman); three animal heads (one snake, one horse, and one boar); or else she traveled with a three-headed black hound. At night during the dark moon, Hecate walked the roads of Greece with her howling hounds, visiting cemeteries and leading shades to the underworld. The daughter of Titans, Zeus shared with Hecate—and only Hecate—the power to grant (or refuse to grant) the wishes of humanity.

As time progressed, greater focus was placed on Hecate's knowledge of the darker, natural mysteries, and she began to be pictured as a "hag" or a "crone," eventually given the title "Queen of the Witches." During the Middle Ages and the Renaissance, the Catholic Church blamed Hecate (and all "witches") for many unexplained "evil" events; even in Shakespeare's *Macbeth*, she is characterized as the

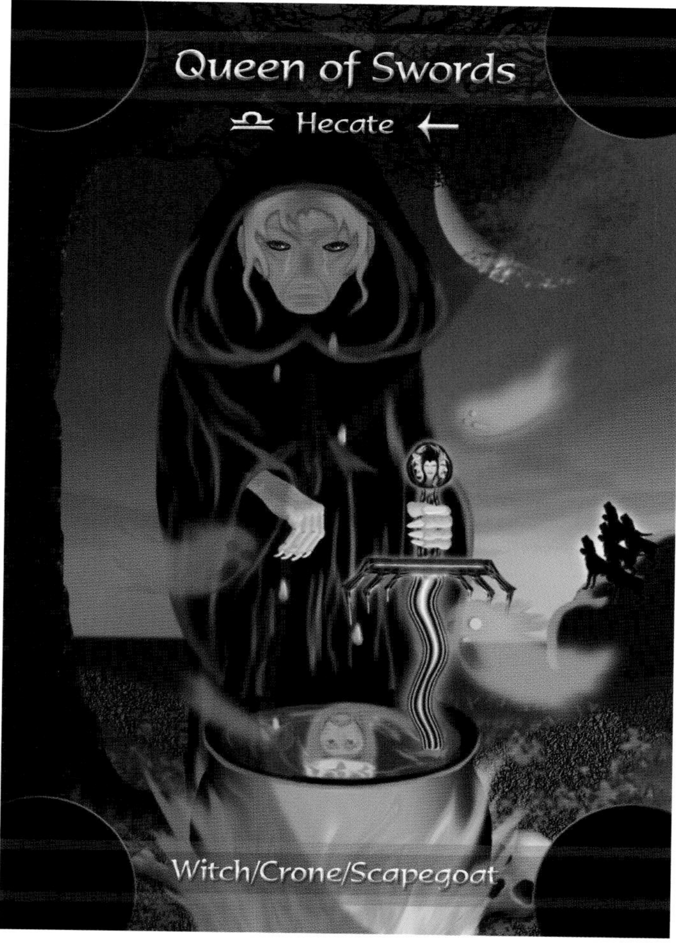

evil goddess of the witches. Instead of embodying the three-faced triple goddess within herself, she eventually assumed the last aspect of the triple goddess, with Persephone (or Artemis, or Kore) as the maiden aspect and Demeter (or Selene) as the mother aspect. Regardless, it is she who helps make transitions and reveals the power of the darkness and shadows.

Dynamic: Thought

Level of Power:

The Queen of Swords slashes with her mighty sword to sway the scales and upset the current balance of things: something is about to end in the querent's life. To identify what is ending, look to the surrounding cards. The querent contains considerable mental resources to succeed in the realms of a communication or a conflict, but the external circumstances are such that now is not the time to act. Wait until things settle down a bit.

Astrological Association: Libra

Type of Sign: Cardinal
Energy of Sign: The Queen of Swords allows the other to fully see her own perspective, immersing the other in the "logical correctness" of the Queen's experience. (Inchange of doing combined with the air element)
Personality of Sign: Harmonizes all around her; appreciates that sometimes one must "harm" in order to achieve harmony. Able to look at all sides of a situation, with an uncanny ability to use logic to influence others towards her own point of view.

Actual People: INTP

INTPs are both architects and magicians; they love intellectual problems and seek to understand and manipulate the people and phenomena around them.

An older woman (or any mother) who excels at mental activities, communication, and handling conflict—also represents a divorcee. May have an air sign (Gemini, Libra, Aquarius) for his sun sign or ascendant.

Prince of Swords
– The Lord of Misrule –

Archetype: Storyteller, Clown, Thinker

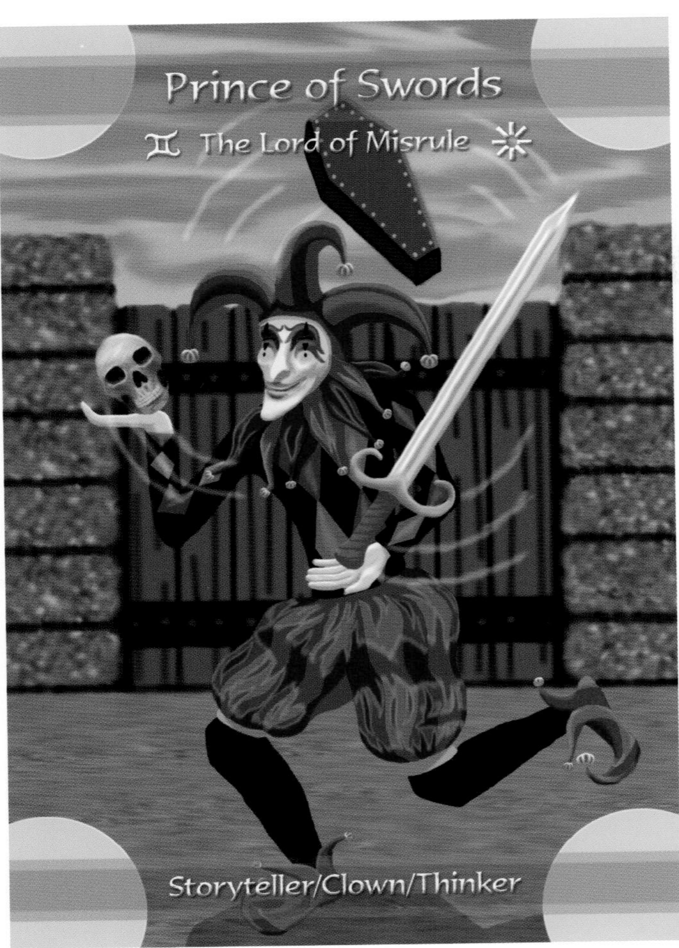

Significance of the Archetype:

The Lord of Misrule (also called the Abbot of the Revels) was the elected master of the winter celebrations in medieval Europe. The peasants would draw lots, and the winner generally began his topsy-turvy reign on All Hallow's Eve and ruled throughout the Christmas season. Wearing a paper crown and the jester's motley, the Lord of Misrule turned everything "upside down," as the ruling noble gave him full license to imbue the holiday season with whatever naughty decadence that he might wish. This tradition can be traced back to the ancient Saturnalia, the Roman celebration of the rebirth of the Sun. During this festival of role-reversals, servants were given equality with their masters and a commoner was chosen as King of the Festival, impersonating Saturn and being treated as royalty throughout the celebration until he was sacrificed on the altar of Saturn at the close of the festival! The Lord of Misrule reminds us to fully enjoy every moment and stop taking life (and death) so seriously.

Dynamic: Coexistence

Level of Power:

The querent has substantial abilities in matters of the mind, communication, or a conflict, but little or no support to succeed. Immediate action garners the only possibility of success; the longer it takes, the greater the chance of failure. The Prince of Swords may also bring an important message or communication into the querent's life.

Astrological Association: Gemini

Type of Sign: Mutable
Energy of Sign: The Prince of Swords maintains a comfortable, detached distance from everyone and everything, rationally emphasizing all the similarities and generalities of experience; he never dirties himself with the depths of specifics or contradiction. (Start of being combined with air element)
Personality of Sign: Astute, clever, witty, adaptable, and quick. Uncanny understanding of the relationships between things and have many interests; however, full of contradictions and constantly changing.

Actual People: INTJ

INTJs are free-thinkers and masterminds; ingenious by nature, they stretch and play with ideas and conventions like taffy.

A younger, single male (probably in his twenties or thirties) who is busily developing his intellect, communication skills, and ability to win conflicts. Because the Prince of Swords corresponds to Gemini, this person may have an important message for the querent, or, if poorly aspected, may be a spy or informant. May have an air sign (Gemini, Libra, Aquarius) for his sun sign or ascendant.

Page of Swords
– Persephone –

Archetype: Victim, Damsel, Ingénue

Significance of the Archetype:

Persephone was the Greek goddess of the spring and daughter of Ceres, the goddess of the harvest, until the Lord of the Underworld, Hades, decided he wanted her. With the help of his brother, Zeus, Hades kidnapped Persephone and carried her down to his dark realm. The Earth became barren as Ceres grieved the loss of her daughter. As Earth experienced its first winter and humanity and all Earth's inhabitants began to starve, Zeus finally commanded his brother to return Persephone to her mother; clever Hades, however, tricked Persephone into eating in the Underworld by taking one single bite of a pomegranate, and since it was decreed that anyone who eats in the Underworld must live there, Persephone was doomed to live six months in the Underworld with Hades and six months on the surface with her mother, never quite fitting into either realm. Persephone became the Dark Mistress of the Underworld, as well as the maiden of the waxing new moon who rules the changing of the seasons.

In Greek mythology, Persephone shares her rulership of the Underworld with Hecate, the Queen of Swords in *The Kingdom Within Tarot*. Both goddesses also represent opposite phases of the Moon—Persephone the new moon and Hecate the full moon. While it is easy to relate Persephone with the

classical image of the Queen of Swords that appears in most decks, she is the Page in *The Kingdom Within Tarot* for good reason: in Persephone we have the maiden forced to grow up before she is ready, the victim who has not yet accepted responsibility for her own life, the damsel who pines for her dreams of perfection yet seems unable to achieve them. Hecate, on the other hand, chooses to rule the Underworld as a result of her Wisdom and Mastery of the Darkness. Persephone must learn to balance the extremes of her ideals with the bitter realities of life before truly realizing her own power—one of the first lessons of all who would call themselves "human."

Dynamic: Mankind

Level of Power:

The situation contains too many conflictive elements that work against each other; the matter will come to little.

Astrological Association: Aquarius

Type of Sign: Fixed
Energy of Sign: The Princess of Swords watches as she induces others to stop against themselves in reaction to her own dynamic expressions of freedom; when others stop around her, the Princess successfully gains more space to be creative and original. (Stop of having combined with air element.)

Personality of Sign: Intellectual, artistic, and the epitome of individuality. Experimental, rational, and idealistic by nature: the quintessential humanitarian who is passionately dedicated to the progress of society, all the while having trouble relating to normal people on an interpersonal level.

Actual People: ENTJ

ENTJs are best at motivating others to grow to new heights; they logically apply their ideals to improve and create their conceptions of a "brave new world."

A child or young woman who has an important message but is struggling with how to logically communicate it amidst opposing forces. May be brilliant and argumentative by nature; struggles with issues of purpose and self-identity. May have an air sign (Gemini, Libra, Aquarius) for his or her sun sign or ascendant.

Chapter Three
The Minor Arcana

The Trinity of the Tarot

While the Major Arcana deal with the grander order of existence—how matter, energy, space, time, thought, and idea interact; astrological influences and impulsions; Qabalistic Pathworking, spiritual progression, and the ultimate journey of the Soul—and the Court Cards handle the levels of power, the focus and implementation of energy through the astrological signs and physics of change, and the relational impact of the people in the querent's life; the Minor Arcana cards, in contrast, handle the here and now, the realm of Earth, and the day to day delight (or drudgery) of being human. The Tarot begins with the transcendent, moves through the dynamic, and ends with the mundane: The Minor Arcana.

The Minor Arcana comprises the final forty cards of any standard Tarot deck. Just like the Court Cards, the forty Minor Arcana are divided into four suits, much like a deck of conventional playing cards. Each card correlates to an astrological planet-in-sign combination.

Wands (similar to clubs) are the **fire suit**, and therefore encompass the fire signs Aries, Leo, and Sagittarius. This suit deals with matters of creativity, desire, and power; Qabalistically speaking, Wands correspond to the Father, Chokmah, and the four Kings of the Court Cards.

Pentacles (like diamonds) represent the **earth signs** Taurus, Virgo, and Capricorn, which discuss the resources (usually career and money) to attain one's goals; they also represent Malkuth, the Materialized Daughter, and the four Pages.

Cups (akin to hearts), also known as the **water signs**, deal with the inner realms of emotion, intuition, love, and mysticism that are attributed to Cancer, Scorpio, and Pisces; Cups are hollow and receptive, like Binah, the Great Mother, and the four Queens.

The **air signs** of Gemini, Libra, and Aquarius are contained in the **Sword suit** (not unlike a spade) focusing on the demesnes of the mind, communication, and conflict; moreover, the hilt of a sword forms a cross, and so the Swords Suit is ascribed to Tiphereth, the Redeeming Son, and the four Princes.

Aces

The Aces embody the root, raw energy of each suit's element in its purest form, often called the "seeds" of each element. There is one Ace for each Tarot suit, and each one has a straightforward interpretation: Aces represent a powerful, new beginning in their corresponding elemental arena. For example, the Ace of Wands might be a new creative endeavor. The Ace of Pentacles suggests a new job or financial venture. The Ace of Cups, on the other hand, would discuss a new relationship or spiritual pursuit. The Ace of Swords shows starting school, a new message, or the beginning of strife.

The Qabalistic Cosmos

At the bottom center of each of the Minor Arcana cards there is half of a colored sphere, representing one of the Sephirah on the Tree of Life. Qabalistically speaking, the number of a Minor Arcana card (or pips as they have often been called) has a correlation to one of the Sephiroth on the Tree of Life. Each Minor Arcana card corresponds to the Sephirotic sphere of the same number: Aces to the first Sephirah, Kether; 2s to the second Sephirah, Chokmah; 3s to the third Sephirah, Binah and so forth.

Obviously the concept of Zero, a fundamental component of mathematics and the Qabalistic system, is represented by The Fool, the Great Dissolver and Wandering Air. In every creation myth, there was "nothing" before there was anything. Qabalah expounds upon this numerical enigma of infinity by describing the triple veil of the negative that exists above Kether on the Tree of Life, as described in the Bible's book of Genesis: *Ayin* (The Primal

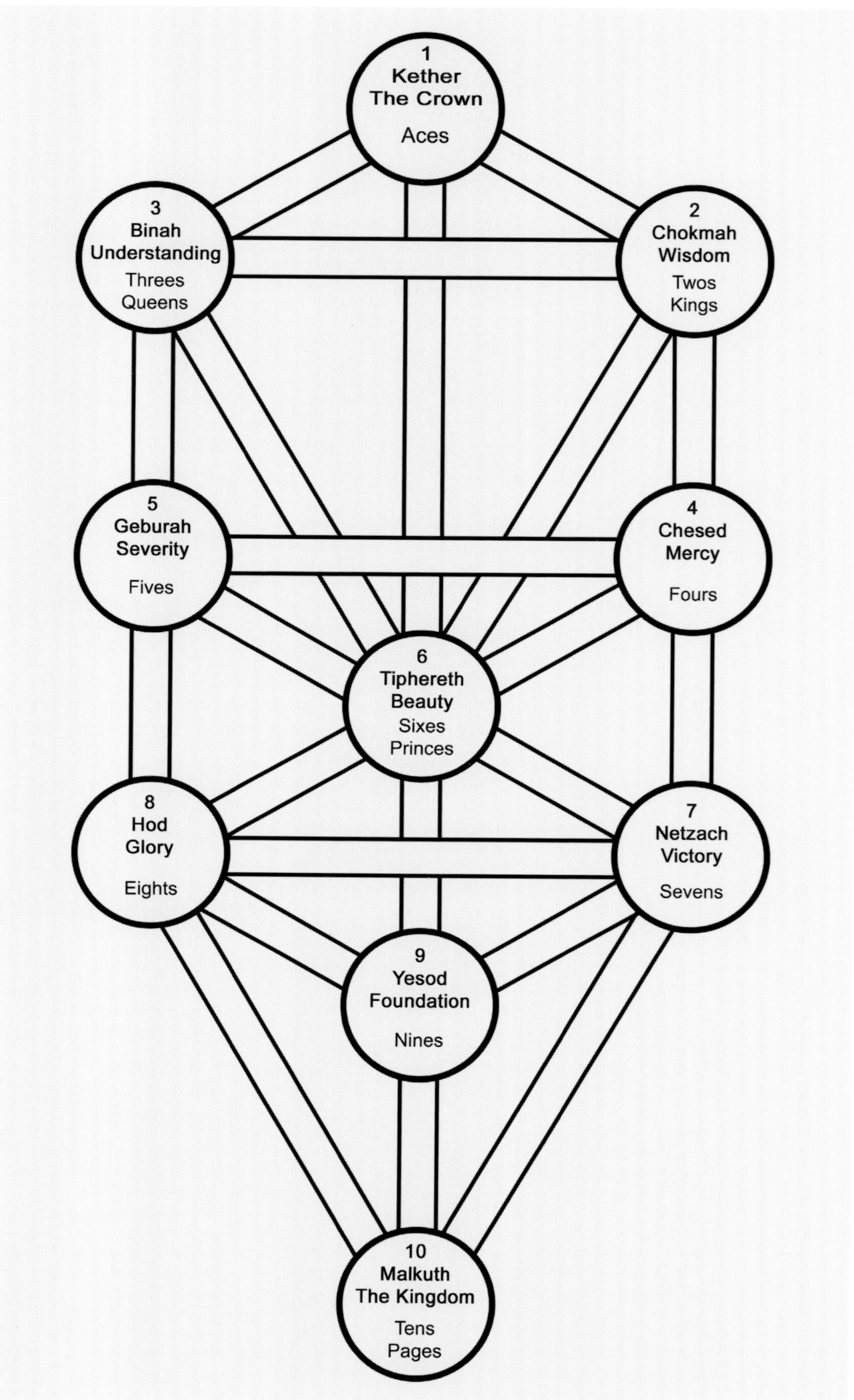

The Sephiroth

Cause, No-Thing, the absence of all known qualities, a conception beyond the possibilities of human thought), *Ain Soph* (Endlessness, Boundlessness, No-Thing Without Limit, a qualified No-Thingness, the Infinitely Great as in contrast to Ayin as the Infinitely Small) and *Ain Soph Aur* (the Limitless Light out of which the universe was molded, not as in contrast to darkness, but as a vibration; the contracting and expanding energies of creation.) Zero is both everything and nothing; it is Absolute Truth.

The Four Worlds

According to Qabalah, there are Four Worlds on the Tree of Life:

Atziluth, the Archetypal World, represented by the Hebrew letter Yod, the element Fire, and the Wands Suit;

Briah, the Creative World, represented by the Hebrew letter He, the element Water, and the Cups Suit;

Yetzirah, the Formative World, represented by the Hebrew letter Vau, the element Air, and the Swords Suit; and

Assiah, the Material World, represented by the Hebrew letter Heh (as in YHVH, the Tetragrammaton), and the Pentacles Suit.

With these attributions in mind, one level of Minor Arcana interpretation is to consider each card as a particular Sephirah working in one of the Four Worlds. For instance, the 2 of Wands might be looked at as Chokmah (2) in the Archetypal World of Atziluth (Wands), just as the Six of Cups might be viewed as Tiphereth (6) in the Creative World of Briah (Cups). In order to better understand these associations, let us commence with a detailed study of the Sephiroth (plural for Sephirah) on the Tree of Life.

Kether and the Aces

The roots of the four elements of the universe—the Aces—correlate to the white Sephirah Kether, called "The Crown," which is Number One at the top of the Tree of Life. (Spirit is the fifth element that serves as both the glue and the limiting factor for the other four; in fact, it could be said that the four elements are simply different levels of crystallization of Spirit.) Kether is the beginning of the idea of existence, for now we have the first postulate (or creative lie) of separation: "I Am." Thus All becomes One, a Point or location from which to gaze outwards, a static, a Singular Being. Kether is the Archetypal World of Plato's Cave, called Atziluth by the Qabalists, a world of Pure Essence without force or form; all the other Sephiroth are emanations from the Number One, just as all the other pips within a suit are emanations from the Ace. The Whirling Motion of the Universe began in Kether.

Chokmah and the Twos

The Two's of each suit correspond to the gray Sephirah Chokmah, Wisdom, called the Father of the Archetypal World of the Zodiac and the Fixed Stars, who is the reflection of Kether. Perhaps the best English word to describe the Sephirah of Wisdom is the idea of Epiphany, for it is only in moments of perfect epiphany, when everything in existence seems to align for one split second as we cry "Aha!" that we abandon the confines of thought and see beyond the curtain of consideration and form.

With Chokmah we have the commencement of dimension, as the second idea that there is another point of existence that is separate from the One is postulated, creating the Line and length. Now there is a separate point from which the One may view its own existence, and as a result we also see the creation of the idea of duality—for there is now the possibility of refusing to accept responsibility (the ability to respond) for What Is. There can be no manifestation without differentiation into pairs of opposites, and thus the Tree of Life (and existence itself) demonstrates this equilibrium.

Chokmah is the dynamic principle and the seat of abstract ideas, the biblical Logos or Word of God, for Wisdom is the Mediator between the Uncreated (Kether) and the beginning of the Created (Chesed, the fourth Sephirah). Just like numerous mythological figures (such as Horus of Egypt and Eros of Greece) Chokmah is the Son that is also the Father—firstly, the Son of the Absolute, Kether, and the Great Mother, Binah; secondly, the husband of Binah and the Father of Tiphereth, the sixth Sephirah and Redeemer. From the earth-bound perspective, Chokmah looks more like the number One than Two, because the ability to view the manifestation of the elements begins with Chokmah; Kether remains wholly concealed. In both Chokmah and the Twos of the Minor Arcana we see the beginning of the Masculine, the Transmissive, the Active, the Will. The Twos accordingly epitomize the manifestation of the element in its most untainted, balanced form; their action is swift, intense, and consuming.

The Shekhinah

One of the most significant aspects of the Qabalistic Tree of Life is that it restores the vital Shekhinah (Hebrew for the feminine face and aspects of God) to the generally misunderstood apparency of an otherwise lop-sided, male-dominated system of beliefs. The Tree of Life has three "pillars"—the center pillar of Harmony and balance with a left and right pillar, each respectively attributed to the female and the male. The God of Qabalah is All, and therefore hermaphroditic rather than masculine. This restoration of the divine feminine (the Shekhinah) begins with the third Sephirah, Binah. Each Sephirah receives the influence of the previous one and in turn conveys its nature to the next; hence, each Sephirah has both a positive, transmissive and a negative, receptive quality. As Chokmah receives the influence of Kether, so it transmits its own nature to the third Sephirah, Binah, which in turn receives its influence and in turn transmits its own nature to the fourth Sephirah, and so on.

Binah and the Threes

The Threes coincide with Binah, the black Sephirah of the Great Mother of "Understanding." In Binah a third Point is postulated, and the dimension of distance or surface is created; now there is space between the two points, and so, geometrically, we have the Plane, the Triangle. When Genesis records that the "Spirit of God was moving over the surface of the waters," it is referring to the Great Waters of Binah, the Giver of Form; Binah gives form to Chokmah's force. Together, Chokmah and Binah shape the Creative World where the living substance of creation waits for impregnation by the Will or Life of the Father, called Briah by the Qabalists; Binah is the Feminine, the Receptive, the Passive, the ideal yin to Chokmah's yang.

With Understanding we attempt to bring into agreement two varying viewpoints (that, ironically, were originally in Harmony for they were once the same point.) With this third point of view comes the stability of a context from which to differentiate, as well as a gap in proximity and perspective. The labor of Communication becomes necessary in order to achieve Connection and Understanding of the divergent viewpoint, and concept is created. The Threes of each suit still retain the basic power of the Aces and Twos, but in a more passive form; inherent in each is the internal struggle to receive understanding and balance as form is given to two differing points of view. Three is the also number of the planet Saturn, and therefore the threes of each suit bring opportunities of limitation in order to eventually produce, whether in the areas of hard work (pentacles), duty (wands), choice (cups), or loss (swords).

Chesed and the Fours

Below the top three Sephiroth on the Tree of Life are the seven remaining Sephiroth, each a color of the rainbow. It is interesting to note the significance of the number seven, spiritually speaking: there are seven chakras, seven notes on the musical scale, seven planets that can be seen from Earth, and the seven double letters of the Hebrew alphabet. (Recall Gurdjieff's "Law of Seven.") Since the Tree of Life is Jewish in its origin, these seven Sephiroth also mirror the seven days of creation in the first book of the Torah (the book of Genesis in the Christian Bible).

Now we leave what is called the Supernal Triad and cross the Abyss, the invisible Sephirah Da'ath (meaning "Knowledge," also called the "false Sephiroth" that spans the Abyss and attempts to replace the living Wisdom of Chokmah with the deadening knowledge of humanity) on the Tree of Life, which separates the Ideal from the Actual, and enter the Formative World, a realm of symbols where the perfected ideas have taken form but now await a material body, called Yetzirah. The root colors of white (reflecting all colors), gray (mixing all colors), and black (absorbing all colors) are replaced with the primary colors of blue, red, and yellow.

Royal blue Chesed is the fourth Sephirah, the Sphere of Mercy or Love, also called Gedulah. (Gedulah means "Greatness" or "Magnificence" in Hebrew.) With Chesed we add a fourth point, so that we now have the three co-ordinate axes to delineate the position of any point; consequently existence now has substance, becoming Solid. Herein lays the foundation of disagreement and the birth of conflict, for not only can one Point's determinism be in opposition to another Point's determinism, but it may also oppose the Solid (universe) as a whole.

Within Chesed is the concept of covenant, for we now have the Rule of the Law of Love, which in its drive to harmonize begins to dictate the four dimensions of the universe as creation begins to manifest as matter, dominating and stabilizing everything; pure change of postulates is replaced by the need for negotiation, the essence of Law. (Crowley's famous axiom, "Love is the Law, Love under Will" may be understood here as Chesed, the Law of Love, being far junior to the Will of Chokmah; yet Love is the limit of the carnal human's hierarchies.)

The Gnostics called this force the Demiurge, for Chesed is not the actual Father, only His likeness, yet many mistakenly bow down to the Law of Mercy. The Roman god Jupiter, beneficent ruler and lawgiver of the cosmos, is attributed to Chesed for good reason: it is a constant balancing (or juggling) act to bring order to the chaos of existence. Jupiter is also the planet of foundations, spirituality, and blessings that come from obeying the natural laws of the universe. In Chesed, the Law constantly works to balance the contracting power of Love—the great unifying factor of the universe—with the expanding force of Life—the dynamic breaking apart and shattering of existing forms to make way for the progression of existence.

Within the fourth Sephirah (and the Fours of the Minor Arcana as well) we have a temporary reprieve of symmetry as structure and substance walk hand in hand with personal restriction for the good of the collective. Chesed brings the concept that one does not own oneself or one's viewpoints; now authority is found in "we." The Fours use the Law to achieve a stable Harmony, but are simultaneously weighted down by their dedication to agreement with others and the world of forms.

Geburah and the Fives

The fifth Sephirah on the Tree of Life is red Geburah, meaning "Strength" or "Severity;" it is also called Pahad, meaning "Punishment." Appropriately associated with the Warrior planet Mars, Geburah cuts the solid balance of Chesed's solidity of stabilized structure, causing the much needed state of Movement, which produces upset, disturbance, and most importantly, Change. The dynamic principle of Chokmah reflects into Geburah, and so we have a break down of the complex into the simple, releasing the latent, trapped energy of Chesed. We may not like the Warrior's influence, but its pressure and tempests are a necessary part of growth and development. With Geburah, through the addition of Motion, the points now have the capacity of time, change, and sequence; five is the number of a spirit involved in the physical universe (the five points of a pentacle represent this phenomenon), attempting to change the static square of the number four by inserting the individual spirit (and therefore Change) back into the equation.

Frater Achad wrote in *Q.B.L.*, "WILL is that which produces CHANGE which is LIFE. Stagnation or fixity is DEATH. Therefore, fear not CHANGE, but embrace it with open arms, for all change is of the nature of LOVE, which is the tendency of any two things to become ONE thus losing themselves in the process" (Achad 1997, *Q.B.L.*, Chapter 9). Geburah offers the chance of a clean slate from which to escape the heavy, stuck condition of Chesed, but in the smaller playing field of matter, energy, space, and time. The Fives of the Minor Arcana represent great change and upset of a fixed condition as a precursor to revolution.

Tiphereth and the Sixes

Both Chesed and Geburah exist on the same plane in the Tree of Life, but they are reconciled in the sixth Sephirah, golden Tiphereth, which forms the bottom point of the second triad, called the "Ethical Triangle." Where the Supernal Triad is associated with the Father of the Trinity, the Ethical Triangle represents the Redeemer; Tiphereth (which means "Beauty" in Hebrew) is the Son of the Father, for it is the only Sephirah below the Abyss that is in direct communication with Kether. Tiphereth is connected with all the sacrificed deities of mythology, and is the Manifested Son of Binah (the Great Mother) and Chokmah (The Great Father), as well as the Perfect Image of Kether, the Absolute, in a form that can be comprehended by Humanity; Tiphereth interprets the Father in terms that the human mind may grasp. Correlated with the Sun, Tiphereth stands at the center of the Tree of Life just as the Sun is situated at the center of our solar system (and at the heart of most of our world religions).

With Tiphereth comes the tangible form of the Point that is capable of experience, for it finally attains self-consciousness. (Consciousness is quite different from Awareness—or the ability to wholly see, recognize, and know—for if we become conscious of something, there is the intrinsic conviction that in some way we do not entirely know the thing.) The "I Am" of Kether has evolved to the hypothesis that "I Am that I Am." Now the Point is able to define itself and shape an identity within the contexts created by the previous Sephiroth. Six is the Qabalistic number of man, and Tiphereth (and the Sixes of the Minor Arcana) represents man and the elements at their practical best. Thus, each Six signifies great success or victory in the matter at hand.

Netzach and the Sevens

The bottom Triangle, attributed to the Holy Spirit and called the "Magical Triangle," constitutes green Netzach (7), orange Hod (8), and purple Yesod (9); the primary colors of the Ethical Triangle now blend to form their secondary or complementary colors: Chesed and Tiphereth mix to produce the Green of Netzach, Geburah and Tiphereth create the Orange of Hod, and Chesed and Geburah combine to the purple of Yesod. With the progression of this lowest Triangle into matter, the Point begins to have a sensory experience of itself and existence.

In Netzach, meaning "Victory" (or some translate it "Triumph" or "Eternity") in Hebrew, the Point experiences Bliss (the Hindu concept of *ananda*); the seventh Sephirah is correlated to the planet Venus, the planet of Love, but Netzach reveals Venus degraded to an entirely imbalanced state as she loses her heavenly origin as the Morning Star and falls into the Veil of Illusion (what the Hindu call *maya*.) The Motion of Geburah now reflects into Netzach, often called the Lady of Nature and Sphere of Illusion, which contains the chaotically free-flowing, elemental, inebriating Dionysian wildness of the forces of Nature, as well as the natural birth of reflexes, instincts, emotions, group mind, and the essence of thought forms that are the creations of the created; in Netzach we discover the sensual use of the arts, dance, sound, color, and the senses in the medium of Natural Mysticism. Here lie the Forces of Attraction and Repulsion. Netzach (and the Sevens of the Minor Arcana) is a powerful, unbalanced, primal force that can only be steadied by the contrived intellect of Hod. The Sevens of the Minor Arcana epitomize a basic state of messy imbalance, and expose the greatest weakness of each of the respective suit's element.

Hod and the Eights

Opposite to Netzach we have Hod, meaning "Glory" or "Splendor." Attributed to the Eights of the Minor Arcana, Hod ironically is just as imbalanced as Netzach and the Sevens, only Hod's imbalance is in reaction to that of Netzach's and errs on the extreme opposite end of the spectrum. In contrast to Netzach's reflection of Geburah, Hod is the reflection of the balancing Law of Chesed, only beneath the Veil of Illusion. Thus Hod, the Lord of Books and Learning, is the realm where the cold, deadening, concrete force of the human mind has its origins as it conceives its hierarchical forms and structures. Associated with Mercury, in Hod the Point experiences Thought (the Hindu concept of *chit*) and, at its best, Intellectual Mysticism—crucial for controlling the emotional chaos of Netzach. Conversely, a state of mutual reciprocity exists between the seventh and eighth Sephiroth: For Hod needs the raw power of Netzach just as much as Netzach needs the commanding authority of Hod if anything is to be both experienced and accomplished below the Veil of Illusion. The Eights of the Minor Arcana, therefore, demonstrate an extreme reaction to the imbalanced state of the elements in the Sevens, and because the Eights are so low on the Tree of Life, they have almost completely lost their initial elemental energy.

Yesod and the Nines

Yesod, the ninth Sephirah, aptly means "Foundation," for it is in Yesod (and in its corresponding planet, the Moon) that we find the crystallization of energy (and spirit) into manifestation as Yesod unites the imbalances of Netzach and Hod through the illuminating influence of Tiphereth. Yesod is the stuff that dreams (and imagination, the ability to perceive a reality beyond the physical world) are made of, for it is the realm of our subconscious. Because Yesod is the final Sephirah in Yetzirah, the formative world, the Nines of the Minor Arcana demonstrate the full manifestation of the elemental force within the stability created by the constant cycle of change—for change is what ultimately keeps existence stable.

The Zohar (*Book of Splendor or Radiance*), one of the fundamental texts of Qabalah, tells us that everything in the material world has its foundation in the spiritual and must, eventually, return to its foundation; all energy ultimately returns to the foundation (Yesod) from which it proceeded before being birthed afresh into a new (if briefly) altered state. We are born into a human body from Yesod, all of us return for our nightly partaking of possibilities as we dream, and when we die we shall ascend to it once again. In Yesod we find psychicism, the astral plane, and the ethereal double, for here is the birthplace of the Point into Being (the Hindu concept of *sat*), pretending that this "briefly altered state" is Actual. Now the hunger, passion, and drive of Being becomes paramount, as the awareness of Truth becomes a dream within a dream. Nines disclose the crystallization into form of each of the elements.

Malkuth and the Tens

Finally, we come to Malkuth, the "Kingdom," represented by four equal colors of russet, navy, citrine, and olive, which hangs from the trinity of triads like a many-colored pendant. Malkuth is the end of all energy emanations as the mixing (or some say muddying) of all the elements into material manifestation creates Assiah, the world of Action where the fruit of the former three worlds now manifest into a tangible form. Malkuth is the Kingdom of Earth and most humans' concept of Reality.

There is a weightiness to this world as the vast collection of manifested Points must continually train their focus upon the physical universe in order to maintain its persisting substance, as well as a danger of each Point getting caught up in Beingness and simply playing out its assumed roles rather than using the games, boundaries, and sensations of Assiah to discover Itself. The sacred gift of Malkuth, however, is the chance for the Points to evolve and transform, for each Point is actually a Star. The number Ten (1-0) is symbolic of the Unity (1) returning to Zero. The corresponding Tens of each suit are both positive and negative, for although they demonstrate the full manifestation of each particular element into the physical plane, each Ten is equally about to utterly lose its elemental identity in the mixture of Malkuth; every Ten shows completion of the matter, but contains a heaviness as imminent destruction of the concluded area is just around the corner.

Qliphoth and the Averse Sephiroth

In Qabalah, Assiah is also referred to as the world of the Qliphoth, which often is translated "Demons" but is perhaps best translated as "Shells" or "Husks." In *The Zohar*, the root of Evil seems to have been the act of separation (reminiscent of the teachings of our modern western religions, which believe that Hell is eternal separation from God), and the limits between one thing and another were regarded as "shells." Over time these "shells," devoid of the Light that once enlivened them, began to desperately leech energy from any place or any being possible; thus Malkuth, with its divisions and separations, became a sort of hellish empire of shells imprisoned in their own distinctions.

In 1925, T.S. Eliot—whether intentionally or not—best described the realm of the Qliphoth (and much of Malkuth) in his poem, *The Hollow Men*, when he said:

> "Shape without form, shade without colour,
> Paralysed force, gesture without motion;
> Those who have crossed
> With direct eyes, to death's other Kingdom
> Remember us—if at all—not as lost
> Violent souls, but only
> As the hollow men
> The stuffed men."

Accordingly, there is an alternate Tree that mirrors the Tree of Life but contains the Evil or Averse Sephiroth, each an empty emanation or "shell" of form without force, the dead residue that is left after Life has departed its corresponding Sephirah. Some Qabalists attribute this disparity to humanity's historic preference for the Tree of Knowledge over the Tree of Life (see Genesis, Chapters 2 and 3). Rabbi Luria, a highly esteemed Jewish scholar from the 1500s, theorized that in the process of creation, a "shattering" of forms occurred that caused each of the four worlds to slip down on the Tree of Life, so that the bottom world of Assiah "fell" into the world of the Qliphoth; thus, Luria taught that the primary goal is to free the shards of the divine spark, not simply from being in the realm of shells, but from their trapped condition here.

Although the Qliphoth are generally described as "evil," they seem necessary at times, much like the rind of a fruit or shell of a seed serves the temporary purpose of protection during vulnerable stages of development. Deliberate access to the Qliphoth and the Averse Tree comes through the false Sephirah Da'ath. Eventually, it becomes necessary for every person who would cross the Abyss to confront the Qliphoth, but only with the aid of his or her Holy Guardian Angel (or True Self); everyone must confront those aspects of themselves that are scattered throughout existence and bring us "dis-ease," for only in wholly embracing the Ecstasy of Awareness can we discover the Absolute.

Card Analysis Classification

Every Minor Arcana card image of *The Kingdom Within Tarot* has been crafted to incorporate within its imagery the astrological correlation, Qabalistic association, seasonal celebration, and spiritual cycle story that relate to each suit. Therefore, after a brief explanation of the significance of each Suit's symbol (Pentacle, Wand, Cup, or Sword), each section will outline the subsequent information:

Setting and Color Scheme:
Each suit takes place during one of the four seasons of the year and has a matching color scheme.

Astrological Correlation:
Each suit contains three corresponding elemental astrological signs.

Seasonal Celebration:
Each suit encompasses a seasonal celebration.

Cycle Story:
Each suit has a universal, divine spiritual story that it represents and that has been commemorated and re-enacted throughout the world in our religious festivals and customs.

Court Card Characters:
The King, Queen, Prince, and Page of each suit are actively involved in the illustrations of the pips.

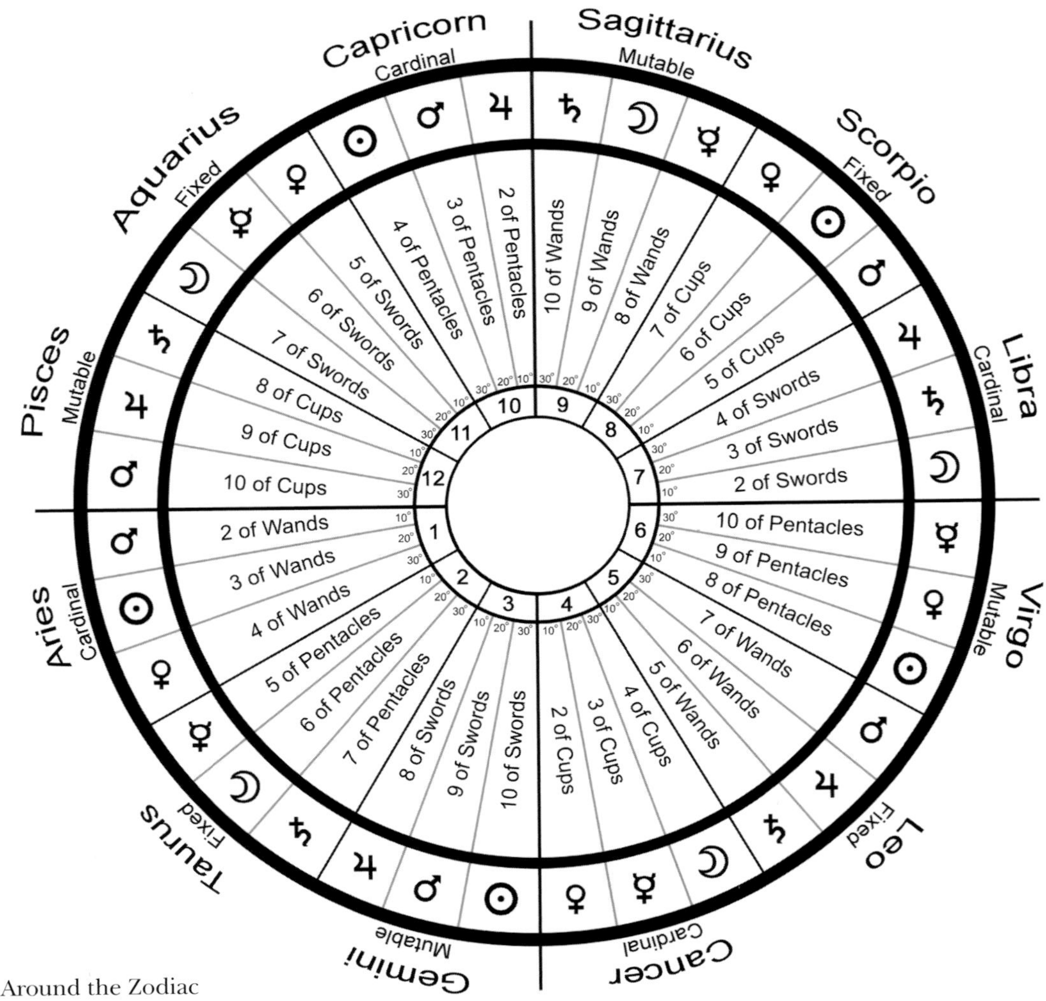

Minor Arcana Around the Zodiac

Astrological Correlations of the Minor Arcana

In addition to the Qabalistic correspondences, each of the remaining thirty-six cards, numbered two through ten for each suit, is a combination of a particular planet working in a zodiacal sign appropriate to the elemental energy of the suit; because the Minor Arcana deal with the more mundane aspects of life—while the three outer planets deal mostly with worldwide and generational issues—the planets Uranus, Neptune, and Pluto are not utilized in the astrological combinations of the pips. Although every planet-and-sign combination is obviously not represented in the thirty-six suit cards, the addition of the Major Arcana and Court Cards allows for all possible astrological combinations. For the reader interested in learning basic astrology, these thirty-six pips demonstrate important astrological energy combinations; with the addition of the Major Arcana, the chance for all possible planet-and-sign combinations (including Uranus, Neptune, and Pluto) become possible, yet prevents the deck from becoming unwieldy and cumbersome.

Each astrological sign is used three times in the pips. Some of the combinations identify the planet as being the **Ruler** or in **Exaltation** in that particular sign, or else the planet may be in **Detriment** or **Fall**. Simply put, the basic energy of a planet is strongest and unfettered in a sign of which it is the Ruler; generally this is a good thing, but with certain planets it is often preferable that their energies are hindered, such as with Mars or Saturn. A planet's energy is hampered, yet still somewhat functional, when in Fall. In Detriment, the planet is behind the curve, not able to manifest on its own. In Exaltation, a planet is being encouraged to act, but not given free reign to do so. There are two "classical" rulerships mentioned in the card descriptions; before the discovery of Uranus, Neptune, and Pluto, ancient astrologers considered Saturn to be the outermost limit of the solar system and thus assigned the rulership of Scorpio to Mars, Aquarius to Saturn, and Pisces to Jupiter. Now, astrologers consider Pluto to be the higher vibration, or more extreme expression, of the energy of Mars, Uranus to be the higher vibration of Saturn, and Neptune to be the higher vibration of Jupiter; thus, we say that Scorpio, Aquarius, and Pisces "share" rulership with two planets.

But why, you may wonder, were these particular thirty-six planet-and-sign combinations assigned to the pips out of all of the possible astrological combinations? Each of the thirty-six pips rules one *decan* (or ten degrees) of the zodiac. Not including the Aces, the Minor Arcana is organized according to the classical arrangement of the planets in order of the speed of their orbit as first observed by the ancient Chaldean astronomers, called the "Chaldean Order," beginning with the Two of Wands (Mars in Aries). The Minor Arcana repeats the descending Chaldean Order (Saturn, Jupiter, Mars, Sun, Venus, Mercury, Moon) around the Wheel of the Zodiac, with Mars being repeated at the beginning and at the end of the solar year (for Mars cuts the old year in order to begin the new). The Cardinal Signs (Aries, Cancer, Libra, Capricorn) are the 2's, 3's, and 4's; the Fixed Signs (Taurus, Leo, Scorpio, Aquarius) are the 5's, 6's, and 7's; and the Mutable Signs (Gemini, Virgo, Sagittarius, Pisces) are the 8's, 9's, and 10's:

Minor Arcana Around the Zodiac

2 of Wands: Mars in Aries (Cardinal Sign)
3 of Wands: Sun in Aries (Cardinal Sign)
4 of Wands: Venus in Aries (Cardinal Sign)

5 of Pentacles: Mercury in Taurus (Fixed Sign)
6 of Pentacles: Moon in Taurus (Fixed Sign)
7 of Pentacles: Saturn in Taurus (Fixed Sign)

8 of Swords: Jupiter in Gemini (Mutable Sign)
9 of Swords: Mars in Gemini (Mutable Sign)
10 of Swords: Sun in Gemini (Mutable Sign)

2 of Cups: Venus in Cancer (Cardinal Sign)
3 of Cups: Mercury in Cancer (Cardinal Sign)
4 of Cups: Moon in Cancer (Cardinal Sign)

5 of Wands: Saturn in Leo (Fixed Sign)
6 of Wands: Jupiter in Leo (Fixed Sign)
7 of Wands: Mars in Leo (Fixed Sign)

8 of Pentacles: Sun in Virgo (Mutable Sign)
9 of Pentacles: Venus in Virgo (Mutable Sign)
10 of Pentacles: Mercury in Virgo (Mutable Sign)

2 of Swords: Moon in Libra (Cardinal Sign)
3 of Swords: Saturn in Libra (Cardinal Sign)
4 of Swords: Jupiter in Libra (Cardinal Sign)

5 of Cups: Mars in Scorpio (Fixed Sign)
6 of Cups: Sun in Scorpio (Fixed Sign)
7 of Cups: Venus in Scorpio (Fixed Sign)

8 of Wands: Mercury in Sagittarius (Mutable Sign)
9 of Wands: Moon in Sagittarius (Mutable Sign)
10 of Wands: Saturn in Sagittarius (Mutable Sign)

2 of Pentacles: Jupiter in Capricorn (Cardinal Sign)
3 of Pentacles: Mars in Capricorn (Cardinal Sign)
4 of Pentacles: Sun in Capricorn (Cardinal Sign)

5 of Swords: Venus in Aquarius (Fixed Sign)
6 of Swords: Mercury in Aquarius (Fixed Sign)
7 of Swords: Moon in Aquarius (Fixed Sign)

8 of Cups: Saturn in Pisces (Mutable Sign)
9 of Cups: Jupiter in Pisces (Mutable Sign)
10 of Cups: Mars in Pisces (Mutable Sign)

Key Phrases

The ten Key Phrases of each suit of the Minor Arcana express the spectrum of four crucial elements of what it is to be human: Wands encompass our Will and Force, Swords our Interactions and Intellect, Cups our Emotions and Aspirations, and Pentacles our Matters and Manifestations—

Wands: Will and Force

Ace: Power of Fire
Two: Aggressive Conquest
Three: Established Strength
Four: Apparent Perfection
Five: Conflict
Six: Victory
Seven: Valiant Resistance
Eight: Fleeting Force
Nine: Boundless Potential
Ten: Oppression

Swords: Interactions and Intellect

Ace: Power of Air
Two: Harmony
Three: Separations
Four: Partnership

Five: Longing
Six: Fresh Horizons
Seven: Futility
Eight: Shortsighted
Nine: Cruelty
Ten: Ruin

Cups: Emotions and Aspirations

Ace: Power of Water
Two: True Love
Three: Abundance
Four: Blended Pleasure
Five: Heartbreak
Six: Sensuality
Seven: Poisonous Illusions
Eight: Abandoned Success
Nine: Indulgence
Ten: Happiness

Pentacles: Matters and Manifestations

Ace: Power of Earth
Two: Successful Change
Three: Triumph After Toil
Four: Acquisition
Five: Financial Troubles
Six: Prosperity
Seven: Discontent
Eight: Fixation
Nine: Inopportunity
Ten: Concrete Accomplishment

For deeper insight, it is also helpful to consider each of the numerical groupings by Key Phrase:

Aces (Influenced by Kether): Power of Fire, Air, Water, and Earth

Twos (Influenced by Chokmah): Aggressive Conquest, Harmony, True Love, and Successful Change

Threes (Influenced by Binah): Established Strength, Separations, Abundance, and Triumph After Toil

Fours (Influenced by Chesed): Apparent Perfection, Partnership, Blended Pleasure, and Acquisition

Fives (Influenced by Geburah): Conflict, Longing, Heartbreak, and Financial Troubles

Sixes (Influenced by Tiphereth): Victory, Fresh Horizons, Sensuality, and Prosperity

Sevens (Influenced by Netzach): Valiant Resistance, Futility, Poisonous Illusions, and Discontent

Eights (Influenced by Hod): Fleeting Force, Shortsighted, Abandoned Success, and Fixation

Nines (Influenced by Yesod): Boundless Potential, Cruelty, Indulgence, and Inopportunity

Tens (Influenced by Malkuth): Oppression, Ruin, Happiness, and Concrete Accomplishment

A final method to think about when looking at the arrangement of the 2-10 of each Suit of the Minor Arcana is to consider each triplicity (set of three: the 2, 3, and 4 of Swords are the triplicity of Libra, the 8, 9, and 10 of Wands are the triplicity of Sagittarius) as **cycles of action**. The first card in a triplicity is the strongest expression or conception of the zodiacal sign, the second card is an alteration of the original energy of the sign (with the goal to preserve or continue the initial idea), and the third card is the end product of the sign (wherein the initial cycle is given significance, all the while containing the seed of its own destruction):

WANDS:

The Cycle of Power (Aries):
2 of Wands—Aggressive Action
3 of Wands—Established Strength
4 of Wands—Apparent Perfection

The Cycle of Success (Leo):
5 of Wands—Conflict
6 of Wands—Victory
7 of Wands—Valiant Resistance

The Cycle of Ambition (Sagittarius):
8 of Wands—Fleeting Force
9 of Wands—Boundless Potential
10 of Wands—Oppression

SWORDS:

The Cycle of Relationships (Libra):
2 of Swords—Harmony
3 of Swords—Separations
4 of Swords—Partnership

The Cycle of Ideals (Aquarius):
5 of Swords—Longing
6 of Swords—Fresh Horizons
7 of Swords—Futility

The Cycle of Mind (Gemini):
8 of Swords—Shortsighted
9 of Swords—Cruelty
10 of Swords—Ruin

CUPS:

The Cycle of Love (Cancer):
2 of Cups—True Love
3 of Cups—Abundance
4 of Cups—Blended Pleasure

The Cycle of Loss (Scorpio):
4 of Cups—Heartbreak
5 of Cups—Sensuality
6 of Cups—Poisonous Illusions

The Cycle of Acceptance (Pisces):
8 of Cups—Abandoned Success
9 of Cups—Indulgence
10 of Cups—Happiness

PENTACLES:

The Cycle of Work (Capricorn):
2 of Pentacles—Successful Change
3 of Pentacles—Triumph After Toil
4 of Pentacles—Acquisition

The Cycle of Wealth (Taurus):
5 of Pentacles—Financial Troubles
6 of Pentacles—Prosperity
7 of Pentacles—Discontent

The Cycle of Synthesis (Virgo):
8 of Pentacles—Fixation
9 of Pentacles—Inopportunity
10 of Pentacles—Concrete Accomplishment

The true interpretation of the Minor Arcana takes these many layers into consideration and combines them, in order to fully comprehend the meaning of each card. Just as Shakespeare's Hamlet said to his friend, "There are more things in heaven and earth, Horatio, Then are dreamt of in your philosophy," so there is much, much more to the humdrum events of the Kingdom of Earth than is generally perceived.

The Pentacles Suit

The Symbol

The Pentacles Suit represents the receptive earth element. A pentacle is the symbol of a pentagram (five-pointed star) engraved within a perfect circle or a coin. Earliest Tarot decks use a coin for this suit, and it was not until the late 1780s that Comte de Mellet changed the suit from coins to pantacles (meaning talismans), which Eliphas Levi and other ceremonial magicians later reworked into pentacles. Some people are bothered by the image of a pentagram, conditioned to misunderstand it as "satanic" or "evil" in some way, much as modern western society now views the swastika—a mythological solar symbol of light—as the twisted symbol of Nazism. Actually, the pentagram is the ancient representation of the spirit incarnated or "ensouled" upon the Earth. Each of the elements is represented by the four lower points of the pentagram—from right to left the points represent water, fire, earth, then air—with the upper point representing spirit, which (ideally) remains senior to the other elements.

The reversed pentagram is often associated with Satan—whose namesake's origins may be traced to the Egyptian Adversary Set, the Sumerian moon god Sin, or the Greco-Roman Lord of Time and Matter, Saturn—whose goal is to ensnare us in the flesh and the limitations of the physical universe. The reversed pentagram is the symbol of a spirit enmeshed or trapped within a body. Having relinquished sovereignty, the being is enslaved by the body's desires, weighed down by the demands of the world, and has lost the memory of its divine origins. This so-called "Sign of Baphomet" (because of it's similarity to the goat's head associated with the Adversary) was first recorded in history during the Inquisition's persecution of the Knight's Templar.

The Pentacle, however, is an upright five-pointed star with a circle around it. Traditionally, circles are a symbol of eternity, for they have no beginning and no end; the circle is also a symbol of the cyclical nature of existence. Circles simultaneously contain and protect. In Medieval times, the five-pointed star was used as a symbol for the five wounds of Christ; Sir Gawain, the gallant knight of King Arthur, employed the five-pointed star as his personal symbol, representing the five knightly virtues. Even the Chinese sometimes represent the five elements in their system of the cosmos (wood, fire, air, metal, water) with the image of a five-pointed star. Also called the "Star of the Microcosm," when a human being stretches out both arms and feet (just like Leonardo da Vinci's famous sketch) the head, two arms, and two legs form the five points of the pentacle, symbolizing man as the microcosm of the macrocosm, a visual depiction of the hermetic axiom, "As Above, So Below" as well as the biblical "kingdom within."

The Pentacle is the perfect representation of both the macrocosm of the Kingdom of Earth—the constantly varying interchange of the elements as they move into and out of solidified form—as well as the human body, the material vehicle of the spirit. Of course, the symbolic goal of the pentagram or pentacle is to become the six-pointed hexagram, commonly known as the Star of David, for just as the five-pointed star represents the microcosm of man, so the six-pointed star (as two triangles laid on top of each other—one reaching upwards, and one reaching downwards) represents the union of man with God as well as the macrocosm of the Divine.

Setting and Color Scheme: Snowy, winter landscape; earthy, muted colors

Astrological Correlation: The earth signs Taurus, Virgo, and Capricorn

Seasonal Celebration: Christmas, Yule, Winter Solstice

Cycle Story: When the God is born of the Virgin Goddess

Court Card Characters: Father Time, Mary, Oak King (Holly King), Newborn King

Ace of Pentacles
Root of Earth / Kether of Assiah

Key Phrase: Power of Earth

Practical Divinatory Meaning:

- Success in money and job
- Material satisfaction
- Don't wait—start now
- Establish a firm, safe, and secure foundation for yourself

Astrological Combination and Qabalistic Influence:

The Ace of Pentacles represents the root of the earth element in the raw, pre-manifestation state of Kether; each crystallization of the material world retains the shadow of its origin in Kether. When Kether is in Assiah, significant action in the physical universe underlies all intended endeavors.

Two of Pentacles

Jupiter in Capricorn (Fall) / Chokmah of Assiah

Key Phrase: Successful Change

Practical Divinatory Meaning:

- Prosperity in work and resources
- You will win in the current situation, even if the other party is more deserving
- Success will come if you act now
- Triumph for the body at the expense of the spirit

Astrological Combination and Qabalistic Influence:

When Jupiter is in Capricorn, the querent is driven by a never-ending ambition to control the material world and change his or her status through achieving ever-greater positions of authority. A person with this planet-and-sign combination will often have a prominent position in society and a strict ethical code, but this success in the material world generally interferes with family life, intimate relationships, and individual spiritual growth. (Spiritually speaking, this combination might breed a Cardinal of the Catholic Church or a Reverend Jim Bakker, instead of an Anchorite or a Mother Theresa.) There is a tendency towards parsimony in minor matters, excessiveness in great ones, and an impulsion to win at another's expense. The influence of Chokmah adds the pure force of the earth element in its most untainted, balanced form, therefore promising swift, intense, and consuming increase in the physical realm.

Three of Pentacles

Mars in Capricorn (Exaltation) / Binah of Assiah

Key Phrase: Triumph After Toil

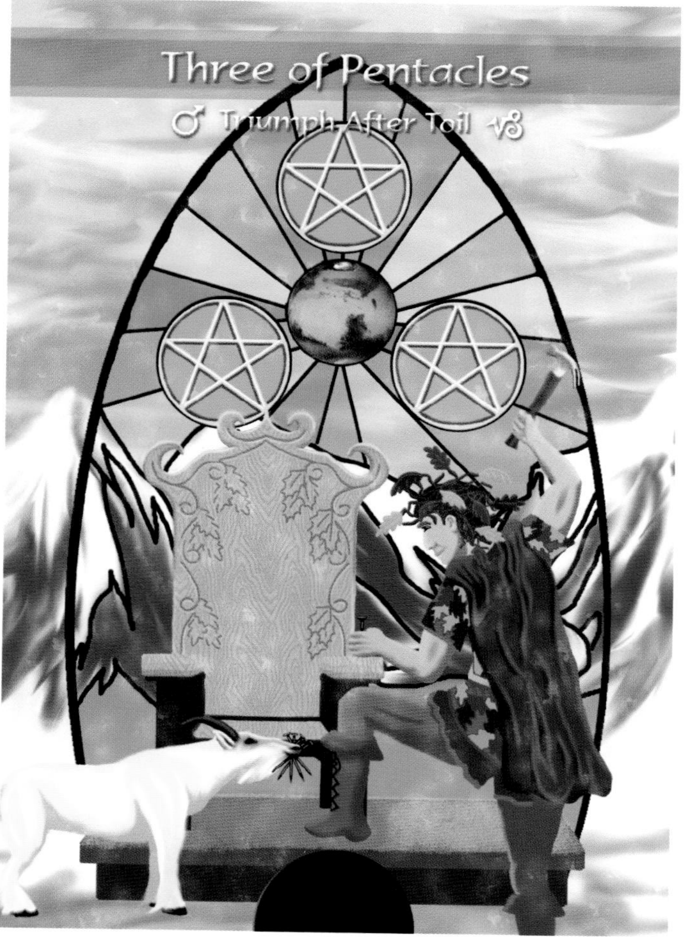

Practical Divinatory Meaning:

- You can succeed if you are willing to work very hard
- Don't miss opportunities just because you feel tired and restricted by your current circumstances—you will only be defeated if you give up
- What you're thinking of doing is a good idea, but be prepared for quite a challenge

Astrological Combination and Qabalistic Influence:

Mars is strong in Capricorn, giving the querent vast resources to accomplish his or her ambitions. The querent is driven by the desire for power at all costs, and takes control by asserting authority. The influence of the Sephirah Binah, however, places limitations upon the prospects themselves so that the querent must work hard in order to utilize his or her innate power and achieve a successful outcome, therefore immense self-control and restraint is required of the querent.

Four of Pentacles

Sun in Capricorn / Chesed of Assiah

Key Phrase: Acquisition

Practical Divinatory Meaning:

- Material attainment; job satisfaction; stabilization of finances
- Accolades and Recognition
- If poorly aspected, confront your fears about wealth and lack, for only those who are willing to give will be able to receive

Astrological Combination and Qabalistic Influence:

Sun in Capricorn brings the ability to rise to the top in the material realm. People with this planet in sign combination tend to be assiduous organizers and attain an impressive position both financially and in the community; they are patient and cunning in their plans as well as willing to exploit their advantages for profit. The influence of Chesed in the realm of Assiah gives stability and security to this card, as well as a remarkable ability to actively create agreement between all aspects of the matter to acquire material goods.

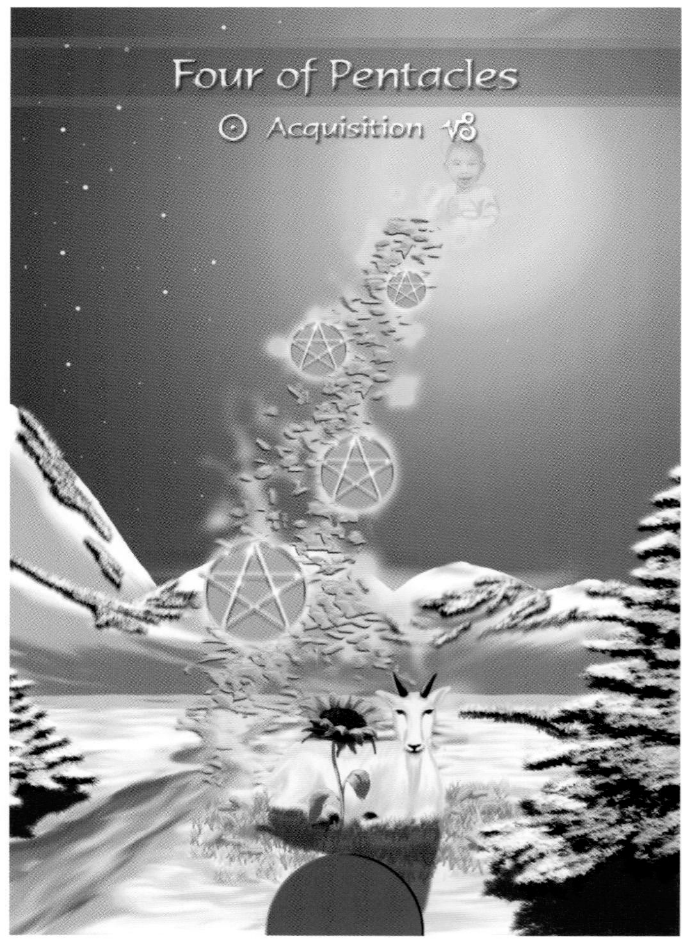

Five of Pentacles

Mercury in Taurus / Geburah of Assiah

Key Phrase: Financial Troubles

Practical Divinatory Meaning:

- Act now, or mounting debt will become too much to handle
- Stop worrying and pretending the bills will go away—consult an expert
- The current advice you're receiving is flawed—get a second opinion
- Focus on future financial goals

Astrological Combination and Qabalistic Influence:

When Mercury appears in Taurus, there is an overriding fear of financial failure, preoccupation with concerns about career, as well as general security issues that make any new ideas or possible changes seem threatening. The influence of Geburah of Assiah adds an active shattering of the existing condition: things need to change, to get shaken up if they are to improve, regardless of the discomfort it may bring.

Six of Pentacles

Moon in Taurus (Exaltation) / Tiphereth of Assiah

Key Phrase: Prosperity

Practical Divinatory Meaning:

- Follow your financial hunches
- Increase of wealth and prosperity
- Happy family matters

Astrological Combination and Qabalistic Influence:

When the Moon appears in Taurus, there will be great security and luck in financial matters. Everything in the material realm will seem to flow the individual's way, naturally. Tiphereth of Assiah only strengthens this card, reflecting the original Greek of Romans 8:28 when it says, "for those who love God, all works together for good by the purpose called being." The very nature of the individual transforms the common into the sublime.

Seven of Pentacles

Saturn in Taurus / Netzach of Assiah

Key Phrase: Discontent

Practical Divinatory Meaning:

- Your hard work isn't enough because of insufficient resources
- Watch out for contractual troubles, cutbacks, and layoffs
- Don't sign any contracts or make any commitments right now—you don't have all the facts
- You will run out of money, time and resources if you keep pursuing this venture

Astrological Combination and Qabalistic Influence:

Saturn and Taurus intrinsically disagree; there is a lack of resources to finish the task at hand, regardless of the considerable effort that has already been invested. An obsession with lack of returns and fear of losing underlies every decision, covered by a desperate need to show off and appear magnanimous. The additional unbalanced state of Netzach makes it impossible to render an equitable resolution at this time.

Eight of Pentacles

Sun in Virgo / Hod of Assiah

Key Phrase: Fixation

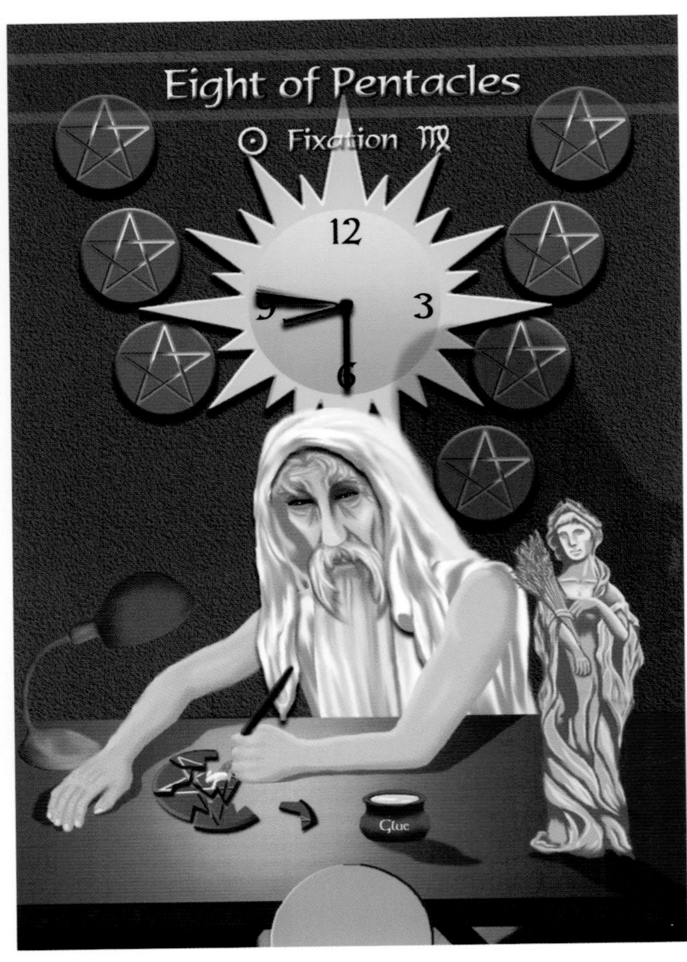

Practical Divinatory Meaning:

- Fixation on the insignificant to avoid the facts
- Stop obsessing about what's not working and move on

- Your current investments will not pay off
- Look at things objectively rather than subjectively—think big picture to get your perspective back

Astrological Combination and Qabalistic Influence:

The Sun in Virgo is able to focus upon the minutest details, categorize any system, and create order out of apparent chaos. The darker side of this critical attention to intricacy, however, is the tendency towards fixation that is often devoid of any perspective of the grander design. Just as the Sun governs our general vitality and constitution, Virgo rules both health and work, for we must feel well in order to work well. Thus, with regards to issues of health, the Sun in Virgo will be consumed with every aspect of an acute illness. Hod in Assiah adds a propensity to over-intellectualize all concerns and pursuits of the moment, to the exclusion of exceptions, future repercussions, and concrete results. Therefore, this card epitomizes the logical construction that the mind generates to re-fashion the external world to match the internal orderings of the querent. The Golden Dawn used the saying "penny wise but pound foolish" to describe this card.

Nine of Pentacles

Venus in Virgo (Fall) / Yesod of Assiah

Key Phrase: Inopportunity

Practical Divinatory Meaning:

- Don't start anything new—especially a romantic relationship
- Be careful of ill-timed opportunities at work
- Watch out for unreliable partnerships and enticing temptations
- You're missing something—be careful

Astrological Combination and Qabalistic Influence:

Where the Sun in Virgo over analyzes the details of a given situation, Venus in Virgo over analyzes emotionally and relationally, with little connection to the hard, cold facts of the matter. This often results in extreme selectivity and illusions with little basis in reason or reality. This planet in sign combination is notorious for falling in love with those with whom they work, often with disastrous results. The additional influence of Yesod of Assiah brings a dreamy lack of reality to the card, further muddling the emotional filter through which judgments are made.

Ten of Pentacles
Mercury in Virgo (Ruler) / Malkuth of Assiah

Key Phrase: Concrete Accomplishment

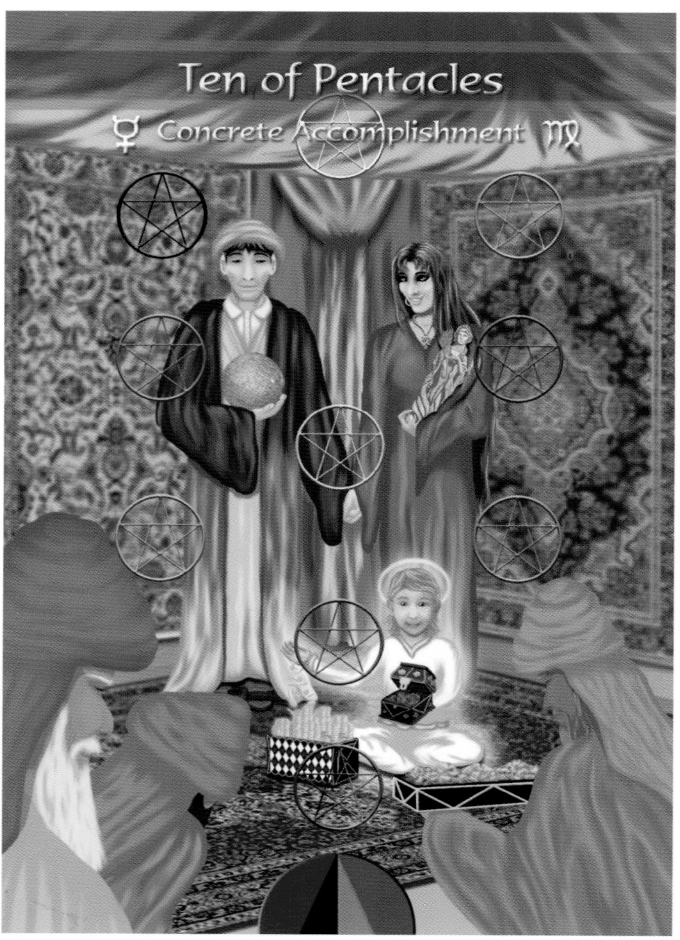

Practical Divinatory Meaning:

- Enjoy the fruit of your labors—you've earned it
- The financing you need is coming
- A good time to move on or up
- Contentment in the material plane

Astrological Combination and Qabalistic Influence:

Mercury learns discipline in meticulous Virgo, thus the intelligence of Mercury combines favorably with the well-ordered work ethic of Virgo to create a multi-skilled craftsman in his or her chosen business field(s). This combination brings a talent for written and oral communication as well as in networking in the workplace. This is the best planet-in-sign combination for productivity, bringing well-deserved tangible rewards on the physical plane. Malkuth is strongest in Assiah, therefore this card represents the complete manifestation and action of the earth element in its most solid and enduring form. As with all Tens, inherent in this card is a bittersweet double-edge, for as one reaches completion in any area on the material plane, there will soon be an ending and destruction of the structure of success in order to prepare for the next conception.

The Wands Suit
The Symbol

Conjure the image of the legendary Merlin of King Arthur's Camelot or else Gandalf from J.R.R. Tolkien's *Lord of the Rings* trilogy. What crucial instrument of power was neither mage ever without? A long piece of wood that each used to channel his extraordinary powers. The legendary magical wand (or staff) of the mighty wizard serves as the symbol for the transmissive fire element of the Wands Suit. Why are wands typically fashioned out of wood? Wood serves as the ideal conductor for the destructive and transformative power of fire. In tales of myth and legend, the magic wand graphically portrays this powerful combination of phallic masculinity with fiery force. Just as the magician masters the art of change in conformity with the will, so the wand is traditionally his (or her) most well known tool for transformation; therefore, Wands govern the realms of creativity, desire, and power.

Setting and Color Scheme: Spring's awakening life; vibrant, bright colors
Astrological Correlation: The fire signs Aries, Leo, and Sagittarius
Seasonal Celebration: Ostara (Vernal Equinox), Easter
Cycle Story: When the God travels to the Underworld and returns to reunite with the Beloved
Court Card Characters: Risen King, Eostre, Dionysus, Mary Magdalene

Ace of Wands
Root of Fire /
Kether of Atziluth

Key Phrase: Power of Fire

Practical Divinatory Meaning:

- Potent action to achieve desires will succeed
- Achievement of goals and creative endeavors
- Long term plans come to fruition

Astrological Combination and Qabalistic Influence:

The Ace of Wands represents the root of the fire element in the raw, pre-manifestation state of Kether; because Kether is pure in Atziluth, this Ace is the most powerful of all the Aces.

Two of Wands
Mars in Aries (Ruler) /
Chokmah of Atziluth

Key Phrase: Aggressive Conquest

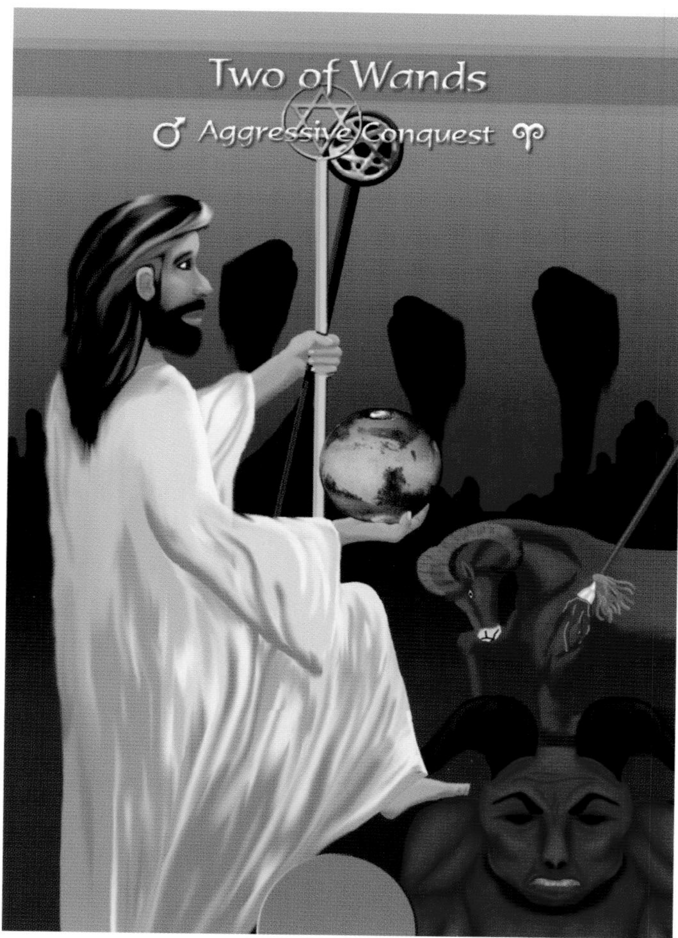

Practical Divinatory Meaning:

- Make it happen, take charge, take the plunge—you will triumph
- Wavering and second-guessing will bring failure
- The others will follow you

Astrological Combination and Qabalistic Influence:

Mars rules Aries, bringing strength and success in impulsive, forceful action. In this combination there is an inclination to embark upon many undertakings and proceed before thinking them through, but the sheer power of this combination seems to always carry one to victory. Mars loves to divide and conquer in Aries, preferring to work alone, as it is too aggressive to partner. The influence of Chokmah in Atziluth adds even greater forceful power to the equation for triumphant conquest.

Three of Wands

Sun in Aries (Exaltation) / Binah of Atziluth

Key Phrase: Established Strength

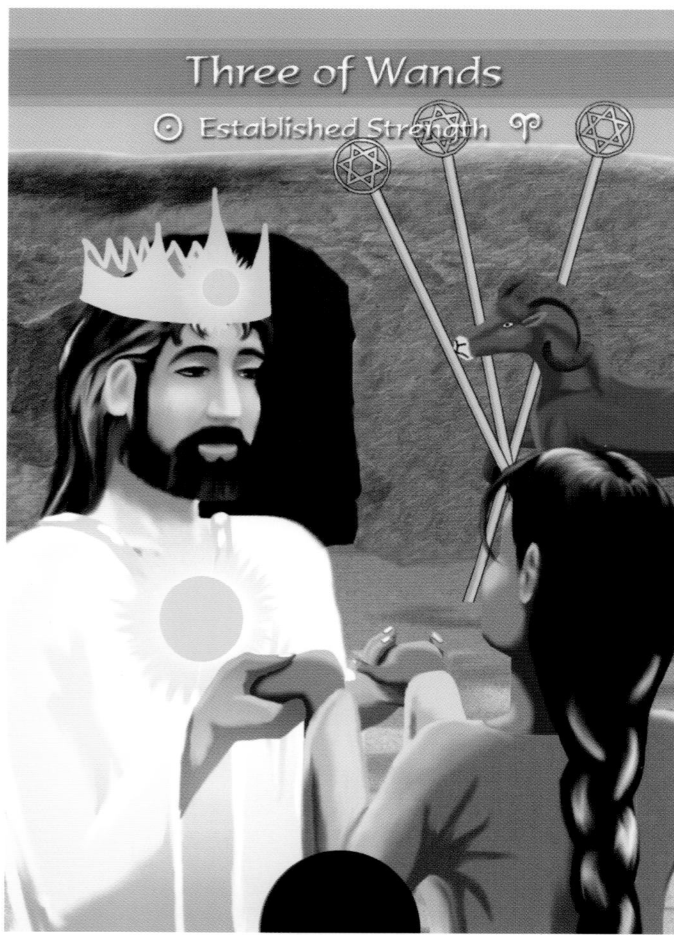

Practical Divinatory Meaning:

- You hold the winning position of power and control in the current circumstances
- Leadership is handed to you, so wield it nobly and justly
- If poorly aspected, watch out for family or group dissension

Astrological Combination and Qabalistic Influence:

The Sun exalts in Aries, behaving as royalty established on the throne. This combination acts assertively in contrast to the aggression of Mars in Aries, as one who has already established his or her strength and has no need to prove it, although there is still a strong drive to lead and impress. The Sun in Aries loves change, but benefits from careful consideration before action. Binah of Atziluth, however, adds the limitation of the differing viewpoints of others challenging one's existing position of leadership, thus calling for constant defense of one's position.

Four of Wands

Venus in Aries (Detriment) / Chesed of Atziluth

Key Phrase: Apparent Perfection

Practical Divinatory Meaning:

- Everything seems wonderful, but it's a lie
- You are making poor decisions everywhere—at home, at work, and in love
- Stop treating those around you as obstacles rather than individuals

Astrological Combination and Qabalistic Influence:

The femininity of Venus clashes with the masculinity of Aries, creating an innate incongruity. The Morning Star merrily seems to twinkle in Aries, but "all that glitters is not gold." This apparent splendor beguilingly covers a desperate need for attention, competitive ownership in partnerships, and an insistence that everyone else play a prescribed part in one's own movie…or else. Chesed of Atziluth brings a drive to achieve the ideal of agreement to the detriment of the reality.

Five of Wands

Saturn in Leo (Detriment) / Geburah of Atziluth

Key Phrase: Conflict

Practical Divinatory Meaning:

- There will be conflicts, disagreements, and dissension
- Problems with the boss at work or other authorities
- Attend to emotional burn out and deteriorating physical health issues resulting from over-doing

Astrological Combination and Qabalistic Influence:

The restrictive maturity of Saturn simultaneously weakens and is weakened when combining with the youthful virility of Leo; the resolute willpower of Saturn applies itself to acquire awards and accolades in a leadership position that affords both control and public recognition, like stage or production management. These same skills, however, breed friction in both professional and personal relationships because of Saturn in Leo's dangerous combination of being righteously over-bearing yet constantly in need of approval; often the individual cannot resolve the discord and will, dejectedly, ultimately end up alone. Geburah in Atziluth adds the destruction of all existing forms to the mix, promising arguments, fights, and continued hostilities until something (or someone) changes.

Six of Wands

Jupiter in Leo / Tiphereth of Atziluth

Key Phrase: Victory

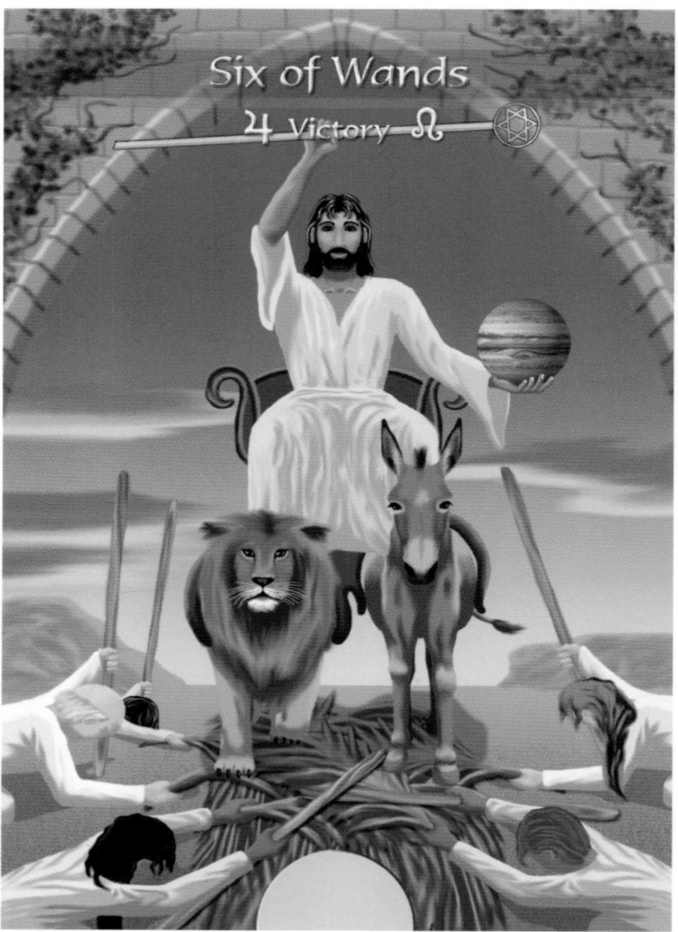

Practical Divinatory Meaning:

- Success in all endeavors
- You will prevail over your problems
- Even in a really negative reading, this card provides the good luck to be victorious

Astrological Combination and Qabalistic Influence:

Jupiter is triumphant in Leo. The public loves them, they expand to rise to any position or occasion, and they love a good show. Even their children adore them. Tiphereth of Atziluth only increases the good fortune of this card, making it quite possibly the most positive card in the deck!

Seven of Wands

Mars in Leo / Netzach of Atziluth

Key Phrase: Valiant Resistance

Practical Divinatory Meaning:

- There will be constant barriers to accomplish your goals
- The harder you push, the harder you will be pushed back
- There may be loss of credit, job, or relationship
- Don't put off going to the doctor right now
- It's a lost cause

Astrological Combination and Qabalistic Influence:

Mars in Leo brings great strength, but also great antagonism from others. There is an egotistic quality to this planet-in-sign that is both potent and pathetic. An overriding sex drive in combination with a competitive spirit seems to invariably impel one to heroic acts, yet simultaneously others obstruct accomplishment in some way. There is a motivation to direct, yet at the same time destroy. Netzach of Atziluth only heightens the out-of-control sexuality at the root of this card, all the while encouraging the more natural, animalistic urges to reign supreme.

Eight of Wands

Mercury in Sagittarius (Detriment) / Hod of Atziluth

Key Phrase: Fleeting Force

Practical Divinatory Meaning:

- Impulsiveness in all matters as a result of preoccupation with long term ambitions
- Slow down or you'll get a speeding ticket
- Tendency to rush and not complete things
- Surprise visit from afar

Astrological Combination and Qabalistic Influence:

When Mercury enters Sagittarius, we have a clash in breadth of vision: Mercury makes superficial connections and quickly covers short distances, while Sagittarius is solely concerned with depth of wisdom and long-term goals. Thus, with this planet-in-sign combination we have far-reaching inspiration, but short-term follow through. There is a great interest in discovery, but an inclination to be easily swayed by other people's opinions as well as the philosophical fad of the moment. The individual is adept at maneuvering the tides of public opinion and popularity, but rarely delivers on his or her promises. Hod of Atziluth bestows this card with greater beliefs in one's own intellectual prowess along with an attempt to attain too much, too quickly.

Nine of Wands

Moon in Sagittarius / Yesod of Atziluth

Key Phrase: Boundless Potential

Practical Divinatory Meaning:

- Boundless potential is yours to achieve your aims
- A long voyage, significant move, or long term goal will soon be realized
- No matter how poorly aspected, this card brings optimism to the outcome

Astrological Combination and Qabalistic Influence:

Child of optimism, idealism, and honesty, the Moon in Sagittarius is a delightful combination. Bursting with confidence and foresight, this visionary realizes far away lands, distant goals, changing scenery, and expansive truths. Yesod of Atziluth brings stability in the midst of change, making the seemingly impossible, possible for this individual—the more radical, the better.

Ten of Wands

Saturn in Sagittarius / Malkuth of Atziluth

Key Phrase: Oppression

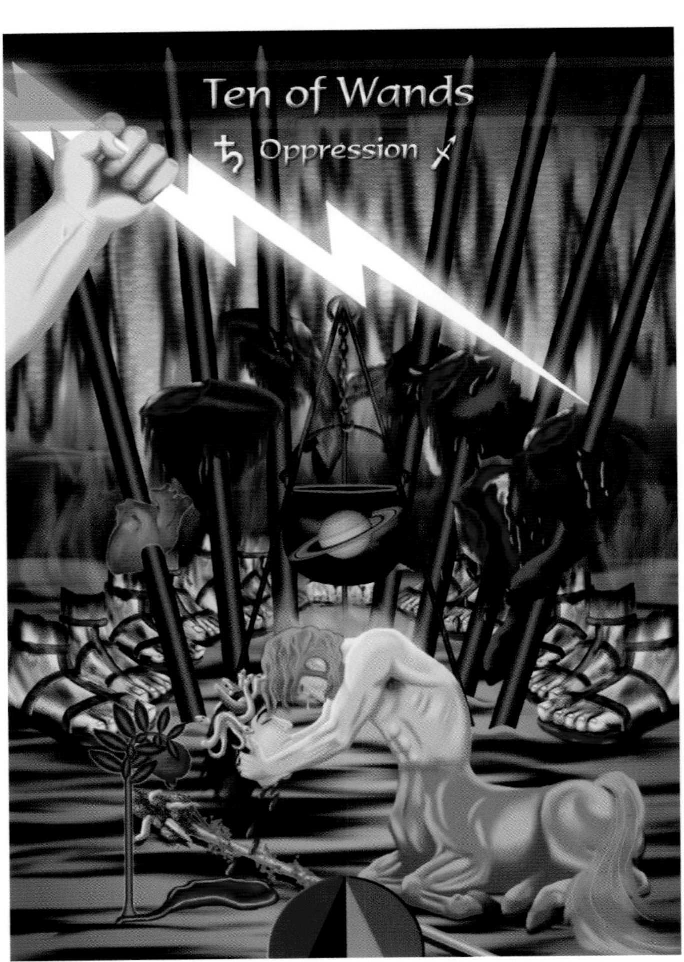

Practical Divinatory Meaning:

- Anxiety and oppression from unforeseen sources
- A confrontation is coming with a suppressive person or group
- Stop blaming yourself for things you can't help
- If you don't STOP, you could have a nervous breakdown

Astrological Combination and Qabalistic Influence:

The heavy limitations of Saturn are ultimately at odds with the broadening spirituality of Sagittarius, forming a rather schizophrenic fusion of traits. All of a sudden the expansive and freeing qualities of Sagittarius begin to suppress and oppress the individual. For example, one might travel to a foreign country that represses individual freedoms, feel inundated by the overwhelming abundance of choices for the future, or else could get involved in a strict religion that insists that its way is the only way. Malkuth of Atziluth demonstrates the blind force of fire almost completely disconnected from spirit, thus exhibiting itself in crude devastation. At least, as with all Tens, there is the promise of the coming destruction of the current situation to make way for the new…it can't get any worse.

The Cups Suit

The Symbol

For most people, the legend of the Holy Grail is either a subject for movie magic—from the comic *Monty Python and the Holy Grail* to the action-adventure *Indiana Jones and the Last Crusade*—or else a dim memory of Arthurian Legend from high school and college literature courses. Tradition has it that King Arthur lost most of his Knights of the Round Table when they embarked upon the Quest for the Grail, fabled to be the very cup from which Jesus drank at the Last Supper and which Joseph of Arimathea later used to catch Christ's blood as he hung on the cross. However, with the current popularity of Dan Brown's novel, *The DaVinci Code*, the Holy Grail has returned to the public forefront as something very different: a symbol of the Divine Feminine. The characters in *The Da Vinci Code* discover the "secret" of the Holy Grail: that the Grail was the literal womb of Mary Magdalene—the sacred "chalice" that carried the divine blood, or child(ren), of Jesus—who allegedly settled in southern France after the crucifixion.

Regardless of our personal preferences and prejudices about its significance, the Holy Chalice or Grail is a vast and complex symbol of literary, historical, mythological, and spiritual import. This Chalice serves as the perfect symbol for the Cups Suit, which represents the receptive Water element. Just as Wands and Swords are tall, piercing, prominent phallus-like symbols, so the hollow depths of the Chalice represent the female vagina and womb, waiting to receive the masculine force which sparks its process of creation through the sacred merging and bliss of sexuality, as the two become one with a greater whole. Cups signify the fertile substance of the universe that unites in order to create, and so rules issues of emotion, intuition, love, and spirituality.

But what, exactly, is the historical significance of this Suit's symbol? The origins of the Grail are diverse and wide-ranging. Experts offer three possible linguistic foundations for the curious term grail. The first is Latin, *gradale*, a dish used in various courses of the meal, and the second is Old French, *gradule*, a wide plate. The third theory is that it originated from the French *sang real* or Sangreal, meaning Royal Blood, which eventually changed to San Graal, and finally Saint Grail. The proposed range of past sources for the Grail as a spiritual icon is vast. Some of these include:

- Egyptian roots in the Pomegranate cup of the cult of Isis.
- Celtic roots in the healing and life-giving cauldrons of the gods Dadga and Bran, or even the Celtic goddess Cerridwen, who had a cauldron that created a potion of inspiration and knowledge called greal.
- Asian roots in the begging bowl of the Buddha.
- European roots in the Communion cup of Catholic transubstantiation.
- Arabic roots in the Kaaba, a sacred black stone near the Great Mosque of Mecca that the Moslems believe God sent from heaven.

The backgrounds of the Grail knights themselves—Gawain, Galahad, Percival, and Bron—also seem to echo older mythologies, such as the Irish heroes Cuchullin and Finn. Bron's name resembles that of the Celtic god Bran. Percival, generally the primary focus of Grail literature, bears remarkable similarities to the much older Welsh tale of Peredur. Based upon the early accounts of Nennius, Annales Cambriae, William of Malmesbury, and Geoffrey of Monmouth, historians have even established that a chieftain named Arthur really existed, uniting and organizing the Celts against the Saxon invasions of the sixth century.

Key writers about the Grail include the following:

- In the 12th century, the French romantic poet Chretien de Troyes wrote *Perceval*, or the *History of the Grail*. (Note: There are many different spellings of the name "Percival.") Claiming that he was reworking material found in an older manuscript, de Troyes' unfinished work became the primary source for later Grail writers.
- In Wolfram von Eschenbach's (1165-1220) *Parzival*, the Grail is a stone that fell from the heavens. He maintained that his work was based upon a mysterious source from southern France and the Kabbalah of the Spanish Jews.
- 13th century Robert de Boron's poems *Joseph d'Arimathe*, *Merlin*, and *Perceval* asserted not only that the Grail was the Christ's cup, but also that the Grail revealed the true inner teaching of the Christian mysteries.
- In 1469 Sir Thomas Malory wrote his well-known *Morte d'Arthur*, which emphasizes the purity of Galahad as the principal Grail knight.
- Richard Wagner's famous *Parsifal* opened on July 26th, 1882. Wagner's occult leanings are well known, and many authorities consider Wagner's opera to be a symbolic primer into his spiritual ideas.
- Alfred Lord Tennyson's (1809-1892) epic poem, *Idylls of the King*, is replete with metaphysical themes and imagery.
- Arthur Edward Waite's (1909) *Hidden Church of the Holy Graal* was released the same year as his (and Pamela Colman Smith's) famous occult Tarot deck. Waite hints that the Holy Grail lies at the root of the Minor Arcana.
- T. H. White's *The Once and Future King* was first published in 1958. In this account of the Grail, Arthur initiates the Grail Quest in an attempt to halt his Knights' conflicts with each other. Lancelot, Arthur's greatest knight, fails because he lacks the necessary purity. Galahad and Percivale find the Grail and depart with it to Babylon, where the Grail will never be seen again. The only successful knight to return to Camelot is Bors.

Interpretations regarding the true meaning of the Grail can be categorized into three basic types. The first is that it is simply a fanciful literary legend. The second explanation is that the Grail has an historical foundation. For example, one hypothesis is that the Grail represents the alternative apostolic succession of the Celtic Church, evidently established by Joseph of Arimathea with the apostle John and founded over two hundred and fifty years before the Roman Church. Another theory proposed by Sir Laurence Gardner in his book, *Bloodline of the Holy Grail,* is the same as that found in *The DaVinci Code*: that Jesus and Mary Magdalene were the parents of a messianic dynasty—traceable to the Merovingian Kings of Gaul who founded the French monarchy, the Queens of Avallon in Burgundy, and culminating in King Arthur of Britain—who were never rulers of territory, but instead the ordained guardians of the people. Eventually the tradition of the Holy Grail was pushed into the land of legend, conveyed primarily through the Tarot's Cups suit.

The final interpretation is that the Grail Quest is spiritually allegorical; renowned mythologist Joseph Campbell succinctly explains this view in *The Power of Myth:*

> "The theme of the Grail romance is that the land…has been laid waste …And what is the nature of this wasteland? It is a land where everybody is living an inauthentic life, doing as other people do, doing as you're told, with no courage for your own life…The Grail becomes…that which is attained and realized by people who have lived their own lives. The Grail represents the fulfillment of the highest spiritual potentialities of the human consciousness."
>
> (Campbell 1991, *The Power of Myth*, 244)

Frater Achad avows that Wagner's version of the Grail Quest is a "collective tradition of mankind [that] when rightly interpreted, must represent the largest truth…[presenting] the ideal humanity which lies behind the aberrations of individuals, races and period" (Achad 2002, *The Chalice of Ecstasy*, 3). Achad compares Parzival, "the Pure Fool," to Everyman (and Woman) who spiritually transforms by ascending the Qabalistic Tree of Life. He emphasizes that when Parzival wins the Holy Spear from Klingsor's Keep and brings it to the Temple of the Holy Grail, this mirrors the merging of the Spear of Wisdom (Chokmah) with the Cup of Understanding (Binah); only with their joining does existence become "Pure Joy," for Understanding without Wisdom is "Pure Darkness." Parzival's true mission is that of Redeemer as he heals the wound of Amfortas, the Grail King (also called the Fisher King) who possesses the Grail but is unable to use it. Malkuth, the Animal Soul and Fallen Daughter, is represented by Parzival's relationship with the woman Kundry, whom he must also redeem as a necessary part of his attainment. Three things are necessary for Parzival to attain the Holy Grail and, thus, redemption: The purification of the Water, the shedding of the Blood, and the anointing of the Holy Spirit (Kether). Once redeemed, Parzival becomes himself a Redeemer.

Every Cup in *The Kingdom Within Tarot* contains a mixture of both water and blood, for symbolically it is only through the shedding of blood and the cleansing of water that spiritual transformation occurs. The Cup contains a terrifying aspect, for it is associated with the concept that the old must be destroyed in order for the new to begin; wrapped in this symbolism are the blood sacrifices of antiquity and the cyclical mystery of female menstruation. The Cup contains the boiling, frothing blood and water of alchemical transformation.

Setting and Color Scheme: The beach in summer; pastel colors

Astrological Correlation: The water signs Cancer, Scorpio, and Pisces

Seasonal Celebration: Midsummer (Summer Solstice), Summer Vacation

Cycle Story: When the God is at the peak of his life and the Goddess is heavy with joyful pregnancy

Court Card Characters: Green Man, Gaia, Sir Galahad, Puck

Restored Tree of Life with the Minor Arcana

Restored Tree of Life with the Minor Arcana

Ace of Cups

Root of Water / Kether of Briah

Key Phrase: Power of Water

Practical Divinatory Meaning:

- Success in all emotional endeavors
- Follow your intuition right now
- Heralds a new relationship
- Now is the time for a sacred pilgrimage or rite

Astrological Combination and Qabalistic Influence:

The Ace of Cups represents the root of the Water element in the raw, pre-manifestation state of Kether; when Kether enters the creative world of Briah, we have the might of suppleness, reflection, cleansing, and cohesion to the detriment of distinctiveness—never underestimate the power of the Deluge.

Two of Cups

Venus in Cancer / Chokmah of Briah

Key Phrase: True Love

Practical Divinatory Meaning:

- Harmonious relationships and reconciliation
- You've found true love
- Expansion of family by marriage, birth, or inheritance

Astrological Combination and Qabalistic Influence:

The ingénue and the mother merge when Venus is in Cancer in order to form a "more perfect union." Here comes the nurturing romantic who, out of a deep need for adoration and an unspoken dread of being alone, seeks the stability of a life's companion and the creation of a home to be the primary focus of all his or her energies. Chokmah of Briah demonstrates the power of the masculine and the feminine in perfect harmony, love's union being achieved by mutual annihilation, the consummation of the parts in the creation of a greater whole.

Three of Cups

Mercury in Cancer/ Binah of Briah

Key Phrase: Abundance

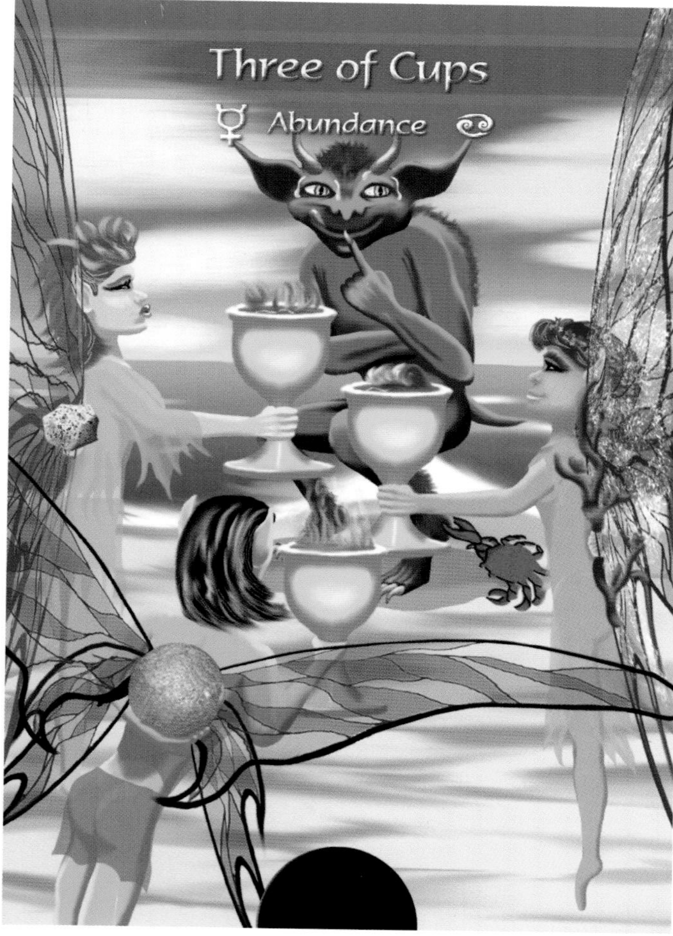

Practical Divinatory Meaning:

- Your are entering a time of abundance—accept and enjoy it
- Increase in lovers, affection, and pleasure
- If poorly aspected, watch out for love affairs and cheating

Astrological Combination and Qabalistic Influence:

Intellectual Mercury is unable to distinguish thoughts from feelings in emotional Cancer—past experiences play far too much importance in present decisions, and the individual reacts with pure emotion to any new idea or circumstance. This fusion forms a general "the more the better" attitude about everything. For example, one may collect multitudes of memorabilia, trivia, and books; find it impossible to choose between lovers; or need to talk incessantly to everyone. Binah is strongest in Briah, lending greater urgency to the unifying impulse of love to embrace each and every encounter. Abundance can lead to ecstasy, but with regards to this card Crowley wrote, "the lesson seems to be that the good things of life, although enjoyed, should be distrusted" (Crowley 1974, *The Book of Thoth*, 197).

Four of Cups

Moon in Cancer (Ruler) / Chesed of Briah

Key Phrase: Blended Pleasure

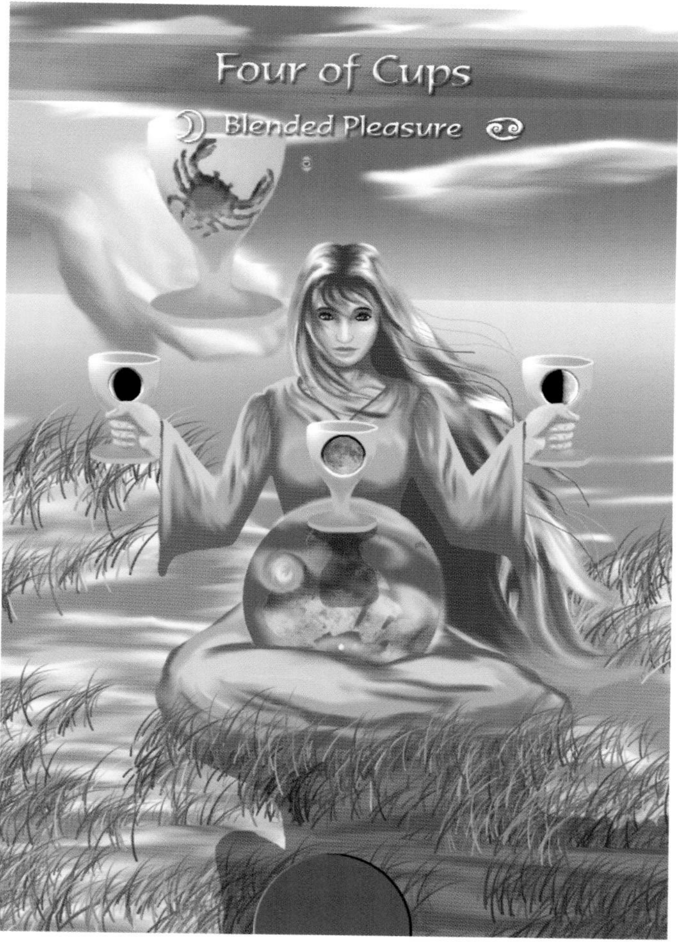

Practical Divinatory Meaning:

- Blended pleasure as you remain in a less than perfect situation
- Dominant feminine influence in one's life
- If poorly aspected, problems with life cycles, hormones, and children

Astrological Combination and Qabalistic Influence:

The Moon rules Cancer, and so we find the greatest strengths and weaknesses of the Moon highlighted in this planet-and-sign combination. Here we have maternal nurturing and extreme empathy; cyclical, emotional perception of the world; an emphasis on home and family; "crabbiness" in times of stress; and a willingness to remain in an imperfect situation for the good of the other. Chesed is weakened in Briah, its stabilizing nature hampered by emotionality. As with all Fours, Chesed of Briah brings Harmony and steadiness—but at what price to the individual who sacrifices for peace?

Five of Cups

Mars in Scorpio (Classical Ruler) / Geburah of Briah

Key Phrase: Heartbreak

Practical Divinatory Meaning:

- Loss of pleasure and desperate avoidance of pain
- Downhill spiral of despair, anger and regret
- Bankruptcy and financial disaster
- Blaming outside circumstances for personal mistakes

Astrological Combination and Qabalistic Influence:

In classical astrology, Mars is strong in all three water signs, called the "watery triplicity"—this strength, however, rarely seems positive from the perspective of those whose lives are affected by it. In Scorpio the emotions are volcanic and bottomless, with many hidden skeletons in the closet, thus when the surgeon Mars enters the scene to "cut" out all the imperfections, he has to cut extremely deep—and it hurts. Individuals with this combination contain tremendous all or nothing passions (and a temper!) that overpowers others and explodes at the most unfortunate times; they often feel like the hero who has failed in his or her life's quest, tending towards depression and sometimes even suicide. The strong Mars causes them to love or hate with equal devotion, either seeking emotional martyrdom on the one hand or Machiavellian revenge on the other. In Briah, Geburah detonates the emotions, creating a walking time bomb.

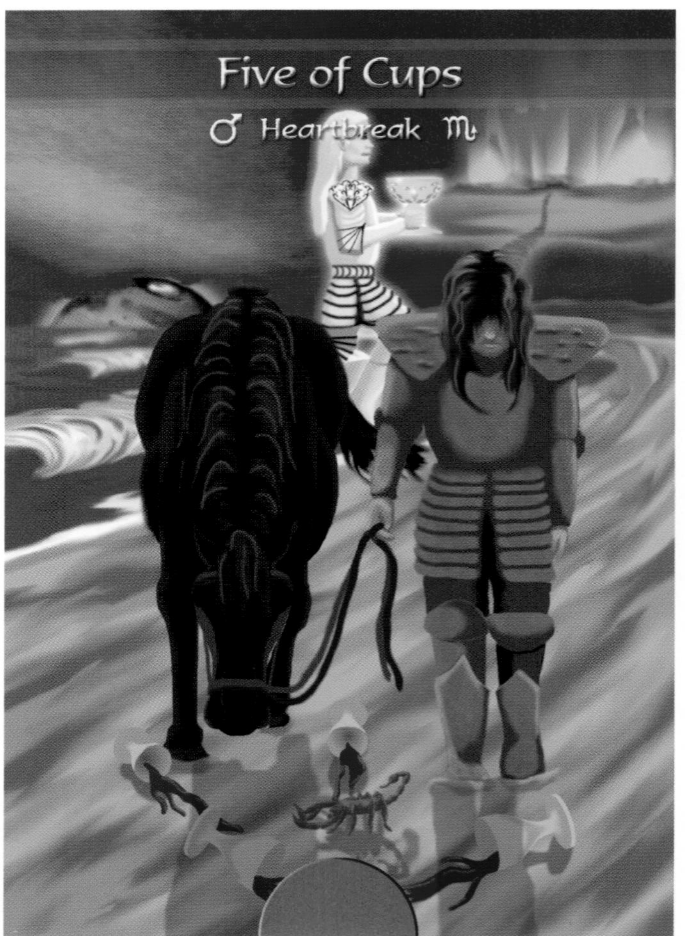

6 of Cups

Sun in Scorpio / Tiphereth of Briah

Key Phrase: Sensuality

Practical Divinatory Meaning:

- Carnal excess and a roller coaster of emotions
- Tendency to give up—DON'T
- Extreme life change, often in resources, debt and taxes
- Difficulty establishing or accepting boundaries

Astrological Combination and Qabalistic Influence:

This card is often called "the Lord of Pleasure," and for good reason—this planet-in-sign combination seeks pleasure (especially of a sexual and financial nature) at all costs, for it denotes losing oneself in the extremes of sensation to escape pain. Of course, this chase creates a roller coaster of extremes, the highs of pleasure always followed by the lows of its darker sister, pain. Those with the Sun in Scorpio are passionate yet distant, curious yet secretive, and love any change (initiated by themselves, of course). Most are extremists that believe that the color gray is only an illusion created to obscure the True Black and White of any situation. The extremes of fiery Tiphereth with watery Briah breed a rich fertility and fecundity to this energy, yet always with an underlying transitory character, for the brilliant Sun of Tiphereth will eventually evaporate the creative moistness of Briah, given time.

Seven of Cups

Venus in Scorpio (Detriment) / Netzach of Briah

Key Phrase: Poisonous Illusions

Practical Divinatory Meaning:

- Pretending that minor matters have great significance in order to avoid facing meaninglessness
- More won't make you feel better

- Conflicts, dirty secrets, jealousies, and dangerous partnerships
- Elaborate illusions to avoid painful truths

Astrological Combination and Qabalistic Influence:

Venus becomes messy, muddled, and venomous in Scorpio: externally lovely but internally perverse. This individual is secretive about everything—inner poisons, sexual fantasies, true responses, deep emotional scars. The same dramatic contrasts of the Sun in Scorpio are also exhibited when Venus is in Scorpio, only the extremes have become sick, twisted, and largely hidden from view. The more upset this individual becomes, the more cold and calculating. Illusions and desires are attributed with significance to make the emptiness of sensation have meaning. There is an interest in anything dark or occult, as it serves the addiction to illusions and mystery. Netzach of Briah is completely imbalanced, for as Crowley stated about this card, "the holiest mysteries of Nature become the obscene and shameful secrets of a guilty conscience" (Crowley 1974, 200).

Eight of Cups

Saturn in Pisces / Hod of Briah

Key Phrase: Abandoned Success

Practical Divinatory Meaning:

- Overlooking an important opportunity
- Persevere and you will eventually succeed
- All is not lost—it is not as hopeless as it seems
- The path of least resistance leads to loss
- Inaction as a result of feeling old and useless

Astrological Combination and Qabalistic Influence:

Saturn is the planet of limitations, while Pisces is the sign of restrictions: this combination, obviously, bodes feelings of loss as one is limited and restricted in the current situation. There is a basic indolence resulting from loss of hope or pleasure, with all the accompanying justifications for lack of action. Saturn brings great potential for self-disciplined accomplishment, but the individual is quagmired in the ever-deepening waters of Pisces. Often one is restricted by feelings of old age and the resistance to change that comes from the fear of the unknown. There is an impulse to retreat from the world as well as a tendency to lose oneself in the demands of others and the current situation. Hod of Briah brings an influence that is opposite to the previous card: now the loftiest aspirations of the mind are bogged down by the mass of understanding.

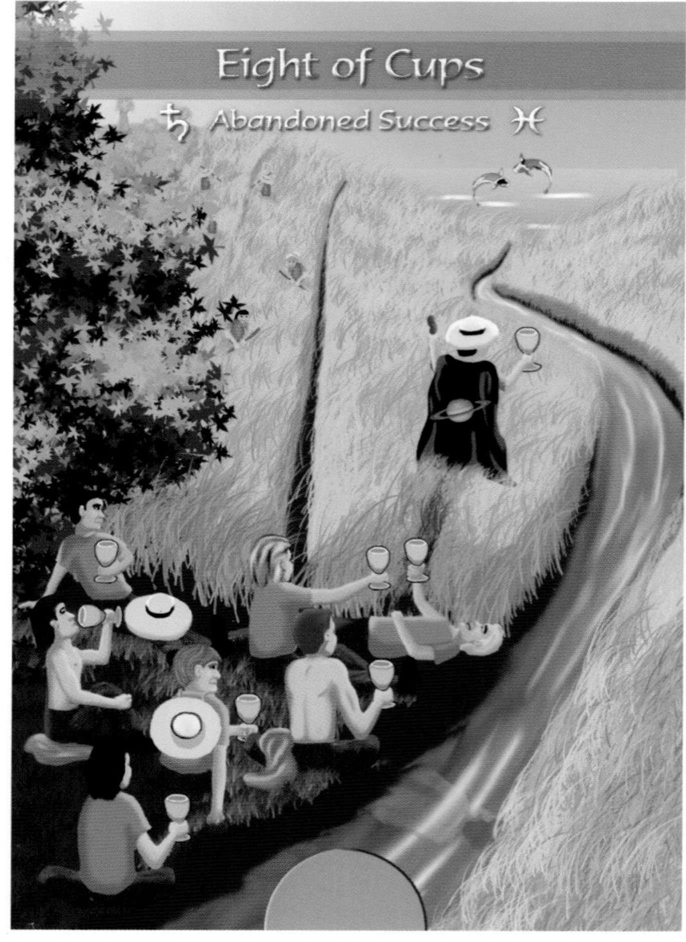

Nine of Cups

Jupiter in Pisces (Classical Ruler) / Yesod of Briah

Key Phrase: Indulgence

Practical Divinatory Meaning:

- Celebration, intoxication, and excess
- Hidden addictions and temptations
- Suffering after overindulgence
- If poorly aspected, watch for concealed intentions and exploitation

Astrological Combination and Qabalistic Influence:

Beneficent Jupiter expands, breaking the restrictive bands of Pisces to bring blessings and happiness, although Jupiter has the tendency to expand over and above in Pisces, bringing too much of a good thing. Pisces, on the other hand, continues to compulsively hide things, so there may be hidden excesses, addictions, deceptions, and ulterior motives—even spiritually speaking. Nines always restore the imbalances of the sevens and eights, and so Yesod of Briah births the steadiest aspects of the Water element, bringing blissful feelings and joyful indulgences—even if the cup does runneth over.

Ten of Cups

Mars in Pisces/ Malkuth of Briah

Key Phrase: Happiness

Practical Divinatory Meaning:

- Achievement of emotional ideals (may not be a positive development)
- Completion and happy endings
- Something hidden in what seems a happy life—warning
- Beware of hidden hostility or manipulation
- Feeling trapped in a heaven of your own choosing

Astrological Combination and Qabalistic Influence:

The destructive warrior Mars attacks the hidden depths of Pisces, but wherever he cuts, more water quickly rushes in to replace the old. At its best, there is a bittersweet Don Quixotic quality to this combination—the blissfully unaware champion who chases windmills yet is useless to this world. Here are two extreme opposite energies—fire and water, aggression and passivity, precision and mystery—that create a bevy of oxymorons. One might help others in order to avoid facing oneself. Someone appears to be a friend, but is really an enemy. Life seems peaceful and idyllic, but this placid exterior hides a mounting desire to escape. There is a grand seeking of elusive ideals to avoid facing the burdens of reality, often manifesting as a dogmatic obsession with the pursuit of happiness and "feeling good" that ultimately enslaves others and oneself. Malkuth of Binah adds a self-satisfied veneer of complacency that further obscures the issue. With the completion of earthy Malkuth in watery Briah, the destruction of all this avoidance is, thankfully, just around the corner.

The Swords Suit

The Symbol

The final Suit of the Minor Arcana is the transmissive Air element, represented by the Sword. To understand the logic behind the choice of this symbol, one has only to look at it: a sword is a phallus crafted for combat. Its sharp blade slices through the insubstantial air and penetrates to the heart of the matter, giving you the upper edge. Battles have been won or lost, agreements made or broken, by the strength of the Sword. The Swords Suit rules those arenas that are combative, sharp, penetrating, and interested in winning the upper edge—conflict, reason, the mind, and communication. Any matter decided by the Sword (or by conflict, reason, and communication, for that matter) by its very nature is impermanent; it takes constant vigilance to maintain a superior position. Is there perhaps a higher Path that transcends the inherent transience of the Sword?

If you look at the hilt of your average sword, you will probably see that it forms a cross. In his text on the Grail myth, Frater Achad calls this the *Sign of the Cross*, "from which the creative Word issued at the birth of the dawning universe" (Achad 2002, *The Chalice of Ecstasy*, 19). According to Achad's Qabalistic interpretation of the Parzival story, we begin our Quest for the Grail (Understanding) with the Sword of Reason, a lesser skill that is needed until we transform it into the Holy Spear of Will and Wisdom (Chokmah). Only with Wisdom (in contrast to Reason) may we regain awareness of our True Selves, which in turn enables us to directly perceive truth without the fallible structures of inference and deduction.

Setting and Color Scheme: Autumn, as darkness falls; dark, Halloween colors

Astrological Correlation: The air signs Gemini, Libra, and Aquarius

Seasonal Celebration: Halloween, The Day of the Dead, Samhein, Autumnal Equinox

Cycle Story: When the old God dies and the Goddess mourns

Court Card Characters: Mictlantecutli, Hecate, Lord of Misrule, Persephone

Ace of Swords

Root of Air/ Kether of Yetzirah

Key Phrase: Power of Air

Practical Divinatory Meaning:

- A new message, contact, or communication is coming
- Use reason and intellect to confront current situation
- Successful resolution of conflict
- Look for new partnerships

Astrological Combination and Qabalistic Influence:

The Ace of Swords represents the root of the Air element in the raw, pre-manifestation state of Kether; when Kether works in the Formative world, the idea of Order is born from Chaos.

Two of Swords

Moon in Libra / Chokmah of Yetzirah

Key Phrase: Harmony

Practical Divinatory Meaning:

- Harmony in partnerships, but the peace will be temporary because of underlying problems
- Positive settlement of legal disputes and personal disagreements
- New partnership or a higher level of commitment in current relationship(s) is coming

Astrological Combination and Qabalistic Influence:

When the Moon enters Libra, there is harmony and balance. Here we have a comfortable joining of feelings with intellect—the only down side to this combination is that, as a result of the changeable moon, the truce may not last long. These individuals will do anything to keep the peace, possibly sacrificing what may actually be more important (remember that harm-on-y has the word harm in it). Chokmah of Yetzirah sparks epiphanies regarding the other sides of an issue, as well as the intellectual acumen to satisfy any disagreement.

Three of Swords

Saturn in Libra (Exaltation) / Binah of Yetzirah

Key Phrase: Separations

Practical Divinatory Meaning:

- Loss of job, partnership, court case, or argument—even lost valuables
- Grief from separation or ending of a partnership
- Current relationships have a flawed foundation—time to renegotiate

Astrological Combination and Qabalistic Influence:

Most humans do not like the appearance of this card in a reading, but it is actually a crucial experience from a broader perspective. Saturn exalts in Libra, limiting Libra's unions and partnership, bringing constriction in agreement and therefore endings, separations, and general sorrow because of the refusal to let go of the achieved balance and order that is past. Although Saturn increases the ability to judge and arbitrate in legal matters, that same skill of judgment can wreak havoc in relationships. To truly understand this card, the influence of Binah of Yetzirah demands close inspection: the dark waters of understanding unite with the world of forms to generate rifts in what we conceive to be the natural order of our lives, creating what seems to us to be the fiendish realities of division and pain. These "fiends" have been with us all along, however; the entire gamut must be embraced in order to find deliverance.

Four of Swords

Jupiter in Libra / Chesed of Yetzirah

Key Phrase: Partnership

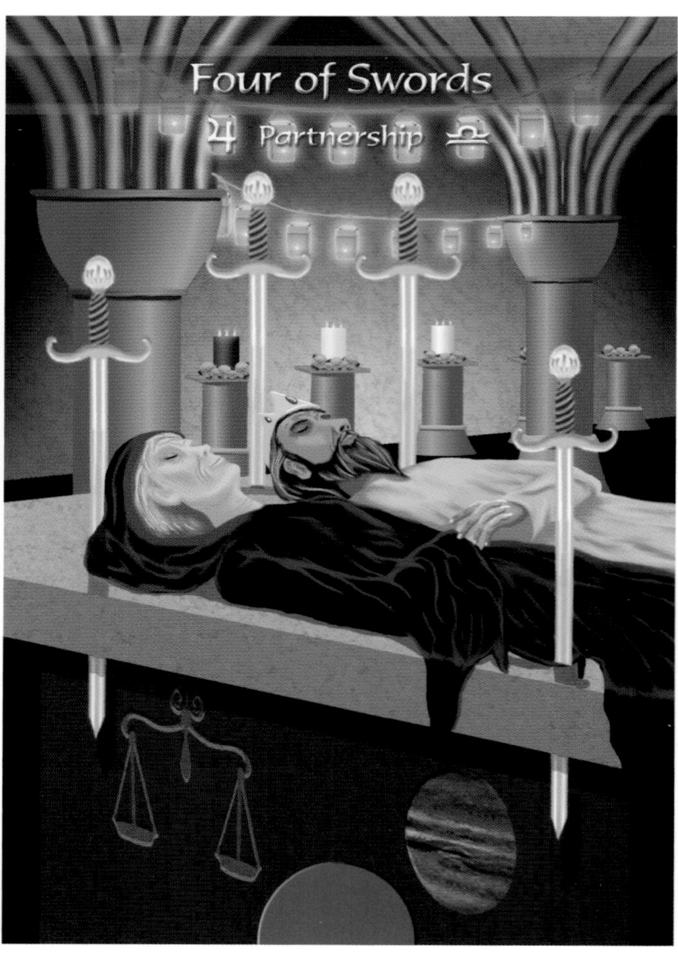

Practical Divinatory Meaning:

- Rest from current strife
- Success in all forms of partnerships
- The professional(s) you consult will provide excellent advice
- Business and financial negotiations will go well, especially if you resolve them yourself
- Personal interactions will only improve your life right now

Astrological Combination and Qabalistic Influence:

Jupiter expands the potentials and possibilities of Libra's partnerships, opening the way for everything from lucrative businesses to soul mates. These individuals will find their success through partnerships, both materially and spiritually. Chesed of Yetzirah is the perfect combination for tranquil stability of all forms.

Five of Swords

Venus in Aquarius / Geburah of Yetzirah

Key Phrase: Longing

Practical Divinatory Meaning:

- What once seemed perfect, has now spoiled and turned rotten
- Dreams become delusions
- Betrayal in partnerships and loss of reputation
- Poor investments of a personal nature as well as a financial one
- New relationships will fail
- If very well aspected, profiting from another's loss

Astrological Combination and Qabalistic Influence:

The beneficial aspects of Venus are diluted in Aquarius, and the cleverness of Aquarius is additionally weakened by the sentimentality of Venus. Sweet Venus becomes aloof, bringing a bittersweet detachment as well as timidity and duplicity. There is a tendency to cling to ideals or causes, for people cling to generalities when they fail at specifics. These individuals seem gracious enough, but underneath is the puzzling amalgamation of avidly seeking one's ideals combined with the fear that those same dreams have already passed by. This commonly leads to a lack of stable partners in the individual's life, as well as a perpetual struggle with feelings of defeat. The real damage comes from Geburah, for here Geburah demolishes through frailty and decadence, rather than force.

Six of Swords

Mercury in Aquarius (Exaltation) / Tiphereth of Yetzirah

Key Phrase: Fresh Horizons

Practical Divinatory Meaning:

- Be ready for good news
- Leaving a bad situation for a better one
- Enjoy your success and the good advice of friends—you deserve them
- Change will bring increase and help you realize your dreams

Astrological Combination and Qabalistic Influence:

Mercury exalts in Aquarius, for now the Multifaceted Genius enjoys a trip through the Sign of freedom, dreams, and humanity. There is great ingenuity and openness to anything new and fresh. A love of avant-garde ideas, science, and technology spurs the individual to ever-greater horizons. Tiphereth shines in Yetzirah, bringing equilibrium and triumph in all forms.

Seven of Swords

Moon in Aquarius / Netzach of Yetzirah

Key Phrase: Futility

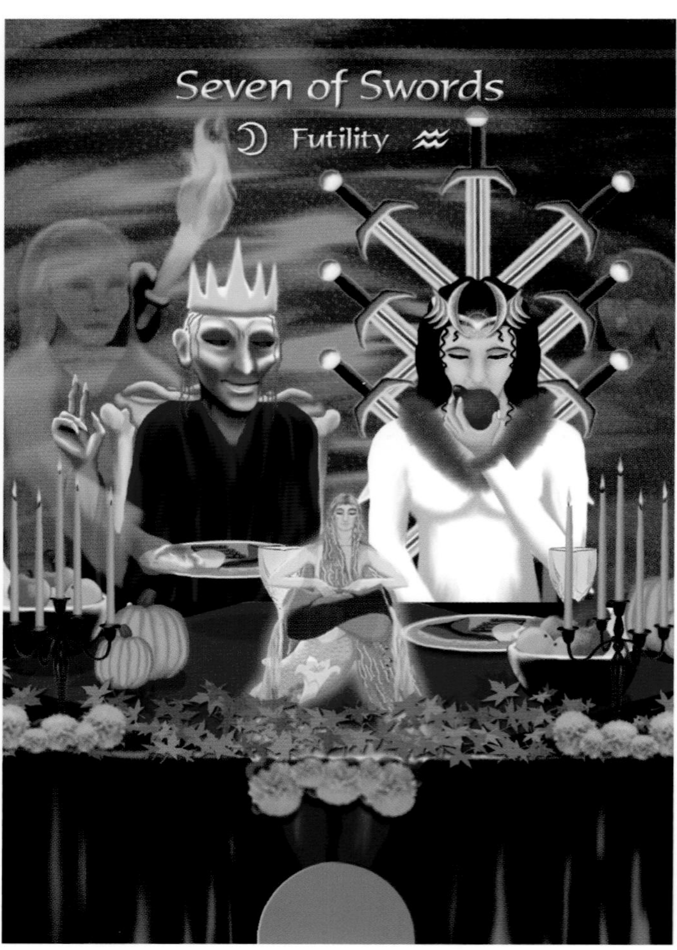

Practical Divinatory Meaning:

- Your good intentions and high ideals are not enough—there's little support for success
- Watch out for betrayal and public mis-information
- Be careful who you trust—thieves and liars surround you
- Any cause you feel drawn to right now is a lost one
- Be careful of investments—promises will not pay off

Astrological Combination and Qabalistic Influence:

People with the Moon in Aquarius tend to lose things—from objects, to relationships, to dreams. Because of the Moon's influence they are changeable, but the high emotions of the Moon are now attached to freedom, ideals, and humanity rather than to groups or individual relationships. They are emotionally independent, detest clingy partners, and tend to align themselves with impossible causes, like world peace. They consider ideals all-important, and are not beyond using deviousness to attain them. Netzach of Yetzirah lends a positive influence, bringing a willingness to compromise and abide.

Eight of Swords

Jupiter in Gemini (Detriment) / Hod of Yetzirah

Key Phrase: Shortsighted

Practical Divinatory Meaning:

- Open your eyes—you're missing something important
- Be careful of snap judgments and groundless conjecture
- Misperception and misapprehension in all arenas
- Focusing upon appearance and image over substance and truth

Astrological Combination and Qabalistic Influence:

When spiritual Jupiter enters superficial Gemini, there is a desire to know about everything, but without any depth. There will be little education or wisdom, but much knowledge of trivia. There will be grand aims, but little accomplishment—much focusing upon small, superficial things to the detriment of grander issues. Jupiter in Gemini is all about the facade of substance, rather than the reality. Hod of Yetzirah is undisciplined at best, further enhancing the lack of follow through.

Nine of Swords

Mars in Gemini / Yesod of Yetzirah

Key Phrase: Cruelty

Practical Divinatory Meaning:

- Explosive arguments with neighbors, siblings, and older women
- Nightmares, loud noises, and trouble sleeping
- Contract disputes and missing paperwork
- Rumors, gossip, and cruel intentions
- Unless someone rises above their own point of view, the fighting will continue

Astrological Combination and Qabalistic Influence:

Warrior Mars becomes fanatical in Gemini—brilliant, brutal, and out for blood, but battling in the realm of communication and the intellect. Gemini's wit is twisted for the purpose of proving superficially perverse half-truths, making one excellent at argument and repartee. There will be inexhaustible energy for gathering proof to substantiate one's case as well as "holy" verbal battles, much like the Great Inquisition. Yesod of Yetzirah imbues order into the disarray of the 7 and 8 of Swords, giving the 9 of Swords a formidable foundation of cunning for the subtle, self-justified cruelty that underlies all this battling.

Ten of Swords

Sun in Gemini / Malkuth of Yetzirah

Key Phrase: Ruin

Practical Divinatory Meaning:

- The current situation is ruined beyond repair
- Your reputation is in danger
- Personal ruin from gossip, rumors, and backstabbing
- A critical communication is coming—watch for it

Astrological Combination and Qabalistic Influence:

Those with the Sun in Gemini may rise up in revolt at the Key Phrase for this card, but please withhold your judgment until finishing this paragraph. The greatest potential enemy of anyone with the Sun in Gemini is failure. Although blessed with quick minds, agile bodies, and admirable flexibility, those with this planet-in-sign combination (perhaps because of their predisposition to be a jack-of-all-trades-but-master-of-none) seem cursed with a proclivity to struggle with finishing anything. If you talk big, wander from interest to interest, are more interested in how things look than what they are, know a little about a lot of subjects, love experiencing more than doing, and rarely see anything to completion—you have a tendency to fail. Stack up failure after failure, and you have Ruin. Multitudes of people born with the Sun in Gemini do not come to ruin, because there are many other things going on in their natal charts (as well as free will) that affect their lives, but this is the basic tendency for those whose Sun in Gemini is poorly placed. Add Malkuth of Yetzirah, and you have the Air element in its weightiest, most gross form—for when logic is disconnected from actuality, free creation is obliterated and replaced with only the mirage of forms.

Chapter Four
Remembering the Art of Interpretation

The Metaphysics and Physics of Astrology

So now what?

Now that we have an extensive understanding of the Tarot cards—what do we do with them?

The *Art of Interpretation* (and it is an art, for not only is it a skill that is attained by study and observation, but it also arises from the exercise of our intuitive faculties as well) is a practice, a skill, and a remembering. We must study and practice all the essentials, honing our developing skills, until our spirit responds with an intuitive remembering of what it has forgotten about itself, the world, and truth. But first, in order to build a firm foundation for accurate interpretation (and prediction), we must add to our current understanding of the Tarot cards themselves the wisdom of the ancient practice of astrology. For astrology teaches not only an extensive ordering of the energies of this solar system, but also a comprehensive method of combining and seeing the interplay of these energies within the Kingdom.

The very mention of astrology invokes an impressive array of responses. Of course, the skeptics consider it to be a lot of out-dated mumbo-jumbo that simply pre-dates modern astronomy. (From an historical perspective, until quite recently "astronomers" and "astrologers" were actually the same people: simply those who devoted themselves to studying the heavens.) Many contemporary astrologers optimistically maintain that an individual's birth chart embodies his or her greatest gifts to the world while acting as an all-knowing teacher through which the individual may confront his or her weaknesses and karmic lessons. The student of *metaphysics* (defined as the branch of philosophy that examines the nature of reality, including the relationship between mind and matter, substance and attribute, fact and value), however, generally tends towards a more prosaic view of astrology: It is the study of the external energies that influence and impel (whether for good or ill) any being living in this solar system. Whether one views this body of flesh as a gift, a teacher, or a curse (or all of the above), the natal chart and subsequent progressions record the astrological impulsions that will continue to rule the individual's body throughout its physical lifetime. Horary and mundane astrology, on the other hand, reveal the astrological impulsions affecting a given event in time, a group, or a worldwide trend.

Astrology is the study of the rhythms, the patterns, and the continual changes of our solar system. Imagine for a moment a large piece of fabric stretched as taut as possible. This is much like the cosmos of existence. Now, imagine that one tiny portion of this vast expanse jiggles ever so slightly—the entire fabric responds to the change by moving as well. Yet, to anyone who is unaware of the original shift of balance, this movement might appear "mysterious" or "unexplainable." So it is with most of humanity. Trapped inside our own narrow point of focus (and our own minds), we do not grasp the grander design of the fabric of the cosmos. The symphony of the spheres plays a jarring note, and we see only the "problems" that result for us on a personal level, not realizing that discordance is an essential part of dynamic harmony. Every quark, every atom, every star, every galaxy has joined together to form an intricate web, but often we feel like the trapped fly at the mercy of the dreaded spider. The study of astrology can help us move beyond our limitations and broaden our understanding of existence.

Astrological impulsions are akin to a river of energy in which the individual (or group) is currently swimming, conveying all its contents towards a specific direction—if you carefully dam a river on one level, you still have to deal with the mounting pressure, a pressure that will inevitably express itself in another area of your life. While some may view these astrological energies as life enhancing, I propose that they are a type of prison—for even the best of birth charts is a restriction of free creation and individual will. An astrological chart is simply a record of the energy moves that are blocked or enhanced by outside forces, imprisoning the individual spirit in a pre-conditioned body of flesh. In my opinion, the goal of studying Astrology is not to appreciate one's natural abilities and learn necessary lessons, but to release oneself from this prison of prescribed impulsions. How is this possible? To the degree that one does not see, "free will" is only an elaborate delusion. To the degree that an individual spirit is associated with his or her body and believes that she/he is the body—a belief firmly rooted in *avidyā*—is the degree to which the astrological impulsions have sovereignty. The more one has *vidyā* (correct understanding) and actually sees, the more one can release oneself from the restrictive programming of the physical universe and his or her own conditioning, laziness, trauma, and avoidance. To break the energeric conditioning of your natal chart, practice behaving (or emoting) in directions other than those to which your chart impels you.

It is natural to ask the two-fold question, "Where do these astrological energies come from and what is their purpose?" While there are myriad theories, I would like to propose only the most obvious. These energies were created by a being (or beings) vastly beyond the perceptivity of most of humanity today, obviously for the purpose of placing physical controls and limitations on any spirit incarnated into the material universe.

Beyond this simplistic answer, I suggest that the individual continue to hone his or her seeing, for once one sees accurately, the answers to this question soon reveal themselves. The second question that naturally follows the first is, "All things considered, why do astrologically-based Tarot at all?" Ah, HERE is the key. For Tarot with a strong astrological foundation assists the reader to see the impulsions, cycles, and trends of which she/he may not be aware. A Tarot reading based upon the wisdom of astrology is not "fortune telling;" it is a snapshot in time of the energies that surround the querent (and issue forth from within the querent) which reveals the probable future that will result from the current impulsions, cycles, and trends if nothing is changed. Free will is a result of *vidyā*, and thus the very act of doing this type of reading gives the querent crucial information that she/he needs in order to act appropriately in his or her life's circumstances.

The physics of astrology are fairly straightforward, although much challenged by certain sectors of society. Today, some scientists claim that we have outgrown the "simplistic" astrological/alchemical basis of the universe upon the four elements. However, it is a workable system of classification that was invented by ancient Chaldean, Arab, and African (or Egyptian) astronomers, who systematically observed the heavens while recording cycles of change, daily events, and natural phenomena. These "astrologers" (which simply means those who study the stars) divided the Sun's path through the heavens into twelve quadrants, now called the zodiac, choosing a cluster of "fixed" stars that were easily recognizable for each quadrant and giving that cluster a name to identify it—thus the twelve signs. Some opponents to astrology point out that today some of these fixed star clusters are not actually in the same place at the same time relative to the Earth as they were in ancient times (for example, the constellation Pisces is still in the sky when the constellation called Aries has supposedly ascended), but this demonstrates a marked misunderstanding on their part: the constellations were convenient markers to identify observable changes, they do not cause the changes themselves.

There is both a literal and an evocative aspect to the four elements—for although fire can be viewed as another name for the state of matter called "plasma," it also epitomizes the nature of a particular form of energy as it materializes in the physical universe—hot, fast, purifying, destructive, and transforming. In contrast, water (like the state of matter called "liquid") is cool, changeable, cleansing, and healing. As I discussed earlier in Chapter Two, the twelve astrological signs of the zodiac are really the four elements (or states of matter) of the universe—fire (plasma), air (gas), water (liquid), and earth (solid)—combined with the three expressions of energy—start, change, and stop. The Cardinal Signs (Aries, Cancer, Libra, Capricorn) combine each element with change, the Mutable Signs (Gemini, Virgo, Sagittarius, Pisces) with start, and the Fixed Signs (Taurus, Leo, Scorpio, Aquarius) with stop. Thus the zodiac summarizes the dynamics of the solar system, and astrological charts reveal which dynamics are encouraged or limited in our lives.

The ancients noticed that certain visible heavenly bodies (the two luminaries and the five inner planets) moving through the zodiac seemed to have predictable correspondences to phenomena here on Earth, their influence either being strengthened or weakened by their movement through certain signs. Out of these observations, the characterization of these "planets" and their "essential dignities" in certain signs was born. (More recent astrologers have added the outer planets to this list as they were discovered by humanity.)

Essential Dignities

As stated in Chapter One, each planet rules, like a King or Queen, one or two signs, called its **Domicile**—the basic energy of the planet is strongest and unfettered in its own Kingdom. When a planet moves through a sign that is opposite to the one it rules, it is in **Detriment**. Here, the planet is behind the curve, not able to manifest on its own. All but two planets also have an **Exaltation**, a sign wherein the planet is encouraged to act, but not given free reign to do so, sort of like visiting the home of your best friend. When a planet appears in a sign that is opposite to its Exaltation, it is in **Fall**. A planet's energy is hampered, yet still somewhat functional, when in Fall, sort of like being the guest of a person who doesn't really like or trust you. Before the discovery of Uranus, Neptune, and Pluto, ancient astrologers considered Saturn to be the outermost limit of the solar system and thus assigned the rulership of Scorpio to Mars, Aquarius to Saturn, and Pisces to Jupiter. Now, astrologers consider Pluto to be the higher vibration, or more extreme expression, of the energy of Mars, Uranus to be the higher vibration of Saturn, and Neptune to be the higher vibration of Jupiter; thus, we say that Scorpio, Aquarius, and Pisces "share" rulership with two planets.

Planet	Ruler (Domicile)	Exaltation	Fall	Detriment
Sun	Leo	Aries	Libra	Aquarius
Moon	Cancer	Taurus	Scorpio	Capricorn
Mercury	Gemini/ Virgo	Aquarius	Leo	Sagittarius/ Pisces
Venus	Taurus/ Libra	Pisces	Virgo	Scorpio/ Aries
Mars	Aries/ Scorpio	Capricorn	Cancer	Libra/ Taurus
Jupiter	Sagittarius/ Pisces	Cancer	Capricorn	Gemini/ Virgo
Saturn	Capricorn/ Aquarius	Libra	Aries	Cancer/ Leo
Uranus	Aquarius	Scorpio	Taurus	Leo
Neptune	Pisces	n/a	n/a	Virgo
Pluto	Scorpio	n/a	n/a	Taurus

Aspects

Besides Essential Dignities, the ancients also observed that the planets themselves seemed to have dramatic influences upon each other, calling these "aspects." The Major Aspects are as follows:

Major Aspects

The most obvious example of these aspects that we observe every twenty-eight days is the Sun and the Moon. When the Sun and the Moon are in **conjunction**, we cannot see the moon in the sky, called the *new moon*. Two times in the moon's cycle the Sun and Moon **square**, the *quarters of the moon*. When in **opposition**, we observe a *full moon*. One exception to the general negativity of an opposition is when two planets are in *mutual reception*, a rather unusual aspect that is created when two planets appear in the sign that is ruled by the opposite planet (for example, the Moon appears in Capricorn while Saturn is in Cancer). When this occurs, the energies of the two planets balance each other out, making their energies both harmonious and stable.

Type	Distance Apart	Effect Upon the Planet's Energy
Conjunction	0 Degrees	Emphasis, intensification, merging of energies
Sextile	60 Degrees (2 signs)	Opportunity, attraction, ease
Square	90 Degrees (3 signs)	Challenge, tension, resistance
Trine	120 Degrees (4 signs)	Flow, balance, harmony
Opposition	180 Degrees (6 signs)	Problems, conflicts, opposition

The Twelve Houses

While the zodiac separates the Sun's ecliptic into twelve signs, creating a scale for measuring the location of a planet in space from Earth's viewpoint, the twelve Houses are a method for measuring the location of a planet from a specific point on the Earth's surface as the Earth rotates. As the Sun appears to rise and set each day, so the planets appear to rise and set as well, and the ancients developed a system of twelve sectors of the sky, called Houses, to reveal if a planet at any given time is rising above the horizon, passing overhead, setting below the horizon, or passing underneath on the opposite side of Earth. Because of these daily changes, the Houses change more quickly than any other portion of an astrological chart. Where the signs are fixed quadrants out in space, the Houses are relative to the point upon the Earth's surface from which the astrologer casts the chart.

The First House begins on what is called the *Ascendant*, the eastern point on the horizon from which the Sun rises. The sign on a person's Ascendant (also known as the *rising sign*) reveals the mask or persona that the individual presents to the world. The Twelve Houses continue from the Ascendant, counter-clockwise around the circle of an astrological chart, until the Twelfth House ends right back on the Ascendant for a total of three hundred-sixty degrees. Astrologers call the cusp (beginning) of the First House the Ascendant, since this is where the aun "ascends;" the cusp of the Fourth House is the IC (abbreviation for *imum coeli*, "lowest heavens" in Latin), as this is the lowest or northern point of the chart; the cusp of the Seventh House is the *Descendant*, for this is the western horizon where the Sun "descends;" and the cusp of the Tenth House is the *Midheaven* or MC (abbreviation for *medium coeli*, "middle of the heavens" in Latin), as it is the top or southern-most point of the chart. These special Houses on the four major cusps (Ascendant, IC, Descendent, and MC) became known as the four Angular Houses. These Houses correspond to the four Cardinal Signs, and contain incredible energy and potential for action. The Second, Fifth, Eighth, and Eleventh Houses are the Succedent Houses, and correspond to the Fixed Signs. Succedent Houses are more stable than the Angular, but have considerably less energy. The Third, Sixth, Ninth, and Twelfth Houses are called Cadent Houses; corresponding to the Mutable Signs, they have less stability, but have the additional attribute of flexibility and adaptability.

The Astrological Houses

Just as each sign has a planet that rules it, so each House has a planet that is Lord. For greater understanding of each of the Twelve Astrological Houses, the following information will be given for each House:

The House
Lord of House
Natural Ruler (corresponds to a sign of the zodiac)
Type of House
Key Activities of the House
Some **Important Placements** of the Planets Within This House (This is not an exhaustive list.)

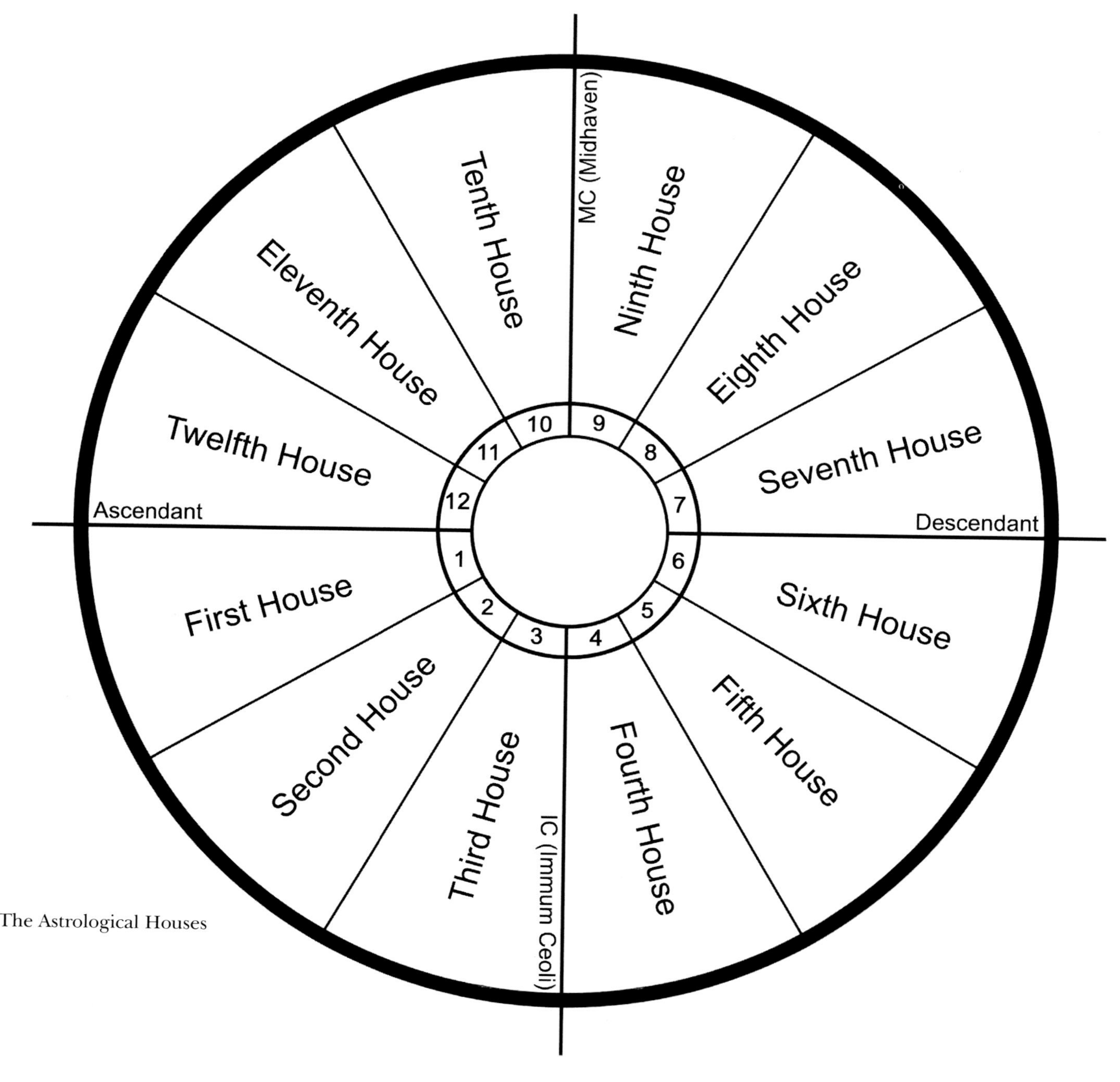

The Astrological Houses

First House

Lord of the 1st House is Saturn
Natural Ruler is Mars, ruler of Aries
Angular House

Key Activities:

The querent's present incarnation, identity, personality, the self...his or her overall health, physical appearance, and body. New beginnings, immediate past and future, and the head. The nature and quality of the querent.

Important Placements:

- **Saturn** shows intelligence, generally promises a ripe old age, and suggests many afflictions early in life because of the father; with regards to a specific question, Saturn restricts and freezes all action pertaining to the matter
- **Mercury** does well in this House, and suggests an imaginative person with excellent communication and public speaking skills
- **Mars** suggests a difficult birth (in any of the Angular Houses) and choosing the hardest road, but succeeding; regarding a specific question, there will be disagreement and rushing into a situation before the proper time
- The **Sun** promises the limelight through charm and appeal (in any of the Angular Houses)
- **Neptune** brings delays, confusion, and deception; possibly even suggests that there is nothing to be done about the matter
- **Uranus** brings an unexpected event and unpredictability on the part of the querent

Second House

Lord of the 2nd House is Jupiter
Natural Ruler is Venus, ruler of Taurus
Succedent House

Key Activities:

The querent's possessions, finances, lawsuits initiated by the querent, money lent to the querent, business associates, resources on all levels to accomplish the querent's goals. The querent's values and security.

Important Placements:

- **Jupiter** in the second House increases wealth
- The **Sun** or **Mars** predicts dispersion of wealth
- **Mars** cuts income and damages possessions
- The **Moon** here reveals that the querent is concerned about/ focused upon money
- **Saturn** grants the discipline to save and hoard money, but also requires a strict budget in order to avoid financial troubles because resources themselves are limited
- The **Sun** brings publicity based solely on merit (in any Succedent House)

Third House

Lord of the 3rd House is the Moon
Natural Ruler is Mercury, ruler of Gemini
Cadent House

Key Activities:

Image. Any place that image is most important, like fashion or movies. Anything short term, like infatuation or short journeys. Communication, information and any place or device used expressly for these purposes (i.e., telephones, libraries, computers). Primary schooling, two children, brothers and sisters, twins, cousins, neighbors, two of anything, moving and wandering, messengers and messages.

Important Placements:

- The **Moon** suggests a short trip or change of local residence
- The **Sun** causes one to work behind the scenes rather than in the spotlight (in any Cadent House)
- **Saturn** slows everything down here, bringing dissatisfaction and lack of support, although the matter will eventually be concluded
- **Mars** brings disturbing news, arguments, and personal attacks

Fourth House

Lord of the 4th House is the Sun
Natural Ruler is the Moon, ruler of Cancer
Angular House

Key Activities:

The determination or end of the matter, something ending, the conclusion. The nurturing parent or parent who had the greatest influence. Family, home, foundations, and inheritances. Property and real estate. Governors and small groups. Place of burial.

Important Placements:

- The **Sun** declares that the querent was blessed with a noble father, but while growing up felt outshined (and intimidated) by the father's success and natural leadership ability; the Sun also suggests that the querent's home will be his (or her) castle.
- **Jupiter** promises a large home and stable family with a religious foundation
- **Mars** suggests strife or division in the home of origin or separation from a parent; with regards to a specific question, Mars often shows the foundation of the question itself to be flawed, or else predicts an unexpected change that will make the question inapplicable

Fifth House

Lord of the 5th House is Venus
Natural Ruler is the Sun, ruler of Leo
Succedent House

Key Activities:

Self-esteem, love affairs for sex's sake, the health of the entire system of the body and the life force itself. Children, pregnancy, and illegitimate children. Pleasures and amusements. Fame, politics, and publication. Entertainment and places of entertainment, bars and pubs, the arts, and gambling. Groups formed purely for the sake of having fun. Ambassadors.

Key Placements:

- **Saturn** and **Mars** here suggest disobedient, spoiled children; also parents who withhold the necessities from their children
- **Mars** in a woman's reading may indicate an abortion or miscarriage
- **Mars** may also indicate seeking release through pleasure, as well as warn of the possibility of an accident in a place of pleasure (like a theatre or an amusement park)
- **Saturn** suggests a general dissatisfaction and bitterness towards the pursuit of pleasure, sometimes leading to sexual inhibitions and dysfunctions
- **Neptune** can show infidelity; if poorly aspected, Neptune warns of a dangerous, unstable and possibly violent relationship
- The **Sun** or **Venus** indicate an attractive and charismatic individual
- **Venus** also suggests temptation or enticement

Sixth House

Lord of the 6th House is Mars
Natural Ruler is Mercury, ruler of Virgo
Cadent House

Key Activities:

Service (whether given or received in work or trade) and servants. Tenants. Commerce. Hospitals, doctors and nurses; acute illnesses. The Stock Market. Uncles and aunts. Pets.

Important Placements:

- **Mars** assures that the surgeon is competent
- The Sign of this House indicates the length of an illness
- When the planets appearing in the 6th House are stronger than those of the 1st House, the individual has a weak vitality and will struggle for a long time against the illness
- **Venus** brings a love interest at work
- **Jupiter** brings digestive disorders, indulgences, and spending too much money on servants and pets
- **Mars** suggests that the individual is a workaholic who overlooks the toll that his or her lifestyle is inflicting upon the body's health; Mars may also warn that there is danger from a pet or animal
- **Saturn** takes on too much responsibility and work, without enough profit or appreciation to satisfy

Seventh House

Lord of the 7th House is the Moon
Natural Ruler is Venus, ruler of Libra
Angular House

Key Activities:

The Other; the querent's business and marital partnerships. Marriage, divorce, war, contracts, open enemies, love affairs for love's sake. Fugitives. The judgment on all love questions. Grandparents. Anyone who acts on the querent's behalf. The defendant in a lawsuit, another bringing a lawsuit against the querent, and all quarrels. The Tarot reader.

Important Placements:

- **Mars** or **Saturn** here show an unfortunate marriage (and if in Scorpio, possibly the death of a partner)

- The **Moon** suggests a change of partnership or ownership
- The **Moon in Cancer** (4 of Cups) in this House says that the querent wants a mate who mothers/nurtures him or her
- **Mars** brings strife, lawsuits, breaks agreements, and makes plans of war
- **Neptune** makes one idolize his or her mate, as well as suggests that the partner is hiding something in the shadows
- **Uranus** dissolves partnerships

Eighth House

Lord of the 8th House is Saturn
Natural Rulers are Pluto and Mars, rulers of Scorpio
Succedent House

Key Activities

Support received from other people. The Other's money or lawsuits initiated by another. Change. Death and type of death. Taxes, insurance, trusts and wills. Legacies, transformation, endings, karmic lessons. Surgery and sexual organs. Predators, danger, and violent rages. Toilets and waste disposal.

Important Placements:

- **Saturn** suggests financial gain through inheritance or alimony, as well as death late in life
- **Mars** can indicate surgery, inner turmoil, or a sudden change to a situation
- **Venus** suggests problems with credit debt and generally spending other people's money to "feel good;" if poorly aspected, the Other may be used and financially devastated by the individual's expenditure of resources without repayment

Ninth House

Lord of the 9th House is the Sun
Natural Ruler is Jupiter, ruler of Sagittarius
Cadent House

Key Activities:

Goals, anything high or long (long journeys as well as long time spans). Higher institutions (like the university, court of law, or big business). Imports and exports. Spirituality, philosophy, science, psychology, books, and higher learning. (Called "the House of God.") The spouse's family. Foreigners, foreign countries and the Middle East. Clergy and grandchildren.

Important Placements:

- **Jupiter** in this House says that the querent is devoutly religious
- **Mars** suggests the individual attacks another religion or spirituality in general
- **Saturn** suggests the individual has dismissed spirituality and religion
- **Mars** suggests that there is danger in a foreign land, possibly death
- **Mars** is extreme in drive and temperament here, persevering to accomplish seemingly impossible goals; for example, some extraordinary athletes have had Mars placed here
- The **Moon** gives one an intuitive spirituality, but also causes one to rush towards goals and take risks, bringing much enthusiasm but little constancy

Tenth House

Lord of the 10th House is Mars
Natural Ruler is Saturn, ruler of Capricorn
Angular House

Key Activities:

The querent's prestige or reputation, his or her calling and ambitions in contrast to what she/he does "just to make ends meet" (6th House). Parent who is the wage earner and authoritarian. Authorities, governments, and employers. The House of the Judge and paying dues for what's been done. Royalty or esteemed people. Also army commanders, professional jobs, kingdoms, empires, and countries.

Important Placements:

- **Jupiter** and the **Sun** here suggest fortunate outcomes for work or profession and great luck
- **Mars** says one will suffer disgrace which is unmerited
- **Saturn** brings many quarrels with an authoritative parent and authorities in general, as well as unresolved disappointment and suppression

Eleventh House

Lords of the 11th House are Venus and Jupiter
Natural Rulers are Uranus and Saturn, rulers of Aquarius

Succedent House

Key Activities:

Dreams, hopes, wishes, friendships, large groups or gatherings. Humanitarian concerns. This House frees from prison, from disease, from money troubles. Things fall in this House. Outer Space, the sky, and space in general. Any new invention or technology that goes beyond current conceptions, like computers or spaceships. Fidelity, falseness, and public opinion are revealed here. The government's allies and resources, as well as its ammunitions and soldiery in wartime. Step-children, foster children, and adopted children (the children and family of the Other.)

Important Placements:

- **Mars** may predict falls or dog bites, fallen idealism, and lost dreams
- **Saturn** outlives most of the family, leaving one embittered and solitary
- The **Moon** here shows a dreamer, an idealist

Twelfth House

Lord of the 12th House is Venus
Natural Rulers are Neptune and Jupiter, rulers of Pisces
Cadent House

Key Activities:

Anything that's hidden or restricted. Prisons, the past, past lives, hidden enemies. Family scandals, large institutions (like churches or bureaucracies), organized religion, mysticism, secrets, clandestine affairs, the subconscious, denial, self-undoing. Jungles.

Important Placements:

- **Saturn** brings mischief, affliction, and self-undoing as well as alienation from the father or possible danger from an unseen older person
- **Venus** indicates a hidden lover
- **Mars** brings many trials and tribulations, as well as a preference to toil alone
- The **Sun** shows an element of self-absorption

At this point your head may be spinning as you inquire, "Why do I need to know anything about astrological Houses when I'm interested in simply interpreting a Tarot reading?" Allow me to explain. The most comprehensive, thorough, and accurate predictive Tarot spread (which the next chapter outlines in detail) is *The Kingdom Within Spread*. This unique spread involves dealing the entire deck into thirteen equal piles—one for each astrological House, and one final pile for *The Kingdom Within* the reading. What grants this particular spread such accuracy is its very basis upon the Twelve Houses and the incredible depth it allows as the reader and querent investigate the truth.

As you consider the House information delineated above, you will have probably noticed (in case you weren't already aware) that there is a natural affinity between certain signs and Houses that follows the natural order of an astrological chart. Aries has similarities to the first House, Taurus to the second, Gemini to the third, Cancer to the forth, Leo to the fifth, Virgo to the sixth, Libra to the seventh, Scorpio to the eighth, Sagittarius to the ninth, Capricorn to the tenth, Aquarius to the eleventh, and Pisces to the twelfth. If the Emperor card (Aries) comes up in the first House in the Kingdom Within Spread (explained in Chapter Five: Tarot Spreads for Divination), the combination stresses the importance (and strength) of their shared energies to the question at hand. An effective way of ordering the interaction of planets, signs, and Houses within a reading is to consider the **planets** as the *basic energy that is currently manifesting in an individual's life*, the **signs** as the *character or direction of that energy*, and the **House** as the *circumstances surrounding the manifestation of a particular energy and where it will manifest*. For example, suppose that the Two of Swords (Moon in Libra) appears in the Twelfth House. There is a basic energy of the Moon (change, manifestation, or femininity), which is acting in the character or direction of Libra (balance of opposing forces, legal proceedings, or partnerships), and the circumstances surrounding the matter (or where it will manifest) is the Twelfth House (anything hidden or restricted, past lives, or large institutions).

If information gleaned from reading the Twelve Houses conflicts in some way, it often helps to consider the general strength of the houses and signs in order to discover which energies will, ultimately, triumph. For example, if the Seventh House indicates that the querent will be unlucky in love, but the Fifth House indicates that the querent will experience a rewarding love affair, which is it? The strength of the Houses and signs, from strongest to weakest, is as follows:

First House:	Aries
Tenth House:	Capricorn
Seventh House:	Libra
Fourth House:	Cancer
Eleventh House:	Aquarius
Fifth House:	Leo

Ninth House:	Sagittarius
Third House:	Gemini
Second House:	Taurus
Eighth House:	Scorpio
Sixth House:	Virgo
Twelfth House:	Pisces

Obviously, any matter of the Seventh House will be stronger than matters of the Fifth House. The querent will experience a rewarding love affair (Fifth House), but ultimately the pleasure derived from it will not last (Seventh House).

Using Aspects in a Reading

The introduction to the Major Arcana (Chapter One) briefly discussed how to determine whether a card is *well placed* or *poorly placed*. Now, however, with this basic foundation in astrology we may delve into this facet of interpretation much deeper. The technical aspects of astrology—such as conjunctions, trines, and sextiles—become apparent when laying the Tarot cards into a spread. If the Tower is opposite the World in a spread, we have Mars and Saturn opposing each other and therefore rivaling the full manifestation of each other's powers. If two cards appear in the same House, we may suppose that they are in the conjunction, and therefore empower each other's energies. In the Kingdom Within Spread, sextiles, squares, and triunes can also be utilized. For instance, if a card is placed two Houses away from another card, the planets are sextiling, and thus bringing each other ease and opportunity.

Also, the *essential dignity* of the planets in their signs (and Houses, in *The Kingdom Within* Spread) gives deeper insight into the details of a particular energy. For example, the Empress (Venus) might appear next to the 3 of Swords (Saturn in Libra); although Saturn in Libra generally brings sorrow and separation, Venus is the Ruler of Libra, either promising a beautiful new relationship in the future, or else that this present sorrow will reap positive results.

There are two additional classical methods of combination, called Elemental Dignity and Planetary Friendship and Enmity. With regards to the Tarot suits, Wands (fire signs) are friendly with Swords (air signs) because both are transmissive and masculine in nature, while Cups (water signs) are friendly towards Pentacles (earth signs) by virtue of their common receptive, feminine nature. Wands and Pentacles are ambivalent to each other, as are Swords and Cups. However, there is enmity between Wands and Cups, as they are elementally opposed, and Swords dislike Pentacles for the same reason. Suppose that the Ace of Cups (a beautiful card) shows up, but it is surrounded by four Wands cards. This suggests that there is great power obstructing the Ace of Cups in some way; to know what that power is, consider the meaning of each of the four Wands cards. Conversely, let's say that the Ace of Cups is surrounded by four cards of the Pentacles suit. Now, not only is nothing blocking the Ace, but it is actually being assisted.

The second method of classical combination to consider is Planetary Friendship and Enmity. In classical astrology, the five inner planets and two luminaries also have their own traditional relationships:

Saturn likes Jupiter, the Sun and Mercury, but dislikes Mars and Venus.

Jupiter likes all planets except Mars.

Mars, the Sun, and Venus like all planets except Saturn.

Mercury likes Saturn, Jupiter and Venus, but abhors the Sun, Mars and the Moon.

The Moon has no close friends, but only dislikes Saturn and Mars.

If the High Priestess (the Moon) appears next to the Wheel of Fortune (Jupiter), then Jupiter will encourage the Moon's manifestation while the Moon will neither help nor hinder Jupiter. However, add the Tower (Mars), and both the Moon and Jupiter will work to oppose Mars' energy, even though Mars does not oppose them.

Key Phrases in Interpreting the Houses

When considering all the Houses in relationship to one another, a general pairing of opposite attributes becomes apparent:

Next, let's consider how each planet affects the House in which it appears:

- Wherever the **Sun** appears, it emphasizes the matters of the House, focusing upon the core of one's self-identity and ego.
- The **Moon** brings mood swings, emotionality, great change, and over-reaction to the House in which it appears; it also indicates where one finds rejuvenation and internal strength.
- **Mercury** always communicates that the matters of this House need to be critically examined and thoroughly thought about before taking any action.
- **Venus** beautifies everything she touches and kindles desire, therefore the matters in this House will generally work out as well as reveal what the querent really wants.
- **Mars** brings substantial activity and initiative to the matters of its House, along with struggle and conflict.
- **Jupiter** makes everything better in the matters of its House—perhaps excessively so.
- **Saturn** limits, causes delays, and creates dilemmas for the matters of the House in which he appears.
- **Uranus** introduces instability, innovation, and unexpected events to the matters of its House.
- **Neptune** initiates a drive for ideals and imagination, but also a danger of being fooled and defrauded. The querent's awareness of the key issues of this House are confused and distorted.
- **Pluto** purifies and transforms the matters of its House through intense change and upheaval.

One final way to utilize the Houses in a Tarot reading involves obtaining additional information about another person who has appeared in a reading. If more information is needed about a person (let's say the querent's brother) who appears in the 3rd House of the Kingdom Within Spread, the reader may treat the 3rd House as the 1st House of the brother's astrological chart. For example, the next House (the 4th) will act like the brother's 2nd House, reveling his resources, while the 10th House will disclose matters of the brother's 7th House, revealing his partnerships.

1st House	The Querent
7th House	The Other
2nd house	The Querent's Resources
8th House	The Other's Resources
3rd House	Issues of Immediacy
9th House	Long-Term Aims
4th House	Querent's Private Life
10th House	Querent's Public Life
5th House	Pleasure and sex
11th House	Ideals and Friendship
6th House	Health of the body and ability to function in the physical world
12th House	Health of the spirit and ability to function in eternity

Key Phrases for Planet-and-Sign Combinations:

Below you will find some key words for planet-in-sign combinations that are not already explained in the Minor Arcana. These are very general, included only to give the reader the basic sense of these energy combinations. Remember that just as each sign has a natural House correspondence, so a planet working in a particular Sign will behave similarly if in the Sign's corresponding house. (For example, the Sun in Aries is similar in energy to the Sun in the First House.)

Many beginning Tarot readers have a difficult time distinguishing between the energies of Saturn, Uranus, and Mars. Saturn stops things, blocking progress through denial, dissatisfaction or dissension. Uranus unexpectedly disintegrates existing arrangements, precipitating accidents and electric-like impulses to be free. Mars collapses and violently destroys, cutting away vital components of success.

Because the three outer (or generational) planets (Uranus, Neptune, and Pluto) remain in a particular sign much longer than the inner planets, I will list the closest time period that each of these three planets have been (or will be) in a sign so that you may see the planets, not only as influencing us personally, but also on a global scale.

	The Sun Emphasizes in...
Aries	see 3 of Wands/ Emperor (Exaltation)
Taurus	see Hierophant
Gemini	see 10 of Swords/ Lovers
Cancer	see Chariot
Leo	see Strength (Ruler)
Virgo	see 8 of Pentacles/ Hermit
Libra	see Justice (Fall)
Scorpio	see 6 of Cups/ Death
Sagittarius	see Temperance
Capricorn	see 4 of Pentacles/ Devil
Aquarius	see the Star (Detriment)
Pisces	see the Moon

	The Moon Changes in...
Aries	caring dominance (sometimes enforces help), moody, quick starts and changes, solitary, usually close to mother
Taurus	see 6 of Pentacles (Exaltation)
Gemini	versatile, superficial, coldly logical, restless curiosity, short-lived emotions, a dislike for routine
Cancer	see 4 of Cups (Ruler)
Leo	risk-taking, action out of insecurity, pleasure seeking, competitive
Virgo	control freak, reads into everything, occupational interests likely to change many times, getting mired in details leads to slow decisions, compassion for those who need help
Libra	See 2 of Swords
Scorpio	possessive, distrusting, hides deepest emotions, sexual fixations, debt, refinancing, loan-seeking and issues with credit (Fall)
Sagittarius	See 9 of Wands
Capricorn	ambitious, self-esteem heavily influenced by professional reputation, valuing career over family, cautious (Detriment)
Aquarius	See 7 of Swords
Pisces	emotionally sensitive, psychic phenomena, hidden motives, secret love affairs, an emotional experience built on a partial picture

Mercury Educates In...	
Aries	impulsive decisions, argumentative, ego-driven intellect, unsympathetic thoughts, enforced communication, rationalization
Taurus	see 5 of Pentacles
Gemini	unbiased consideration of other points of view, eloquent communication, playful wittiness, analytical, effective manipulators (Ruler)
Cancer	see 3 of Cups
Leo	flirtatious, game player, walks the dangerous line of desire (and usually gets burned), intellectually combative and condescending, impulsive communication (Fall)
Virgo	see 10 of Pentacles (Ruler)
Libra	inspired by others' communication and ideas, strong diplomatic skills, effective researchers, prefers balanced viewpoints, tends to follow rules, legal settlements, contract negotiations
Scorpio	seeks what lies beneath the surface, excellent investigators (good at poking into other people's business), attracted to darkness and mystery, possible early sexual experiences, a tendency to hold grudges and deep beliefs from others
Sagittarius	see 8 of Wands (Detriment)
Capricorn	directing communication, seeks positions of leadership and greater authority, good at professional posturing, prefers practical communication that gets things done, straight shooting and to the point, uses words and intellect to accomplish career ambitions, condescending, traditional and grounded
Aquarius	see 6 of Swords (Exaltation)
Pisces	largely affected by the thoughts of other people, impractical and dreamy realities, melancholy, out of touch, pontification without practicality, inability to decide or commit to a belief or course of action, rarely actually changes anything, usually insecure (Detriment)

Venus Loves In...	
Aries	see 4 of Wands (Detriment)
Taurus	likeable, prefers security and predictability in relationships, loyal, sensual (Ruler)
Gemini	relationally fickle, many dates with many different people, seeks new experiences, amiable, persuasive, doesn't like to be pinned down, playful
Cancer	see 2 of Cups
Leo	charismatic, proud, affectionate, conquering, passionate, a penchant or pleasurable sexual encounters and theatrical love affairs
Virgo	see 9 of Pentacles (Fall)
Libra	harmonious relationships, tasteful, in love with love, attractive, strong drive for companionship, anticipates what others want, agreeable (Ruler)
Scorpio	see 7 of Cups (Detriment)
Sagittarius	prefers new and exhilarating to stability and comfort, exciting, flirtatious without the desire to possess, needs and finds freedom in relationships, the sharing passionate experiences with another, a loves for philosophy or higher education (not necessarily schooling), openness
Capricorn	conservative and practical when choosing partners, establishes social roles and rules of conduct, significant relationships must support the pursuit of professional status and/or wealth, attracted to professionals/authorities
Aquarius	see 5 of Swords
Pisces	protected romantic ideals, enticing sexuality tempered by considerations of propriety, hidden infatuations, secret desires, forbidden love (Exaltation)

Mars Excises In...	
Aries	see 2 of Wands (Ruler)
Taurus	a cut in resources, loss of income, insufficient resources to accomplish a goal, a stubborn pursuit for more and more, sudden usage of credit (Detriment)
Gemini	see 9 of Swords
Cancer	quick to strong emotions, zealous, family fights, an early separation from one or both parents, fiercely independent to the detriment of family, a flawed foundation for stability in any matter (Fall)
Leo	see 7 of Wands
Virgo	a workaholic, obsessively about details and/or work ethic, overwork or accidents bring illness, disciplined, dedicated, detailed operations (from accountancy to operations)
Libra	legal problems, a shattered relationship, fights, separation, divorce, open conflicts with another (Detriment)
Scorpio	see 5 of Cups (Ruler)
Sagittarius	extreme points of view, extravagance, strong ideological or religious disagreements (up to and including violence), desires to get far away, major conflict resulting from incompatible paradigms
Capricorn	see 3 of Pentacles (Exaltation)
Aquarius	revolutionary, ideal-driven, fervent leaders, dislike of tradition, a fight for freedom, impersonal in their dedication to ideas over individuals, can indicate the end of friendships with each going their own way
Pisces	see 10 of Cups

Jupiter Increases In...	
Aries	magnanimous, egocentric, inspirational, optimistic, a love of indulgence, weight problems, big plans and dreams, aiming very high
Taurus	an increase in resources (e.g., pay-raises, won lawsuits, etc.), positive financial situations, a fixated love of money and luxury, indolent after success, pompous
Gemini	see 8 of Swords (Detriment)
Cancer	generous regard for family, overeating, success in real estate, strong foundation for an endeavor, trustworthy and optimistic (Exaltation)
Leo	see 6 of Wands
Virgo	noble ideals, sees many trees clearly but sometimes misses the forest, excellent health outside of the tendency to over-indulge, overestimates the value of personal analyses
Libra	see 4 of Swords
Scorpio	tends to benefit from the resources of others, access to other others' money (i.e., credit or inheritance), too much impulse buying can lead to major credit problems, jealous and possessive of relationships, very sexual, devious when unhappy
Sagittarius	see Wheel of Fortune (Jupiter) and Temperance (Sagittarius) (Ruler)
Capricorn	see 2 of Pentacles (Fall)
Aquarius	the established idealism of a winner, a strong motivation to help or "save" others; well liked by large groups, a driving value of openness and freedom, ideals more important than practicality, well-intentioned but not always grounded in fact, optimistic
Pisces	see 9 of Cups

Saturn Limits In...	
Aries	authoritative, strong sense of self, slow to begin but obstinately committed once begun, disciplined with age, resists control by others, stops others to enliven self, "my way or else," suggests a person had a harsh father (Fall)
Taurus	see 7 of Pentacles
Gemini	communication difficulties, bickering, discontent with job or career path, writer's block, concern about gossip, tension between siblings, arguments with an authoritative parent, trouble in high school
Cancer	motivated by a sense of duty or honor, cautious, conservative, dissatisfied commitment through difficulties, familial obligations, points to difficulties with home and hearth (Detriment)
Leo	see 5 of Wands
Virgo	dedicated, extreme dedication to work, methodical, efficient, thorough, professional, a tendency to over-think and worry about things, can also point to a digestive and/or chronic ailment
Libra	see 3 of Swords (Exaltation)
Scorpio	a samurai-like sense of honor, a disciplined dedication to see things through, opinionated, paying off taxes or accumulated debt with great effort, a strong sense of duty and/or morality
Sagittarius	see 10 of Wands
Capricorn	see The World (Saturn) and The Devil (Capricorn) (Ruler)
Aquarius	work with the public or large organization, older friends, lonely, withdrawn
Pisces	see 8 of Cups

Uranus Upsets In...	
Aries	(1928-1935) pioneer, non-conformist, leader who brings radical changes, wild
Taurus	(1935-1942) radical innovations in finances and marketplace, money loss. (Fall)
Gemini	(1942-1949) educational upsets, problems with siblings, shocking messages, breakdown in agreements, major changes in electronic recording and broadcasting
Cancer	(1949-1956) upsets/changes in home or real estate, the reinvention of familial roles, faltering foundations, wandering
Leo	(1956-1962) upsets in love affairs, explosive antagonism, notable developments in the entertainment industry, sexual promiscuity, fizzling potential, self-destructive distraction (Detriment)
Virgo	(1962-1968) unusual scientific achievements, problems with work or health, striving for freedom from work contracts, the desire to freely serve
Libra	(1968-1975) a possible divorce due to one or both partners desiring more freedom, problems with partnerships, open relationships, volatile agreements
Scorpio	(1975-1981) upsets with taxes, debts, sex, or death; unexpected violence and internal upheavals, the meltdown of "black or white" dualities (Exaltation)
Sagittarius	(1981-1988) rebellion against established culture and orthodoxy, foreign adventures, radical concepts of religiosity and higher-educational pursuits, the unstable pursuit of distant goals
Capricorn	(1988-1995) sudden upsets/changes with authorities; unexpected changes in government, career, and professional reputation, the redefinition of business in an electronic age
Aquarius	(1995-2002) radical reform, openness to change, expansive ideas extolling freedom, "new world" thinking, the exponential growth of technological innovation (Ruler)
Pisces	(2003-2011) breaking the bonds of closed beliefs, the collapse of barriers, surprising conflicts with idealistic extremism, careening recklessly into the unknown, the blind pursuit of ideals, seeking new worlds (whether real or imaginary), reactionary escapism

Neptune Blurs In...	
Aries	(1861-1875) illusions of power, self-delusion, possible insanity, taking things too far, confusing the mind's movie screen for a window
Taurus	(1874-1888) illusions about resources, financial criminality, losing possessions easily, hidden motives
Gemini	(1887-1901) vague communications, a con artist, dishonest communication, an impractical grasp of short-term possibilities
Cancer	(1901-1915) idealistic about home and country, refusal to see family problems, foundation built upon dreams and wishes but lacking substance
Leo	(1914-1929) dreams of happiness for all, refusal to see downsides of pleasure, sex without conventional boundaries, imagined competition, unrealistic self-estimations
Virgo	(1928-1943) deception by technicalities, blurring details out of self-interest, small obstacles, neurosis and fixation (Detriment)
Libra	(1942-1957) detrimental illusions in partnership and interpersonal judgment, easily influenced by others, untrustworthy, difficulty with unwavering commitment, overtly manipulative
Scorpio	(1956-1970) drug addiction, the blurring of rules and standards, illusions about credit and others' resources, sexual escapism
Sagittarius	(1970-1984) false gurus, philosophical and educational sophistry, a visionary, completely unrealistic aims and long-term plans
Capricorn	(1984-1998) illusions about ambition and responsibility, the idealization of convention, the condescending veneer of professionalism, growing world financial bubbles
Aquarius	(1998-2012) conceptions of a new world, impractical imaginings that feel good to pretend along with, eccentric, mass misrepresentation, reaching for impossible dreams and failing after ignoring inconvenient limitations, betrayal by a trusted friend
Pisces	(1847-1862/ 2012-2026) hidden forces determining an outcome, spiritual growth, religious delusion, the fervor of intoxicating emotion, stumbling into danger or darkness, mystic (Ruler)

Since Pluto was discovered much later than the rest of the planets (in 1930, when Pluto was in Cancer) and stays in a sign anywhere from twelve to thirty-two years, you will find an important historical event that is characteristic of the specific energy combination (revealing the global tendencies) rather than key words to apply to individuals. I will only record the historical events from Cancer through Sagittarius (Pluto is in Sagittarius at the writing of this book). For Capricorn through Gemini I will only list general key phrases for world trends. Remember that Pluto's purification always brings upheaval in some form as Pluto digs deep and purifies through fire.

In addition, a few signs have some interesting relationships:

In Venus, Libra, and Scorpio you'll find information about poison.

Leo, Libra, and Aquarius discuss potential love affairs.

Scorpio and Libra (and Cancer if it happened long ago or to a family member) discuss death and cause of death.

Libra and Sagittarius discuss airplanes and air flight in general.

Additional Aspects of the Moon

Because the Moon is closest to the Earth and its influences change most often, the Moon deserves additional study. In astrology, we often refer to the *nodes of the moon*, the longitudinal points where the

Pluto Purifies In...	
Cancer	(1913-1938) crisis of family and foundations: the stock market crash
Leo	(1938-1957) crisis of pleasure and power: World War II, atomic bomb
Virgo	(1957-1971) crisis of work and health: onset of the computer, technology; Medicare and Medicaid signed into law by President Lyndon Johnson
Libra	(1971-1983) crisis of partnerships: "living together" before marriage
Scorpio	(1983-1995) crisis of debt, other's resources, and sex: AIDS (Ruler)
Sagittarius	(1995-2008) crisis of philosophies: Conflict between world religions and ideologies. USA split in Bush/Gore election; September 11th Terrorist Attacks
Capricorn	(2008-2024) political and professional crisis: The role of government redefined, particularly in reference to control of economic forces. Obama elected first African-American president and Federal Government increases oversight of significant sectors of society—from the airline and automotive industries, to banking, real estate, credit, and even healthcare
Aquarius	(2024-2044) freeing and ideological crisis
Pisces	(2043-2067) crisis of all things hidden and restrictive
Aries	(2066-2094) crisis of the body and the self
Taurus	(2095-2129) crisis of possessions and resources (Detriment)
Gemini	(2129-2159) crisis of image and communication

Moon crosses the Sun's ecliptic. The *north node* (called the Dragon's Head) reveals what will ultimately bring fulfillment. The *south node* (called the Dragon's Tail) reveals what will be the greatest limiting factor that prevents progression. In addition, a *void of course* moon is when the Moon is making no aspects with other planets as it completes its transit through a sign. During this time it is best not to start anything new or take unnecessary risks, as they will amount to nil. As a general rule of thumb, it is best to begin projects during a new moon, build projects as the Moon waxes (grows), complete projects as the Moon wanes (diminishes), and reflect or take stock during the dark moon. Make important decisions at full moon. (The Ascendant and Descendant, the Moon's nodes, and the void of course moon will be applied to Tarot reading in the next chapter, as we learn the Cross Spread and the Kingdom Within Spread.)

Interpreting Reversals

Some Tarot readers don't deal with reversed cards at all, while others often characterize them as negative or as simply being the opposite meaning of an upright card. In astrological Tarot, reversed cards are interpreted more like an astrological *retrograde*—a time when, from our vantage point on Earth, a planet appears to be moving backwards in its orbit. During retrograde, the planet's energy appears to turn inwards, encountering problems in actually manifesting or releasing into the external world. Reversed cards therefore express the internal energy that is originating from the querent or else an energy sought by the querent. An upright card, in contrast, is energy that is external to the querent—that originates from outside the querent, that literally "rains downs" upon the querent's life. For example, let's say that the 4 of Swords (Jupiter in Libra) appears in a reading. Upright, it might say that the person has found a soul mate, but if reversed it suggests that the person is only seeking a soul mate. Obviously, reversals can substantially change the context of a reading. Every reversed card carries an additional, more personal, message for the querent as well—a reversed card demands that the querent pay close attention, for this is a crucial message for the inner life of the querent.

Chapter Five
Tarot Spreads for Divination

The "Mystery" of Divination

"Divination" seems a fascinating conundrum in our society today. Its root word, "divine," means, *relating to, emanating from, or being the expression of a deity*, and the word itself literally means *prediction uttered under divine inspiration*. Yet, ask your average person off the street, and you'll either be told that it's all a bunch of superstitious nonsense—or worse, actually evil. Even for those who are intrigued by or practice a form of divination—from complex techniques such as Tarot, astrology, and the I Ching to the more intuitive methods like palm reading, crystal gazing, or prophecy—most do not even agree with each other as to what is actually happening when they "divine."

There are three basic philosophies with regards to Tarot and its divinatory qualities—some readers use Tarot for the prediction of future events, others choose a more psychological approach as they use the Tarot as a sort of mirror of the wisdom of their true selves about themselves and their world, while still a third group of readers integrate both of these views into their readings. Many professional diviners mystify their own divination, making it seem somehow "beyond" the grasp of "normal" people. My personal goal is to "de-mystify" the Tarot so that anyone can pick up a deck of Tarot cards and discover their own answers to their questions. Those who oppose divination accuse that it's Satan, an evil spirit, or the diviner's own deluded (or defrauding) mind. To further mystify the topic, although there have been many examples of accurate predictions, there are at least an equal amount of inaccurate ones to match.

What's really going on? The mental filters with which people view divination are so diverse and cemented that I could spend the next 500 pages tackling this topic and still not address each one. Instead, I will state what I see, and allow the individual reader to determine his or her own understanding. *Synchronicity* is the idea that all phenomena occurring at any particular moment in time relate to one another (remember the Hermetic axiom, "As above, so below"). It is because of this very synchronicity of existence that we may utilize seen phenomena—such as the symbols of the Tarot cards that have been deliberately crafted to connect the unseen with the seen—to gain knowledge of those phenomena that we cannot see. Any observed phenomena can be a source of divination—from tea leaves in the bottom of a cup, to the reoccurring patterns of stars in the heavens, to the pictures that the clouds seem to form in the sky. However, the more whole and perfect the method of divination, the easier it is to see when using it. The most perfect systems of divination of which I am personally aware are the Tarot and the I Ching, although I in no way am discounting that others exist.

As to what is happening when divining, much depends upon one's viewpoint as to whom (or what) is the source(s) of the information. And yes, there are those who tap into darker forces from which to divine. (Yes, Virginia—there is Evil.) As for the truth or accuracy of the divining, it largely depends upon two variables: the potential for accuracy of the approach and the lucidity of the vehicle (the diviner). Some systems, such as Tarot, astrology, and the I Ching, are comprehensive systems that, if assiduously studied, offer consistently accurate results for the practitioner. Other means, such as reading tea leaves or speaking in tongues, are much more intuitive, and therefore depend considerably more upon the *vidyā* of the diviner. Personally, I would never ask someone to "divine" information for me who was emotionally upset, entangled in human drama, or physically exhausted, for the potential for clarity is considerably weakened by these states. Ultimately, all methods of divination become unnecessary when a spirit regains complete *vidyā*.

Divinatory Spreads

So, how does all this information culminate in a comprehensive predictive reading? Many querents request a General Reading on their lives, which reveals the same basic information that may be found in a natal progression; the rest have a Specific Question that they need answered, such as "Does he love me?"

or "Will I get the job?" Just as a horary astrological chart is a snapshot in time of the planetary answer to the birth of a particular question, so a Tarot reading with an astrological basis will reveal the same inter-weaving of energies at the question's inception. Predictive readings reveal the probable outcomes based upon the current energies and behaviors surrounding the querent; however, I always stress to every querent that there are numerous influences upon any given question, and that usually the reading will focus upon what the querent needs to hear, either preparing him or her for the future or else imparting valuable information that may be used to alter the current trend. A thorough Tarot reading should contain all the information necessary to answer the querent's questions.

There are entire books written upon the subject of Tarot spreads, and I have probably tried them all. For the purposes of this book, however, we will focus upon only the most *consistently* effective spreads for divination. Each of these four divinatory spreads is progressively more detailed and complex, and it is important to choose a spread appropriate to the question being asked, as well as state the question in a format conducive to receiving clear insight. There are two basic types of readings: General Readings in which the querent has no specific question(s) but simply wants insights into his or her life, or else Specific Questions.

How does one state a Specific Question in the best possible format? For the sake of example, let us consider some effective and less effective questions about the ever-popular subject of Love:

Effective Questions:

What do I need to see that I am not seeing in my current relationship?

What will happen in my relationship if I ____________?

Will we get married?

Why have I been unsuccessful in finding a partner?

What do I need to see in order to reach resolution with regards to the break up of this relationship?

Less Effective Questions:

Should I date (or marry) this person?

How can I change my spouse?

How can I get him (or her) back?

How can I get him (or her) to fall in love with me? (...or to marry me?)

How can I get revenge for what he (or she) did to me?

The first set of questions is effective because they seek further information to help the querent see more clearly and make appropriate choices. The second set of questions is less effective because they come from a place of *avidyā*: The initial question asks to be relieved of responsibility and have the cards make the decision for the querent, the next three questions exhibit a desire to gain control of another, while the last question expresses evil intentions. The more effective the question is, the more useful the answer will be.

To begin a reading, thoroughly mix the deck until you instinctively feel that it is time to stop. Sometimes this takes only a few shuffles, occasionally this can go on for a few minutes. What matters here is not how you mix the deck, but that you create a consistent ritual of mixing, so that every time you do a reading you create a sacred space by beginning the same way. Next, have the querent cut the cards.

The Key Spread

This first spread is simple, but profound. Choose one of the following three questions to ask as you shuffle the cards:

What is the Key to solving this current dilemma (name the specific dilemma)?

What Key truth is the querent refusing to see in this situation (name the specific situation)?

Who is the querent (or who is the other) being in this situation (name the specific situation) that is the missing Key to understanding?

Keep your question clearly in mind as you shuffle. After the querent cuts the cards, fan the entire deck out before you and with your left hand choose one card and place it before you. This card reveals the "Key" to unlocking the answer to the question.

The Triangle Spread

The triangle is a shape that creates balance and symmetry between three apparently opposing points, just like the three triangles on the Tree of Life. Shuffle, cut, and fan the cards just as you did in the previous spread, only this time focus upon a particular situation in your life (or the querent's) in which you need guidance. Choose three cards, laying the first card to the left, the second card to the right, and the last card in the center beneath the first two, forming an inverted triangle.

1

The Problem

2

The Way Through the Problem

3

The Outcome

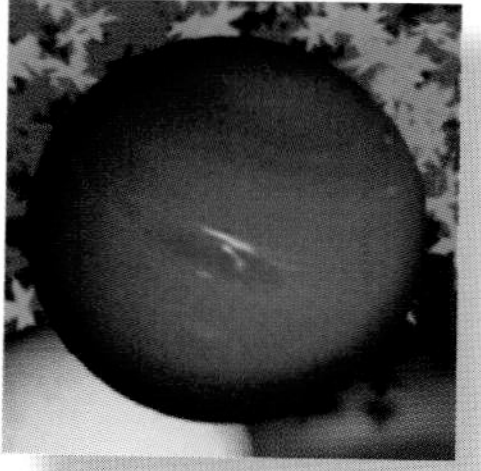

Card One: The Problem
Card Two: The Way Through the Problem
Card Three: The Outcome

Card One reveals the truth that needs to be faced in the current situation. Card Two shows what must be done in order to face and conquer the challenges presented by the first card, while Card Three predicts what will happen in the situation if the recommendation of the second card is followed.

The Cross Spread

The cross is an ancient symbol, much older than the Christian tradition with which it is most commonly associated today, and can be found in numerous sacred traditions throughout antiquity. At its most basic level, it is a symbol of the two intersecting paths that spirits travel upon throughout existence—the vertical axis is one of progression, where each is either on an upward journey towards spirit or a

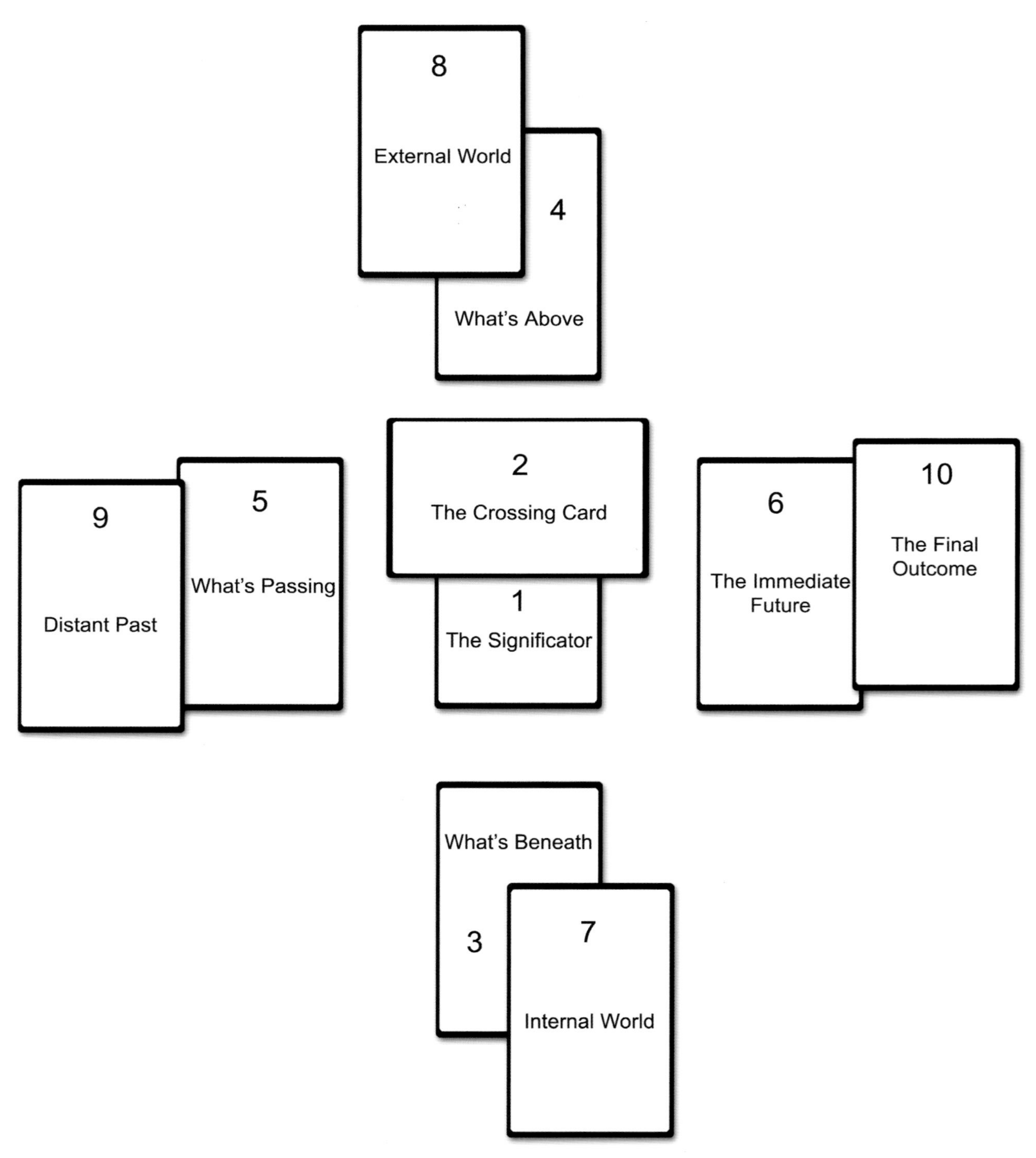

downward journey towards matter; the horizontal axis represents our actions inside the realm of time, justice, cause and effect. The Celts overlaid the basic cross with an additional sacred symbol, the circle of the Sun, representing the circle of life, the cycle of the seasons, and at each place that an axis intersects the circle, we have the cardinal directions—north, south, east and west—as well as the elements—earth, air, fire, and water, with spirit residing at the center. The Cross Spread is thus named because its shape looks like an equilateral cross.

After thoroughly shuffling the deck, cut the deck three times—once for each Triad on the Tree of Life—and from the top of the deck, lay out ten cards in the form of a Cross.

The Significator: In a general reading about a person, this represents the querent; with regards to a specific question, this represents the situation. (This is the Ascendant of the reading.)

Crossing Card: Reveals what is currently "crossing" (blocking, impeding) the querent or the situation. (This is like the South Node of the Moon.)

What's Beneath: What information does the querent already know that forms the foundation of the question?

What's Above: What information is obvious, but the querent currently is not seeing it?

What's Passing: What has occurred recently in the querent's life; what is passing away from the querent's life?

The Immediate Future: What is in store for the querent in the immediate future? (This is the Descendant of the reading.)

Internal World: What is the internal world of the querent? What is she/he bringing to the situation?

External World: What is the external world of the querent? What is surrounding him or her?

Distant Past: What past issue or problem is the querent still carrying in the present that is blurring his or her ability to clearly perceive the situation today?

The Final Outcome: What is the ultimate outcome of this situation? What is the main message that the querent must understand in order to grow? (This is like the North Node of the Moon.)

As you can see, the Cross Spread thoroughly considers all angles of an issue. The first and second cards reveal the heart of the matter. The third and seventh cards show what's going on inside the querent, while the fourth and eighth demonstrate what's surrounding the querent. The fifth and ninth cards tell us about the querent's past, and the six and tenth cards focus on the querent's future and the main message for the querent.

Finally, let us consider the most advanced spread (which not only reveals a far greater picture but also gives substantially more information in all its subtleties): the Kingdom Within Spread. It is crucial to note that the novice Tarot reader should be acquainted with the Key Spread, the Triangle Spread, and the Cross Spread (as well as thoroughly versed in the information from Chapter Four) before trying the following spread. Understand the cards in simpler readings before attempting more complex ones.

The Kingdom Within Spread

For General Readings (or for Specific Questions that are more complex in nature), I suggest initially using a Cross Spread to discover the prevailing energies in the querent's life, followed by the more comprehensive Kingdom Within Spread. Similar to the traditional zodiac Spread, this advanced spread seeks further clarification of a particular card from the Cross Spread or else answers additional questions introduced by the querent as a result of reading the Cross Spread.

After laying out and interpreting the Cross Spread, write down the Cross's ten cards so that you can remember them during the Kingdom Within Spread. Now, randomly place the cards back into the deck, shuffle the deck until you feel that you should cease, and deal the entire deck into a circle of twelve equal piles, with a thirteenth pile in the center of the circle. This is the astrological circle of the Twelve Houses, and the center pile, which is turned over last, reveals the Kingdom Within, focusing upon the *larger truth* that is the heart of the reading. You will have one card remaining after dealing six cards (the number of Tiphereth, the Redeemer) into each pile; place this remaining card in the center pile, for a total of seven cards, for Netzach points the way to Bliss.

Next, look through the pile pertaining to the matters of the First House, carefully searching for any of the original ten cards that appeared in the Cross Spread. Turn over any of these cards that you find in the first pile, as well as the card directly to the left and the right of each original card. Watch carefully for

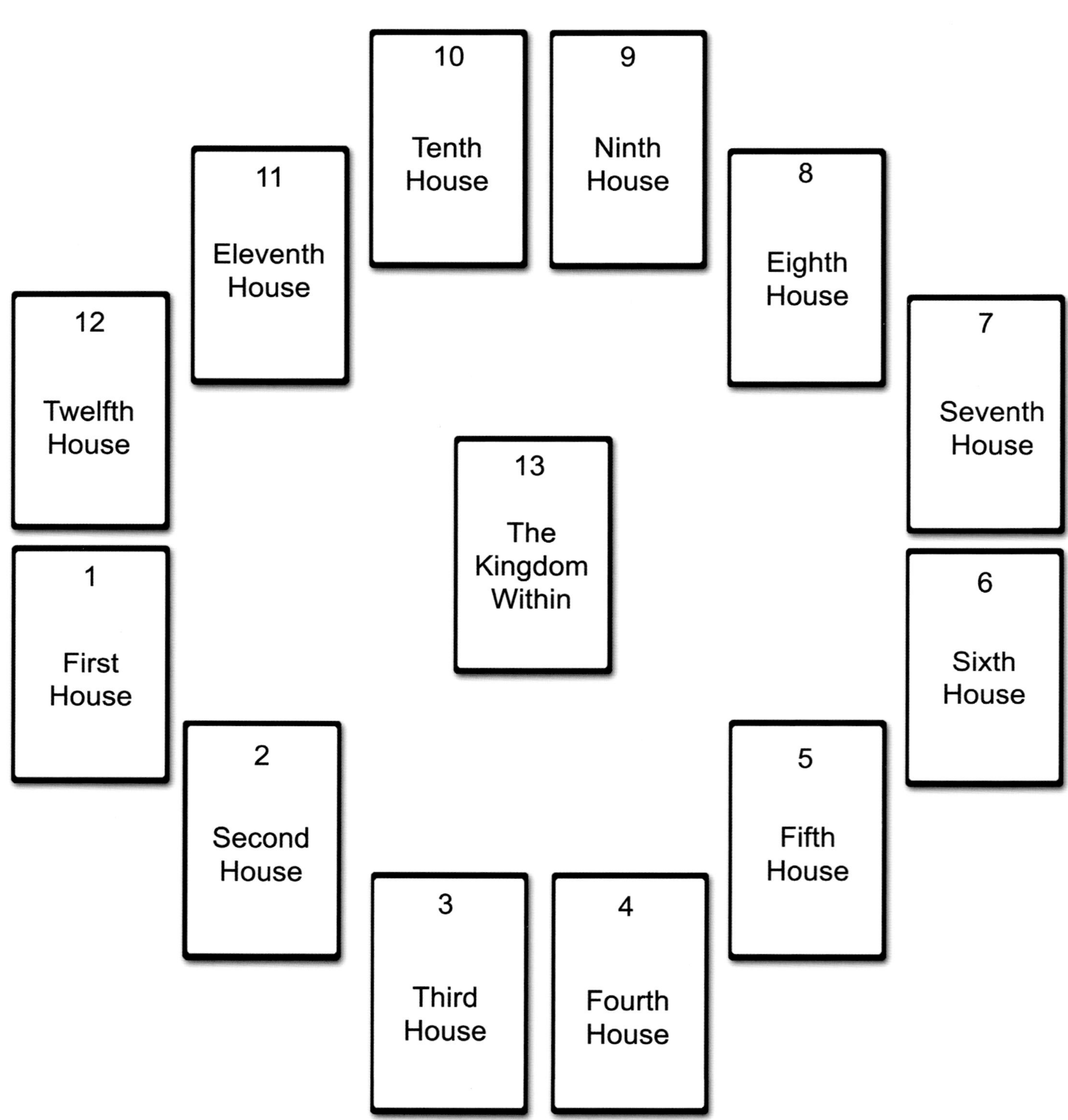
10
Tenth House
9
Ninth House
11
Eleventh House
8
Eighth House
12
Twelfth House
7
Seventh House
13
The Kingdom Within
1
First House
6
Sixth House
2
Second House
5
Fifth House
3
Third House
4
Fourth House

any Sign cards from the original Cross Spread that come up in the First House, for these reveal the Sign that is on the Ascendant, the mask or persona that the querent puts on to face the world (if the central card(s) represents a pure planetary energy, there is no clear Sign upon the Ascendant.)

Continue through the rest of the twelve piles (Twelve Houses), forming groups of three cards each; the two additional cards in each group give vital insights into the meaning of the center card from the original Cross Spread. Do not turn over the center pile until you are finished interpreting the initial twelve.

To understand how to interpret a particular "House of Cards" (forgive the pun), let's pretend that we have uncovered three cards in the First House: The 9 of Cups upright from the initial Cross Spread, surrounded by the Queen of Swords reversed and the 3 of Pentacles upright.

According to the information from Chapter Four, the First House pertains to the querent's present incarnation, identity, personality, and self-understanding, as well as his or her overall health, physical appearance, and body. In the First House we might also find information about new beginnings or immediate past and future events. This House ultimately reveals the nature and quality of the querent.

The 9 of Cups (Jupiter in Pisces) upright in the First House tells us that the querent has little self-control and is lost in a period of excesses and overindulgences; she/he is probably either already overweight and experiencing the health risks from intemperance, or else will soon begin to suffer these repercussions. The Queen of Swords (associated with Receptive Libra) reversed adds additional insight, telling us that the querent desperately wants this problematic lifestyle to end, probably because of a desire for partnership or else to save a current partnership. The 3 of Pentacles (Mars in Capricorn) upright reveals that the querent can and will succeed in the changes that need to be made, but warns that it will require hard work on the querent's part; ending the overindulgence and healing the resulting health problems will not be easy. Mars in the First House (from the 3 of Pentacles) shows the querent choosing a difficult road, as well as having the tendency to rush into a situation before its proper time; however, Mars is determined to cut the excesses. In combination with the reversed Queen of Swords, Mars instructs the querent to make sure that she/he remains passive until the plans and support during the change are firmly in place. The Queen of Swords might even recommend finding a knowledgeable older woman to help facilitate the change.

Additionally, Jupiter does not like Mars, while Mars has no problem with Jupiter. For the querent, this is a good thing because the querent wants to inhibit the excesses of Jupiter while encouraging the activity and initiative of Mars. Also, Cups and Wands have a natural enmity, while Wands and Swords work well together, ensuring that the Wands and Swords unity will overcome the 9 of Cups in this situation. In this particular combination, we have Pisces on the Ascendant (always use the center card from the Cross Spread to reveal the Sign on the Ascendant), presenting the querent's mask or persona as emotional, deliberately mysterious, easily influenced by the emotions of others, and motivated by hidden substance of which they are not aware.

Now use the art of interpretation as outlined in the previous chapter to gain deeper insights about the original ten cards from the Cross Spread. Following are some additional things to consider:

If two original cards appear next to each other in a House, simply turn over the card on either side of the pair (forming a group of four cards) and interpret the two original cards as though they were two planets in conjunction, with the two surrounding cards adding further insight.

If three or more original cards appear in a House, turn over all six cards and interpret the entire group as pertaining to the matters of that House.

If two or more Major Arcana cards appear in a House, this says two things to the querent: that there are powerful forces at work that are beyond the querent's present control and that the querent would benefit from working with the energy of these Major Arcana cards on his or her own.

Remember that an effective way of ordering the interaction of planets, signs, and houses within a reading is to consider the planets as the basic energy that is currently manifesting in an individual's life, the signs as the character or direction of that energy, and the house as the circumstances surrounding the manifestation of a particular energy and where it will manifest.

Key Words to Remember the Houses

1st House: The querent and beginnings
2nd House: The querent's resources
3rd House: Issues of immediacy and appearance
4th House: Home, roots, and the end of the matter
5th House: Pleasure and sex

6th House: Physical health and the ability to function in the world
7th House: The other and partnerships
8th House: The other's resources
9th House: Long-term aims
10th House: The querent's public life
11th House: Ideals and friendship
12th House: Spiritual health and the ability to function in eternity

Generally speaking, the cards representing the outer planets—the Fool (Uranus), the Hanged Man (Neptune), and Judgment (Pluto)—should be interpreted after the rest of the Major Arcana, since they are less specific to the individual and instead broadly influence entire areas or groups.

If the querent asks about taking a particular action and the Moon (either as the High Priestess, 6 of Pentacles, 4 of Cups, 2 of Swords, 9 of Wands, or the 7 of Swords) does not appear in the matter's House, nor is that House making any aspects (conjunction, sextile, square, trine, or opposition) to a House which contains one of the Moon's cards, than the Moon is considered to be Void of Course, meaning that it is best not to act or take any unnecessary risks at this time. Also watch for upright Queens, for they caution the querent to remain passive and wait before acting.

The center (thirteenth) pile of cards is called the "Kingdom Within," for it reveals to the querent the ultimate message that is central to the reading. After interpreting all Twelve Houses, turn over the entire center pile and lay out the cards, in order, from left to right, with the bottom card becoming the first card on the left. If some original cards from the Cross Spread appear in the thirteenth pile rather than in one of the Twelve Houses, don't worry: This means that they are also part of the "Kingdom Within." This final pile tells a sort of story to the querent, summing up the rest of the reading and focusing upon the larger truths that are manifesting in the querent's life. The "Kingdom Within" answers the crucial question, "What must I do now?" Read the six cards in order from left to right, interpreting the cards as they affect each other astrologically; each card is a "challenge" which needs to be faced by the querent: either an action required on the querent's part, or else something that the querent must focus upon in order to see more clearly and discover "the Kingdom Within." The first card on the left is the initial challenge, the second card is the challenge which follows the first, and so forth, with the last card on the right revealing the final outcome of conquering these successive challenges.

Additional Ideas When Reading for Others

It is often useful, when the querent first sits down for a reading, to have him or her look through the deck and choose a card to act as his or her Significator in the Cross Spread, representing either the querent or else the querent's current situation. Make no suggestions and give no information about the "meaning" of the cards at this point—there is no "wrong" reason for the querent to choose a card. Allow the querent to tell you the reason for his or her choice, but do not prod. The reading will reveal all pertinent information. This method is more time consuming, but you may use this period to build affinity, establish a common reality, and ascertain the communication style to use that is appropriate for the individual querent's needs. (If you are limited on time, a shorter version of this is to have your querents spread the deck face-down before them and, without looking at the pictures on the cards, instinctually draw the card that seems to attract them.) Set aside the chosen card, shuffling and cutting the deck normally.

Interpreting Troublesome Questions

The Key Spread, Triangle Spread, Cross Spread, and Kingdom Within Spread provide the means to reliable, accurate divination. However, even for the experienced reader of the Tarot, there are some troublesome types of questions that need to be addressed further: Questions Requiring *Yes* or *No* Answers, Questions of Health, Questions of Time, Lost Items and Locations, and Worldwide Events.

Questions Requiring Yes or No Answers

It is not the purpose of a Tarot deck to tell the querent what to do in a particular situation, but instead to give him or her more information so that she/he may see more clearly, and thus make better decisions. Generally, it is not a good idea to make any decision when emotionally upset, physically weakened—by hunger, illness, or sleep deprivation—or when one knows that she/he is not seeing clearly. However, let's say that you don't have much time, and you just need a quick yes or no to a simple question like, "Is this price quoted by the mechanic the best I will find?"

Shuffle and cut the cards the way you always do, and pull one card off the top of the deck. If the card is upright and positive, the answer is "yes." If the card is reversed and positive, the answer is "Yes—but wait before acting." If, on the other hand, the card is upright but its meaning is either negative or mixed, the answer is "no." If the card is reversed and either negative or mixed, a simple "yes" or "no" is not sufficient to answer the question; thus, a more comprehensive spread is necessary.

Questions of Health

When a person is sick, it is a serious thing and should not be left up to a Tarot reading—a health practitioner should always be consulted as soon as possible. However, there are many questions about health that may be clarified by a Tarot reading. In the Kingdom Within Spread, look to the 6th House regarding information about acute illnesses and any question regarding the quality of hospitals or medical care. Look to the 5th House (and occasionally the 1st) for information about the general vitality and overall health of the body. Hidden illnesses may show up in the 12th House. In questions of possible death, look first to the 8th House (and occasionally the 7th), but please remember—this is a serious matter and the reader must be very sure before uttering one word about such a devastating event. And always seek outside clarification in matters of health—Tarot gives guidance, NOT a diagnosis!

In order to simplify answering questions of health, I have summarized the health issues of the signs and the planets below for convenience' sake:

Health Issues of the Signs...

Aries
The head and face, as well as any related maladies—like headaches, strokes, eye problems (see Gemini for sight problems), toothaches, inflammations, pimples, disfigurements, baldness; also blood and muscles.

Taurus
Illnesses of the throat and neck—like laryngitis or tonsillitis.

Gemini
Lung disorders—like bronchial and respiratory problems, pneumonia, and tuberculosis. Nervous disorders. Failing sense perception, eyesight problems. Problems with arms, shoulders, and hands. Illnesses of the connective systems of the body—like veins, arteries, and nerves.

Cancer
Digestive and gastric ailments. Cancer and tumors. Edema and other disorders from excess bodily fluids. Illnesses of the ovaries, breasts, stomach, or mouth.

Leo
Heart disease and poor circulation. Spinal problems. General vitality problems. Problems with ribs or sides. Fevers.

Virgo
Illnesses of the intestinal and digestive tract—like irritable bowels, diarrhea, and constipation. Also appendicitis, duodenal ulcer, pancreas problems, and hernias.

Libra
Illnesses of the kidneys, diabetes, and skin disorders. Problems with the ovaries, lower back, and buttocks.

Scorpio
Problems with the groin and elimination—like the bladder, hemorrhoids, hernias, descending colon and rectum, prostrate gland, or ovaries.

Sagittarius
Liver disorders. Problems with the hips, thighs, and sciatic nerve. Blood sugar irregularities. Gout. Falls from horses and sports injuries.

Capricorn
Illnesses of the bones, teeth, and knees. Colds, rheumatism, and arthritis. Any chronic complaints. Also skin diseases.

Aquarius
Problems with legs and ankles. Defects of blood circulation. Nervous and spasmodic complaints.

Pisces
Problems with the feet and lymphatic system. Hidden tumors and cancer, problems from alcohol or drugs, asphyxiation, malnutrition.

Health Issues of the Planets...

Sun
Integrity of entire body's system, general vitality, heart, spine, the will to live, the right eye of men and left eye of women.

Moon
Stomach, breasts, the stomach and digestion, the fluids of the body, tear ducts, mucous membranes. The left eye of men and the right eye of women.

Mercury

The nervous system, eyesight, and sense perception. The bronchial tubes, lungs, and respiration. The left hemisphere of the brain. The arms, legs, shoulders, and tongue. Any illnesses of thinking and communication—like a brain tumor, headaches, stuttering, delusions, memory problems, insanity, or dumbness.

Venus

The veins, neck, and throat. The kidneys and thyroid. The skin, back, belly, and female reproductive organs.

Mars

The head, face, brain, nose, and tongue. The muscular system and muscle control. Male sexual organs. Blood and arteries, iron in the blood. Shares a part in high blood pressure. Infectious diseases and epidemics, wounds and cuts, bruises and burns, the adrenal gland, high fevers, migraines, shingles, and frenzies.

Jupiter

The liver, thighs, sciatic nerve, hips, and feet. Cellular growth and weight gain. High blood pressure, blood sugar levels, and the pituitary gland. Any illness resulting from too much good living.

Saturn

The skeletal system, skin, gall bladder, tendons, cartilage, and teeth. Illnesses caused by cold, melancholy, fears, or old age—deafness and arthritis.

Uranus

Some nervous disorders. Any sudden illnesses, growths, or spasms—like epilepsy, convulsions, or a paralyzing stroke. Sudden falls and falls from great heights. Accidents due to electricity, lightning, explosions, and natural disasters. Plays a part in high blood pressure. The pineal gland. Circulation of the blood.

Neptune

Any illnesses that are difficult to diagnose and treat. Poisoning as well as illnesses from alcohol and drugs. Also asphyxiation, insanity, sleepwalking and sleep disorders, weakening or debilitating illnesses. The thalamus and right hemisphere of brain (the seat of creativity and imagination). Lymphatic system and feet.

Pluto

The sex glands and reproductive systems, eliminative organs, DNA and metabolism, any essential but unconscious bodily functions. Enzymes. Also, any response of the body to purify the system—like hives and allergies.

Questions of Time

Invariably, a concerned querent will ask the question, "When?" Although often crucial to a complete answer, be very careful and precise before responding to this question—make sure you know; it is always appropriate to admit that you do not. Then again, an experienced reader can use the Tarot to accurately answer questions of time. Only answer questions of time within the context of a reading; allow a preponderance of information to guide you.

There are three basic methods, and one advanced method, for determining the timing of an event; below I will list and explain them in order of difficulty.

Basic Time Measurement:

1. Seasons of the Year

This method works well for more simple Tarot Spreads. **Each Suit in the Tarot relates to a particular season of the year: Wands are Spring, Cups are Summer, Swords are Autumn, and Pentacles are Winter.** Use the Tarot suits to predict timing within the coming year. For example, if there is a predominance of Wands in a reading (more than half), then the event in question will happen in Spring. The aces of each suit suggests the start of the corresponding season.

Additionally, **each season of the year encompasses three signs of zodiac: Aries, Taurus, and Gemini occur in the Spring; Cancer, Leo, and Virgo arise in the Summer; Libra, Scorpio, and Sagittarius happen in Autumn; finally, Capricorn, Aquarius, and Pisces emerge in Winter.** If three or more zodiacal signs of a particular season appear in a reading, this can indicate that the event will occur during the corresponding season (or even more specifically, if two or cards correlating to one specific Sign appear in a reading, then the event will happen during the corresponding time period attributed to the Sign).

2. Types of Signs

To know how long something will last or how long the querent will have to wait, look for a majority of types of signs of the zodiac in a reading:

Cardinal Signs

(Aries, Cancer, Libra, Capricorn)—weeks/ short time span

Fixed Signs

(Taurus, Leo, Scorpio, Aquarius)—years/ long time span

Mutable Signs

(Gemini, Virgo, Sagittarius, Pisces)—unable to determine/ medium or unknown time span.

3. Using Decans of the Minor Arcana

This is the only method that I have found to be effective when drawing only one card in answer to a question of time. Each of the cards of the Minor Arcana (not including the Aces) rules one *decan* (or ten degrees) of the Sun's yearly 360 degree progression through the zodiac. (See *The Minor Arcana Around the Zodiac*, for a visual representation.) Three of each of the Minor Arcana cards corresponds to a particular sign of the zodiac (i.e., the 2, 3, and 4 of Wands are in Aries). Use these decans to discover the portion of the year in which the event will take place. Since there are three cards for each sign, attribute the first (like the 2 of Wands) to the beginning of the period that the Sun is in the particular sign, the second (like the 3 of Wands) to the middle of the period, and the third (like the 4 of Wands) to the end of the period. For example, let's say that the 3 of Wands is drawn—since the Sun is in Aries from March 20th to April 19th, this indicates that the event will take place in the middle of this time period, between March 31st and April 9th. When using this method, it is important to note that if any card is drawn other than one of these thirty-six Minor Arcana, either the time itself is indefinite or else that this method may not be used to answer the question.

Following is a chart noting the decans of the Sun's progression through the zodiac.

Decans of the Minor Arcana

Astrological Sign	Dates Covering Signs	1st Decan 0-10 Degrees Into Sign	2nd Decan 10-20 Degrees Into Sign	3rd Decan 20-30 Degrees Into Sign
Aries	March 20 – April 19	March 20 – March 30 **2 of Wands**	March 30 – April 9 **3 of Wands**	April 9 – April 19 **4 of Wands**
Taurus	April 19 – May 20	April 19 – April 29 **5 of Pentacles**	April 29 – May 10 **6 of Pentacles**	May 10 – May 20 **7 of Pentacles**
Gemini	May 20 – June 20	May 20 – May 30 8 of Swords	May 30 – June 10 **9 of Swords**	June 10 – June 20 **10 of Swords**
Cancer	June 20 – July 22	June 20 – July 1 **2 of Cups**	July 1 – July 11 **3 of Cups**	July 11 – July 22 **4 of Cups**
Leo	July 22 – August 22	July 22 – August 1 **6 of Wands**	August 1 – August 12 **7 of Wands**	August 12 – August 22 **8 of Wands**
Virgo	August 22 – September 22	August 22 – September 1 **8 of Pentacles**	September 1 – September 12 **9 of Pentacles**	September 12 – September 22 **10 of Pentacles**
Libra	September 22 – October 22	September 22 – October 2 **2 of Swords**	October 2 – October 12 **3 of Swords**	October 12 – October 22 **4 of Swords**
Scorpio	October 22 – November 21	October 22 – November 1 **5 of Cups**	November 1 – November 11 **6 of Cups**	November 11 – November 21 **7 of Cups**
Sagittarius	November 21 – December 21	November 21 – December 1 **8 of Wands**	December 1 – December 11 **9 of Wands**	December 11 – December 21 **10 of Wands**
Capricorn	December 21 – January 20	December 21 – December 31 **2 of Pentacles**	December 31 – January 10 **3 of Pentacles**	January 10 – January 20 **4 of Pentacles**
Aquarius	January 20 – February 18	January 20 – January 30 **5 of Swords**	January 30 – February 8 **6 of Swords**	February 8 – February 18 **7 of Swords**
Pisces	February 18 – March 20	February 18 – February 28 **8 of Cups**	February 28 – March 10 **9 of Cups**	March 10 – March 20 **10 of Cups**

Advanced Time Measurement

Although this method is potentially the most specific and accurate, it also requires the greatest understanding and finesse as it requires an advanced understanding of astrology. Using the Kingdom Within Spread, you may combine both the Types of Houses (Angular—1st, 4th, 7th, 10th; Succedent—2nd, 5th, 8th, 11th; Cadent—3rd, 6th, 9th, 12th) with the Types of Signs (Cardinal, Mutable, Fixed).

For the purpose of illustration, let us consider a querent who desires to know when she will become pregnant. First, I would look at what is occurring in the 4th House (for the end of the matter and family) as well as the 5th House (for children, pregnancy, and childbirth) in the Kingdom Within Spread.

MAKE SURE that one of these Houses discusses a pregnancy or a child—NEVER attempt to answer a question of time if the matter under consideration is not addressed within the House, or if it IS addressed but the answer is clearly to the contrary.

Suppose that no cards are turned over in the 4th House; the 5th House is a Succedent House, so I would look to see if we have a majority of Cardinal, Mutable, or Fixed signs among the cards that I have turned over. Imagine that in this House we have turned over the 10 of Pentacles (Mercury in Virgo), the Empress (Venus), and the 9 of Wands (Moon in Sagittarius). The key words for the 10 of Pentacles are "Concrete Accomplishment," the Empress is a quintessential card for motherhood, and the Moon, in the 9 of Wands, is a planet often associated with young children and pregnancy. Clearly, this woman is going to conceive. Using the chart above and because of the two Mutable signs (Virgo and Sagittarius) in the 5th House (Succedent), we know that her conception will come to pass within months of the reading.

Angular Houses	Succedent Houses	Cadent Houses
Cardinal Sign—days	Cardinal Sign—weeks	Cardinal Sign—months
Mutable Sign—weeks	Mutable Sign—months	Mutable Sign—years
Fixed Sign—months	Fixed Sign—years	Fixed Sign—unknown

Lost Items and Location

If a querent wishes to know the location of a lost item, the reader should consider both the element of the sign or house as well as the locations ruled by the planet or sign itself. Following is a list of each:

Location by Element of the Sign or House

Fire Signs
Middle height, upper room or midway up in a room, near a wall or partition, fireplace, chimney, heater, oven, or stove.

Air Signs
Highest part of room or house, high shelves, or roof.

Water Signs
Low in room, near plumbing (bathroom, kitchen), water, lowlands or low places.

Earth Signs
Ground level or below, floor pavement, cellar, ground floor, or outdoors.

Angular House
Nearby, in home, office, shop, or room where article is usually kept, or where person works with or uses it, easily found.

Succedent House
Not in usual place, home, or office, but nearby, out of doors, must be looked for and harder to find.

Cadent House
Far off or hidden (third house says in neighborhood), not easy to find, may be lost permanently, out of sight, found only indirectly and usually by another person.

Location by Planet

Sun
Bright places where the Sun shines, grand buildings like theatres and palaces. The center of any place.

Mercury
Places of communication and thinking, like schools, telephone companies, Internet providers, newspaper; pets and veterinarians; any place that moves.

Moon
Any place connected with women or water—rivers, ponds, baths, bogs, etc. Also suggests that you will obtain what you're looking for.

Venus
Any location that is beautiful and alluring—gardens, outdoors, meadows, fountains, bedrooms, beds, wardrobes, cushions, dancing schools, places connected with beauty and art.

Mars
The scene of an accident, competition, or fighting; places of war, bloodshed, and destruction as well as hot, arid places like deserts.

Jupiter
Grand, large places, such as courts, important public places, and foreign places; also spiritual places, like altars, churches, and cathedrals; places of gambling.

Saturn
Places of government, old places, courtrooms; any location that is earthy, dirty, harsh, cold, or dark, such as deserts, deep pine forests, obscure valleys, church yards, holes, ruins, and graves; places that set boundaries, like eaves, doors, fences and thresholds.

Uranus
Places far away and out of reach, power plants, electrical outlets, places after a natural disaster.

Neptune
Places of fog or difficult-to-see places; drug houses and places for treating addiction.

Pluto
Toilets, garbage, waste, and radiation; nuclear power plants; dens of criminality; places of upheaval.

Location by Sign

Aries
Sharp peaks or mountains, pastures, hiding places, isolated places, places of competition and sports; new places.

Taurus
Hidden places of the Earth, like forests, caves, and mines, also farm buildings, pasture, countryside, and cellars.

Gemini
High, airy places, like hilltops, mountaintops, upstairs rooms, and skyscrapers; places of connection like hallways and windows; places of communication like rooms for debating, reading, or writing; also storage places, like chests, boxes, or computer memory; smaller living spaces, like apartments and condominiums; neighborhoods.

Cancer
The home and any place close to the home like the yard or a car; watery places, like lakes, harbors, moving water, beaches, seaside, springs, wells, and marshes.

Leo
Any place that deals in fun, entertainment, or amusement, like stages, bars, theatres, and amusement parks; any places that are wild, rocky, barren or generally accessible to animals but inaccessible to humans; eminent structures like castles, national monuments, and palaces; places where children play.

Virgo
Places of service and work, hospitals and clinics, any institution; offices and studies; anywhere books or merchandise are kept; any place at floor level or low down.

Libra
Airports, high places, windy places, hillsides, mountains, upstairs, and attics. Also, one room within or joined to another.

Scorpio
Places with lots of insects or reptiles as well as poisonous or stinking places; deep, watery, dark locations, like lakes, bogs, and muddy places; kitchens, bathrooms, and any room that contains water; damp places.

Sagittarius
Anything far away, like foreign lands; anyplace open and high, where one can see far in the distance, like the open sea; also wherever large animals live, like hills and fields; upstairs and near fireplaces.

Capricorn
Earthy, dark locations, such as mines and other places that are deep underground; anywhere animals are kept, places where wood is stored, barren fields, dung heaps, bushy or thorny land, and mountains paths; places near a floor or threshold; slums and abandoned places; places of business.

Aquarius
Open, large, pleasant places; places that are hilly, uneven, off the floor, or near a window; places of freedom and technology.

Pisces

Anyplace that is hidden or obscure, like oceans, thick forests, and jungles; places of restriction, like prisons; places of organized religion; large institutions.

Worldwide Events

The prediction and understanding of events on a worldwide scale is an entire study in itself, for the more data and intricacies that are added to the web of a reading, the more finesse it takes to make accurate predictions. However, for those who are interested in pursuing this broader knowledge, here are some important things to consider:

- The 1st House is the side that you support, while the 7th House is the side that you oppose or don't understand.
- If you want to know if a war will start or not, check out the Emperor (Aries) or the 1st House; also sports competitions.
- To determine the final judgment of the matter, as to which country will win a war, who will win the election, or which team will win the game, look to the 4th House.
- The Media and Hollywood are 3rd House matters. The Arts and Entertainment can also be found in the 5th House.
- Find information about ambassadors and diplomacy in the 5th and 11th Houses.
- The Stock Market and Commerce is a 6th House matter.
- Look to the Hermit (Virgo) and the 6th House for employment disputes and union matters.
- The opposing side in any disagreement or war is in the 7th House.
- The IRS, taxes, and national debt are 8th House matters.
- Places or countries that are far away (like the Middle East), wars over ideals and religious beliefs (like terrorism), trials and court cases, universities, and big business appear in the 9th House.
- The 10th House rules matters concerning governments, countries, judges, royalty, military leaders, and all other authorities.
- Humanitarian or environmental efforts show up in the 11th House, as well as a prison release, outer space exploration, technological advances, and the public's opinion. The 11th House is also where you will discover information about the governments' resources, ammunitions, and soldiery.
- The 12th House reveals secrets and denials, spies, imprisonments, large institutions, and scandals.
- Issues of organized religion have to do with the Wheel of Fortune (Jupiter) or the 12th House.
- Drug, alcohol, and addiction coincide with the Hanged man (Neptune).
- With regards to natural disasters, look for the Fool (Uranus)—with regards to accidents and attacks, look to the Tower (Mars).
- With regards to perjury, paperwork, the Internet, or newspapers, look to the Magician (Mercury).
- Air travel concerns Justice (Libra), Temperance (Sagittarius), and sometimes the Magician (Mercury).
- The Fool (Uranus), the Hanged Man (Neptune), and the Judgment (Pluto) suggest generational trends.
- In conflicts between men and women, the Sun (Sun) or Strength (Leo) represent the men while the Empress (Venus) or the High Priestess (Moon) represent the women.
- The Devil (Capricorn) will discuss getting what one deserves, responsibilities, and one's professional reputation.
- Look to the Judgment (Pluto) for the porn industry, criminality, espionage, or psychological warfare, as well as nuclear power or nuclear weapons. Pluto also rules the depravity of Organized Crime, the Mafia, and the corruption of the corporate world.

There are a ridiculous amount of contradictory lists with regards to which Sign rules which country. I have devised a simple rule of thumb that always works: Ask yourself how each country that you are concerned about is currently behaving in the given matter, and you will discover the Sign that rules that country for this reading. For example, the USA is generally ruled by Cancer because of its growing tendency towards conservatism and traditional values (besides the fact that it was "born" on July 4th, when the Sun was in Cancer). However, sometimes the 11th House can rule the USA, especially with regards to its founding values of freedom and democracy.

Chapter Six
Tarot Spreads for Spiritual Progression

What is "Pathworking?"

Pathworking is the process of working with the thirty-two Paths on the Qabalistic Tree of Life (and thus the Tarot) not for the purposes of divination and prediction, but to gain *vidyā* and progress spiritually. One literally works with each Path (the first ten through the Minor Arcana, the crucial four through the Court Cards, and the remaining twenty-two through the Major Arcana) to gain missing insight and break down those barriers that prevent the individual from spiritual progression. Whenever a large number of Major Arcana cards appear in a divinatory reading, consider working with those particular energies during his or her meditation, prayer, and other spiritual rituals; however, there is no reason to wait for this occurrence. There are five basic Pathworking spreads that the reader may use in his or her own spiritual explorations that are explained at the conclusion of this chapter, but before we commence with these spreads there is some final information that is crucial to Pathworking with the Tarot that we shall first consider: The Cyclical Nature of Existence, The Story of the Sacrificial God, and The Hero's Journey.

The Cyclical Nature of Existence

> *"The Leavers and the Takers are enacting two separate stories, based on entirely different and contradictory premises."*
>
> (Quinn 2002, 42).

There are basically two methods of viewing the progression of historical events: the first comes from the Western mindset (and is the viewpoint generally taught by today's academia) that presents history as a linear progression of time. Within this model, there was a beginning to existence, time advances and builds in an orderly manner, and there will someday be a termination to this timeline of existence. End of story. This viewpoint presupposes a logical and hierarchical structure of survival and advancement, and explains the "taker" mentality of the societies who believe it, for if time progresses in a straight line, then the rational goal of both the individual and the group would be to rise to the top, taking what is necessary to attain their goals.

Long before this conception of time, however, (and still in existence in many cultures around the world today) is the model of the Cyclical Nature of Existence. In this model, what we call "time" is simply the record of a series of cycles: the cycle of a day, the seasonal cycle of the year, the cycle of a being's lifespan, the cycle of an Age (or Aeon), the cycle of a sun and its solar system. This "primitive" conception of existence also sees cycles within cycles (for example, one might physically be a mature adult while simultaneously developing a new relationship), but the cycles always share a similar progression: creation/conception, beginning/birth, development/growth, maturity/adulthood, persistence/old age, destruction/death. This cyclical view of history encompasses the rise and fall of dictators, grand civilizations, and even the existence of our own Mother Earth as well. The cyclical nature of the physical universe can be contained and continued through repeated alteration for a time, but never halted completely, for with each creation comes an eventual destruction, making space for the next cycle to begin.

Although both these models contain a level of truth, Pathworking with the Tarot is based upon the Cyclical Nature of Existence; just as history is cyclical, so any event, experience, or goal can also be viewed from this cyclical model. Many of us, tutored in a linear view of time all our lives, tend to emphasize the outcome of any occurrence as being most important; we lose patience with the journey itself and focus only on our destination. However, each occasion in our own life is actually a cycle of stages: from the initial idea, to the planning and steps taken to achieve the desired result, to the outcome itself (whether or not it is what we actually intended), and finally to the long term repercussions, or afterglow, of the effect. Every part of a cycle is important; the wise person considers all stages of a cycle, rather than placing his or her attention only upon the ends themselves. Cyclical thinkers have infinite patience with all aspects of a given cycle, and therefore have a leaver mentality, for it is not so much their goal to change existence to fit their desired outcome, as to experience the fullness of the cycle itself, leaving each to its natural course, clearly seeing all aspects of it and expanding exponentially as a result.

The Story of the Sacrificial God

> *"There is not one people but had its Savior or Messiah, its Avatara or Buddha, who taught and showed them the true pathway of life."*
>
> (Fussel 1999).

From this cyclical view of existence comes the Story of the Sacrificial God (also known as the Dying and Rising God) that underlies the spiritual substance of much of humanity's religions and holy traditions. Sir James George Frazer was the first to research this astounding uniformity in his pioneering text, *The Golden Bough*, wherein he presents the evolution of the moral, ethical, and spiritual values of modern civilization from this simple, yet profound, story.

The Minor Arcana of *The Kingdom Within Tarot* deck specifically uses pictures to tell this Story of the God King who is born of the Great Mother, who willingly dies and conquers Death itself (through resurrection or being reborn as his own child), who returns to humanity with the elixir of life, who unites with his Beloved Bride and rules "heaven on earth" as his Beloved is infused with his likeness or essence (often depicted as being pregnant with his child) until the cycle all repeats itself again.

Many of the Sacrificial God myths lack certain elements from this prior description, as well as signify varying truths to the people who believe them. To some the God King is the God of the Sun and the Seasons, to others the God of Vegetation and Fertility, to others this reconciles the Masculine and the Feminine aspects of God, and yet to others this is the story of Redemption and Salvation; sometimes the death of the God King is literal, sometimes it is symbolic.

In the Tarot, the Sacrificial God is represented by the Hanged Man, the Incarnation of the Logos, the Divine Spirit who descends to manifest the Presence of God and redeem the fallen self by reconciling with Divinity. Not only does the Story explain the natural process of death and rebirth that characterizes life itself, but it is also the ideal model of redemption for those still trapped and believing in the agreements of the physical universe as "real."

The particulars of the Sacrificial God stories vary widely according the traditions of each culture as the myths were spread orally rather than written down, metamorphosing throughout time to suit the needs of each successive culture, breeding substantially divergent specifics—even of a similar deity. From Krishna of Indian mythology, to the Egyptian Osiris and Horus, to the Aztec's Quetzalcoatl and Persia's Mithras...from ancient Mesopotamia's Tammuz and Odin of the Norse, to the Oak King of the Celts and Dionysus of the Greeks...and even to Jesus Christ of Christianity, Sacrificial Gods mythos have had a prominent place in cultures throughout history.

Christians may take umbrage at the inclusion of Jesus Christ on this list of Sacrificial Gods, but Jesus' birth, life, message, death, burial, and resurrection encompass many essential components of the Story of the Sacrificial God King. No religion develops in a vacuum, and the Story of Jesus (whether historical or no) is the amalgamation of the Jewish traditions, Roman environment, Greek philosophies, Persian myths, and Egyptian ideas of the times. Many religions in those times shared similar themes and often the deities themselves became melded together in the minds of their believers. The true difference between early Christianity and the prior Sacrificial God cults was that while the older religions often kept their mysteries secret save for a select few initiates or members, Christianity openly offered the secrets of redemption to the entire world.

In essence, the same rituals, sacraments, teachings, and promises that existed in the Sacrificial God King mythos are also found in Christianity. The concept of Christ or Kristos originated in ancient Egyptian mythology and the Osiris/Horus myths. Five hundred years before the birth of Jesus, the Greek dramatist Euripides described the rites of Baptism and the Eucharist as essential elements of the Orphic Mysteries in his play, *The Bacchae*. The Eucharist (also called Communion or Mass) that Jesus introduced to his twelve disciples at the Last Supper was based upon the ritual consumption of the God King, just like the contemporary followers of such God Kings as Osiris, Dionysus, Attis, and Mithras. Earliest accounts record that the God Kings at first were ritually sacrificed and eaten by their followers, then eventually other humans were sacrificed as "scapegoats" and eaten in place of the God Kings, then animals began to be substituted, until finally it became common to eat grain offerings in the form of bread shaped like the God or else with a cross upon it (think of the traditional Easter treat, hot cross buns). A Central theme in the Christian book of Revelations is that Christ will return for his Church, the "Bride of Christ," and so the Pagan Mysteries also mirrored Christianity's Christ and his Bride through their sacred marriage between the God King and the Bride Goddess, who represented the initiate's incarnate self or "eidolon," resurrected and saved by her "marriage" to Osiris-Dionysus, representing the disincarnate Self or "Daemon" of the fallen individual (Freke and Gandy 2001, 123).

Since the story of Jesus is perhaps best known by Western civilization today, the following are some simple comparisons between the story of Jesus and some of the most famous Sacrificial God mythos:

Mithras of Persia

Perhaps the most analogous to Jesus' own story, this Persian savior was called the "light of the world" and born of a virgin in a cave attended by shepherds and gift-bearing magicians on December 25th. He performed many of the same miracles attributed to Jesus, encouraged his followers to partake in ritual communion at a Last Supper, and his ascension to heaven was celebrated at the Spring Equinox (Easter). The Church Father St. Augustine wrote that the priests of Mithras worshiped the same deity as he did, and the remarkable similarities between these two Sacrificial Saviors was later explained by the Catholic Church as the devil imitating the gospel before Christ's birth, so that people would see the resemblance and doubt Jesus' uniqueness.

Osiris / Horus of Egypt

Died and resurrected to reflect the annual cycle of fertility and renewal of the Spring flooding of the Nile; Horus was known as "the way, the truth, and the life," "the father seen in the son," and "the light of the world."

Tammuz of Mesopotamia

Resurrected each Spring after being buried in a tomb and descending for three days into the Underworld; the Queen of Heaven, Inanna, went to the tomb to mourn the death of her God King only to discover it empty.

Odin of the Norse

The suffering and dying god who through his crucifixion became the "savior of men."

Why, it is natural to ask, are these correlations so often unknown by modern Christians themselves? The record of Jesus Christ and Christianity, unfortunately, has been written (and re-written) by the Catholic Church which, from an historical perspective at least, for a time displaced or defeated all other beliefs in Sacrificial Gods. The Catholic Church began this historical re-working in 325 C.E. through Emperor Constantine, Bishop Eusebius, and their Council of Nicea's insistence that the Son and the Father were *homoousius*, and thus Jesus was one with God and completely unlike and separate from all of creation. This continued in 503 C.E. when the Emperor Justinian and the Council of Constantinople declared belief in reincarnation to be "heresy."

In order to assimilate divergent religions, the Church began to offer a host of "saints" (now numbering in the thousands)—some of whom were patterned after pagan gods and goddesses (like Saint Brigid, Saint Josaphat, and Saint Lucy)—as well as appropriating and renaming the Pagan Equinox and Solstice Festivals as Easter, Christmas, St. John the Baptist's Day, and St. John the Apostles' Day. The Divine Feminine Queen of Heaven that was such a central character in the story of the Sacrificial God was distorted into the Holy Virgin Mary, the Madonna, the Mother of Jesus Christ. During the Dark Ages, the Catholic Church monopolized "the truth" through insisting that each layperson must rely on the mediation of the ordained clergy for salvation and requiring that all scriptures and liturgy be conducted in Latin instead of the common vernacular; the final (and most deadly) blow was dealt by the appalling violence of the Crusades and the Holy Roman Inquisition. A valiant attempt to transform the Christian religion began during the Reformation, but the efforts of the Catholic Church had so altered and obscured the true message that many protestant churches continued to base their beliefs on flawed understanding, resulting from a misguided dedication to the more ingrained interpretations of the Catholic Church along with a refusal to trust their own ability to see.

So what is the significance of the Story of the Sacrificial God? Were the stories of these Rising and Dying Gods pure mythology, or did some (or all) of them actually exist? Probably both. Does the existence of such a multitude of Sacrificial Saviors negate the story's importance? Quite the opposite. In this Story, we discover the "interior truths [that] were wrapped in external and perceptible ceremonies, so that men, by the perception of the outer which is the symbol of the interior, might by degrees be enabled safely to approach the interior spiritual truths" (Crowley 1974, *Gems from the Equinox*, 36). Just as a seed must fall to the ground and die before the life force within may be released to grow into the light, so this Story shatters the husks of the outer rituals of our religions to allow the inner truth to spring free. The Story of the

Sacrificial God is the allegory of the Redemption of Fallen Humanity, of the God King who demonstrates for us the path to salvation—so that we may each, in turn, embark upon our own Hero's Journey.

The Hero's Journey

The tale of the Hero's Quest has been told in every culture and mythos on Earth; all the novels, movies, and computer games that we so adore are structured according to its plotlines. It is the story of a hero (the Protagonist) who faces daunting challenges and obstacles, and yet—after almost succumbing to the seemingly impossible odds—perseveres, overcomes, and triumphs (or in a tragedy, the hero fails). The hero is perhaps the most treasured mythological archetype—each and every one of us relate to his (or her) story, for it is, in fact, our own story. We are the heroes in the myth of our own existence. (The word myth is not used here to mean a fanciful story of explanation, but instead it is a foundational archetypal story that forms the basis for what we believe and how we enact our lives.)

The twenty-three cards of the Tarot's Major Arcana tell the archetypal story of the Hero's Journey—the story of the Way that an individual incarnated spirit in this world may follow in order to discover the Kingdom Within. Although I will explain this monumental journey below, these words are simply the culmination of the toil of those who have come before. The timelessness of the images upon the Major Arcana cards are because each embodies one aspect or obstacle of our own Hero's Journey on Earth. In addition, Joseph Campbell's *The Hero with a Thousand Faces* provides the basic outline for the archetypal Hero's Journey (Campbell 2008, *The Hero with a Thousand Faces*) while Robert Anton Wilson's *Prometheus Rising* suggests the basic stages of an evolving spirit (Wilson 1983, 40-41). Frater Achad's *Q.B.L.* offers insight about the Hero's traversal as she/he climbs the Tree of Life), while his text, *The Chalice of Ecstasy*, discusses the Fool's Redemption in detail.

The Archetypal Fool's Journey

0: The Fool

The Fool is the hero of our story. He is each one of us at the beginning, during, at the end, and after our journey through life. It is no mistake that the Fool is numbered zero—for he is both the beginning of existence, the end of existence, and exists outside and throughout all existences. While the other Major Arcana cards each represent a step (or Path) along the Hero's Journey, the Fool is always with us. Each of us must redeem our selves and remember what we have always known. Most of us begin as Percival (rather than Galahad) on our own Quest for the Holy Grail. (Alas, there are also those who begin believing themselves to be Galahad only to discover that they resemble Lancelot.) The Pure Fool is everything, but doesn't know it—he already has everything he needs, but doesn't see it. It is this very lack of seeing that prevents instant success in his quest, for "as a man thinketh, so he is." [Or as Robert Anton Wilson states, "Whatever the Thinker thinks, the Prover proves" (Wilson 1983, 25).] The Fool has the unadulterated energy and madness of pure Ecstasy, a gift that he must learn to use as he traverses the Path until he becomes the Path Itself. He must overcome his own obstacles and unmask his own illusions. He plays the game of existence, but believes his own lies—his journey is to transcend time and space to find the truth of the Kingdom Within the Here and Now.

The Ordinary World

(Early Experiences, Enemies and Allies, Programming and Conditioning)...

1: The Magician &
2: The High Priestess

The Fool incarnates into the Ordinary World with a few "spiritual governors" already in place. The first is the duality of opposites; the second is the struggle of power, will, and knowledge over intuition, truth, and understanding. The Magician and the High Priestess initiate the Fool into the duality of existence, for one of the first laws of the material universe is that as soon as we name some aspect of a polar experience, we invoke its opposite. (Only in the Purities or Virtues of life do we discover an escape from duality, for you can only undo or contaminate a Purity—it has no opposite.)

Within each of us there is the animus, the inner male personality. This is the Magician who introduces the Fool to the transmissive, positive (often called masculine) side of existence—the world of action through creative force and intellect. The Magician points the Way to controlling the Four Elements through the Higher Will, and is the representative of Chokmah on Earth, the True Man. However, the Fool cannot yet perceive The Magician in himself, and so begins to seek outside himself for a dim reflection, finding only the apparency of a grand illusionist rather than the power of his True Will.

The High Priestess, on the other hand, is the anima, the inner female personality; it is she who tutors the Fool in the passive, negative (sometimes called feminine) side of existence—the womb of his dark, unconscious potential that waits for the active principle to spark it into manifestation. She is the pure muse of the Fool's True Self upon his subconscious mind, and contains both the monsters that the Fool most fears as well as the mysteries that he longs to grasp. She is able to initiate the Fool into the mysteries of Nuit (the Star Universe), but her secrets are trapped in the Fool's subconscious, waiting for the Fool to birth and bring them to life.

3: The Empress

The first being encountered by the Fool on his earthbound journey is his Mother, the Empress. It is she who nurtures him, who introduces him to both sensation and sustenance, who offers pleasure and sanctuary. For the rest of the Fool's lifetime, he will base his concept of "woman" and "security" upon this primary relationship; the Fool has now been imprinted with the concept of that which is good for him, and that which is not. The Empress is also Mother Nature (or Mother Earth), and based upon the Fool's initial positive and negative experiences within the world of the five senses, he will decide what sort of place this world is. Ideally, the Empress offers the Fool the love and devotion that he may use to regenerate the Kingdom, while transmitting the understanding of the Great Mother (Binah). This pivotal relationship can teach the Fool the Path of Unity, the experience of losing the Ego and being absorbed into the Absolute. At her best, the Empress is the True Woman who guides the Fool to discover the Divine Feminine. However, often the Fool's experience with the Empress is less than idyllic, and he is programmed to fear lack and loneliness while learning insecurity and distrust.

4: The Emperor

The second being whom the Fool meets is his Father, the Emperor, who teaches the concepts of Authority, Structure, Hierarchy, Reward, and Punishment. The Fool begins to notice that there is a pattern and order to existence, and that the physical world responds predictably upon further exploration (such as learning not to touch the stove because "hot" hurts). From the Emperor, the Fool learns the rules of power and engagement, and begins to order the world according to that which is higher than him and that which is lower. Rather than a logical realization, this concept of order is an emotional/gut level response and imprinting. However, the Fool can use the harsh lessons of the Emperor to gain deeper insights into the truths of Retribution and Substitution (rather than sacrifice) as well as how to harmonize the Personal Will with the True Will.

5: The Hierophant

Next, the Fool begins to branch out from his home of origin, enrolling in primary school as well as joining other social groups such as church, clubs, or sports. Historically, the Hierophant was a spiritual guide who interpreted the mysteries of life for the initiate, and thus the Fool turns to teachers, ministers, coaches, and other professionals to prescribe how he must live in order to function in society. He is introduced to those aspects of existence that act as the Great Levelers: culture, education, organized belief systems, money, work, patriotism, and, most importantly, conformity. The Fool learns to use language and symbols to communicate, thus labeling and packaging phenomena rather than experiencing each as fresh and alive; the Fool begins to have and own the symbols of others. He toils to establish stability. The Hierophant, familiar with Korzybski's famous words, "those who rule symbols, rule us" (Korzybski 1994, 76), carefully controls the Fool's creative use of symbols with rules and restrictions. However, the lessons of the Hierophant are a necessary stage for the Fool to learn how to balance the influences of the Empress with the Emperor and gain a broader perspective on his journey towards enlightenment.

The World of Labor and Trials

(Inside the Belly of the Whale)...

6: The Lovers

Now the Fool enters adolescence, and as the hormones begin to surge, he becomes aware of the presence of the Lovers in his life. He desires to experience the connection that the Greeks called eros, the love of the Other that reflects one's own beauty. He wishes to make connections and visit another's reality. Our Fool is attracted by image, apparency, and romance, as well as motivated by a fear of being alone with himself. The Lovers offers lessons about the consequences of valuing perception over substance, for what the Fool really seeks in the Other is the missing (or unconscious) part of himself. Now he feels guilt when he cannot measure up to his own or another's desires, based upon the accepted roles of his peers rather than the reality. The Fool must overcome these restrictions as he confronts, in physical form, the oppositions of duality as well as the chimera of appearances.

7: The Chariot

The trumpeting Chariot rides through the Fool's life, heralding him to leave (and often confront) his parents and family while establishing his own chosen home environment. The Chariot calls the Fool to establish self-will and control, building his own base. He takes charge, faces conflict, and makes life-changing decisions. If this challenge is successfully surmounted, the Fool will now hold the reigns to his own life. The Chariot offers to initiate the Fool into the mysteries of Hadit, the center of Life that is everywhere, the flame that burns in every heart and is the core of every star.

8: Strength

Now is the time for the Fool to learn Strength—to confront and tame his fleshly body, his bestial nature, the Fallen Daughter of Malkuth. Strength brings the drives and desires of the body to the forefront, demanding for release—to live lustily, to copulate, to bear progeny, to rip the flesh from the body of one's enemy, and to build a rock solid Ego that is the center of its own existence. With the mastery of Strength the Fool discovers the bliss, rapture, and ecstasy that were always within him.

9: The Hermit

Once satiated, the Fool realizes that the sensual world offers little attraction. He finds himself asking difficult questions: Why is there something rather than nothing? Why does it seem as though something is missing in life? Why are there pain and suffering? The Fool meets the Hermit, who assists the Fool as he searches for these critical answers, considering all the details, leaving no stone unturned in his quest for understanding. The Hermit encourages the Fool to look inwards and seek solitude; the Fool finds himself seeking the alternate path of Severity, that of the Ascetic and the Abstinent. Through the Hermit he learns to temper his excesses and control his impulses. Our Fool realizes there is much, much more than Ego, but does not yet comprehend the grander design.

10: The Wheel of Fortune

The Fool has an epiphany—a moment in time when everything in the cosmos seems to line up perfectly as he envisions the vast Wheel of Fortune. The Wheel reveals the interconnected web of creation that is built around patterns and cycles as diversity and unity merge to produce the Grand Order of the Universe. The Fool begins to understand fate and destiny as well as the God within and beyond the rituals of humanity. The Wheel of Fortune shows him the Life Force that is active in the One Substance, yet differentiated into the Four Elements. He glimpses the mixture that conceals the supreme essence at the root of all duality.

11: Justice

The Fool must now confront Justice and learn her lessons of Harmony and balance, for the order of existence is founded upon the laws of cause and effect, as well as ownership and responsibility. Justice teaches the Fool to carefully measure the facts (rather than feelings) in making his judgments. The Fool observes the true benefits of Equanimity and Partnership, as the Law of Love—that great unifying force—works most effectively only when operating beneath Individual Will.

The Baptism of Initiation

(Descent Into the Under (Inner) world)...

12: The Hanged Man

The Fool begins his descent into the world beneath the lies, apparencies, and dualities of the physical universe; he enters a fog and must be content to face not knowing. He "takes up his cross" and must endure. The Fool's apparent sacrifice, however, is actually his redemption, for he meets the grinning Hanged Man, His True Self, for the first time as he sacrifices his Ego and surrenders to Life itself. The Fool joins the Hanged Man as all that he thought was so, is turned upside down by his new visions. The Hanged Man demonstrates the power of redeeming love in contrast to self-sacrifice, as he tells the Fool, "This is my body which I destroy, in order that it may be renewed." The Hanged Man demonstrates to the Fool that sometimes light must descend into the darkness in order to redeem or enlighten it.

13: Death

Death greets the Fool, bearing his horrifying gifts of change, ending, and transformation. Death eliminates the Fool's apparencies of Ego, Attachment, Fear, and Refusal. The Fool faces his own *avidyā* and befriends the ghoulish spectre, comprehending that Death (and Change) is not a permanent state—it is simply the fabric of the equation upon which the universe is founded: Creation, Preservation, and Destruction. Thus Death, the Great Transformer, teaches the Fool the valuable lesson of Transition.

14: Temperance

Temperance's territory is the scorching desert, vast and empty since few travelers are willing to negotiate its uncomfortable extremes. Temperance avoids excesses, exercising moderation and self-restraint. The Fool now faces the difficult challenge of satisfying two extremes: attaining distant goals as opposed to preserving what is. On the Temperance card of *The Kingdom Within Tarot* deck we find two centaurs, half-human and half-animal, considered the wisest of all for their perfect integration of the animal body with the human mind and spirit. Our Fool meets both the male centaur, whose arrow is the Root of Fire and Chokmah, as well as the female, who preserves the cup of Chesed, the sphere of Water and Regeneration. Temperance offers the Fool the secret to balancing Creation with Preservation: each in its appointed time, and not a moment longer.

15: The Devil

The Devil is only hideous from one vantage point; in most situations, the Devil actually seems sweet, seductive, and captivating. The Twin sides of the Fool (both his masculine and feminine) must face the Law of Karma, for as he has sown his seeds, so he shall reap. To the uninitiated, the Devil appears to imprison the Fool in the material world. Upon meeting the Devil face to face, however, the Fool finally recognizes that he has used the Devil as a scapegoat to avoid recognizing his own actions of delusion and self-annihilation. The greatest lesson of the Devil is not bondage, but release, for once the Fool confronts his own duality and the shame of his own fall, he sheds the illusion of incarnation as a prison and experiences for the first time the ecstatic love and adoration of all things in the physical realm, no matter how marvelous or base.

16: The Tower

Now the Fool must face the most difficult part of his journey through the Underworld: Destruction, in the form of the Tower. The Tower shatters all the Fool's existing forms, forcing him into Crisis, his greatest initiation. His Ego is in ruins. Yet wonder of wonders, as the Fool's world is devastated, he discovers an unexpected revelation: the utter freedom and joy of Destruction, for there is nothing further to fear! Like a phoenix, his True Self rises from the ashes of his Ego! In the Tower the Fool learns the most vital of truths: to become perfected, all must be annihilated.

Our Transcendence and Return

(The Freedom to Live)...

17: The Star

The Fool finally meets the Star, the gift of his own destiny. The water-bearer holds two pitchers—one pours forth the gift of the knowledge of good and evil (duality) leading to incarnation into the physical world and the cycle of birth, life, and death; the second bears the Tree of Life, offering sovereignty of the spirit and eternal life. The Fool finally conjures the dream of the Restored World.

18: The Moon

The Moon immerses the Fool in the shadowy realm of his own subconscious—his illusions, emotions, fantasies, and nightmares. It is time for his True Self to confront and finally see All That Is. Bubbling up from ages past come the Fool's forgotten and repressed actions that have bound him to physicality. He must voyage through his own prejudices, harmful acts, superstitions, and insanities; he must be buried in the bowels of the Earth in order to resurrect and conquer the Underworld once and for all.

19: The Sun

With the acceptance of his entire existence, the Fool now sees (rather than dreams of) the radiant Sun, the representative of the Father in the Kingdom of Malkuth, for the first time. The radiance of the Sun illuminates the darkness, bringing all that was once hidden into the light. The Fool achieves Enlightenment.

20: The Judgment

Once enlightened, the Fool initiates his own Judgment. He is purified by fire, which consumes him and destroys all his lies and refuse, and he crosses the Abyss to be absorbed into All That Is, all the while retaining the truth of himself. The representative of the Father is no longer necessary for him, for he sees the glory and ecstasy of the True Father. He attains the Holy Grail and becomes the Redeemer.

21: The World

This is the final stage in the Hero's Journey, for now the Transformed Fool has integrated all his disparate parts and remembered his True Self that was once shattered throughout this present lifetime and eternity, discovering the Ecstasy that lies beyond both the darkness of understanding and the light of wisdom. For the few who discover the Kingdom Within, the Center of All, the Ever-coming Crowned Child, the World is neither an illusion nor a prison, but truly becomes the Kingdom of Heaven. The Fool is now able to see, understand, and know whatsoever he so chooses. The Fool at last recognizes the true state of the World. He is free to act in any way he prefers, and capably interacts with All That Is. He reflects everything but holds on to nothing. Infinity fills him. The Fool has come full circle, but only now can he see what was always within him: a Hero, a King, a Star.

The Kingdom Within All

(Specific to the Kingdom Within All Tarot deck)

The Hero's Journey is but one adventure that the Fool may choose within the infinite possibilities of the Kingdom Within All.

Pathworking Spreads

Pathworking Spreads are meant to be done alone rather than by another reader or for someone else. Set aside at least fifteen minutes for the Single Seed spread, longer for the other spreads: you will need time to not only lay out the cards and interpret them, but also to work with the energies of the cards so they may assist you in gaining clearer vision.

The Single Seed Spread

Remove the Major Arcana cards from the deck. Shuffle and fan the twenty-three cards in front of you. Close your eyes, quiet your mind, and focus upon the following question:

> "What must I face in order to see more clearly?"

Choose the Major Arcana card that answers this question with your left hand and place it upright before you (there are no reversed cards in this spread). Now, follow these steps:

Meditate upon the images on the card:

- What do you see?
- What do they mean to you?
- How do they make you feel?
- Are you blocking this card's energy from your life in any way?
- Or, conversely, are you immersing yourself in the card's energy to the point of excess?
- Does this card remind you of anyone?
- What is your relationship to this person?
- Is there any closure that is still necessary for you in this relationship?
- Does this card remind you of an experience or a dream?

Next, look up the meaning of this card and read it thoroughly from Chapter One. Sit in a comfortable position for a few minutes and consider the meaning of the card. Compare your instinctive responses to the written ones.

Finally, re-read this card's part in the Hero's Journey. Enter a prayerful, meditative state with the card either in front of you or in your hands, and open yourself to embrace its energy. If it scares you, face this fear. If you have trauma associated with its images, look at the memories thoroughly and they will disappear. If you view this energy as either "good" or "bad," look at the entire energy as it is, rather than putting labels or judgments upon it.

It is a good idea to eventually do the Single Seed spread with each of the Major Arcana cards. One suggestion with regards to meditation: the goal of meditation is to get beyond your mind and body. If you struggle with meditation, it is either because your body wants control or your mind does. If your body wants control, you will feel a need to scratch or move constantly. If your mind wants control, you will either find your mind tends to drift into tangents or else you might create grand mental structures around the images rather than simply looking at them and seeing what is there. In order for meditation to succeed, you must use your spiritual eyes rather than your physical or mental ones.

'Till We Have Faces Spread

I named this unique spread after one of my favorite novels by C. S. Lewis (by the same title) that retells the Greek myth of Cupid and Psyche as a Heroine's journey to spiritual enlightenment. In the final chapter of the novel, the main character, who has cried out in anger at the gods for their silence and inaction, finally comprehends the terrible truth that until we approach the gods with our own face, instead of the many false ones that we believe our selves to have, we can never truly hear their answers.

For this spread, separate the sixteen Court Cards and shuffle them thoroughly. Now, choose the Court

Card which you instinctively feel best represents you in this present moment. If you choose a King, take out the other three Kings and lay all four of them upright before you. If you choose a Queen, lay the four Queens before you; if you choose a Prince or a Page, do the same, so that you end up with four cards in front of you.

It is time to look at the faces or personas with which you mask yourself, as well as look at the deeper truth behind each of these visages. Follow these four steps during your prayerful meditation:

Similarities and Differences

Look at the images upon each of the cards. How are these Characters the same? How are they different? Re-read the information about each one in Chapter Two. Consider which card most attracts you. Why? Which most repels you and why? What can you learn about yourself by comparing and contrasting these four cards with yourself?

Stage of Life

Next, consider the stage of life, level of power, and phase of progression that is represented by the four characters. Do you like the phase that is represented by these cards? Why or why not? In which areas in your life are you currently acting out this stage of life? In which areas in your life are you currently acting out this level of power? In which areas in your life are you currently acting out this phase of progression? What do you need to do to embrace the energies that you perceive in these cards; what do you need to let go of?

Archetypes

Look at the Archetypes associated with these four cards. Are you currently playing any of these games or wearing any of these "faces" in your life? Why and for what purpose? How do these archetypes aid you and how do they hinder you? Have you fallen into the mistaken belief that these "faces" are actually you? Who are you without these masks?

Qabalistic Correlation

Each Court Card has a Qabalistic correlation—Kings to Chokmah, Queens to Binah, Princes to Tiphereth, and Pages to Malkuth. Re-read the section in the Introduction to Chapter Three about the Sephirah that corresponds to the four cards you have chosen. How do these characters reflect the energy of their Sephirah? What can you learn about this Sephirah from these four cards? Strip away all your archetypal faces, and take some time to focus upon this Sephirah, opening to its energy. What beliefs and misconceptions have been clouding your vision of this Sephirah? Channel the energy of this Sephirah to begin to connect with the Divine. Using all that you have experienced and seen during the 'Till We Have Faces spread, ask yourself this final question: How can I open to this Sephirah in my life today?

The Death and Resurrection Spread

Use only the Minor Arcana for this spread. After separating the Minor Arcana from the rest of the deck, shuffle them thoroughly and fan the thirty-six cards before you.

Choose two cards:

The **first card** represents an energy that must be put to death in your life, or what must be destroyed and annihilated in order for your life to transform.

The **second card** is what will resurrect from the ashes of the first card's death, what new birth or blessing will come from the ending and destruction of the energy of the initial card.

Now, pause a moment and reflect upon these two cards. Consider the Sephirah (the colored half-circle) at the bottom of each of the cards in conjunction with each other: do they correlate to a specific Path on the Tree of Life? (For example, if one card has a green sphere for Netzach at the bottom and the other has orange for Hod, this suggests Path 16, the Hierophant.) If the two spheres are not connected by a Path on the Tree of Life, consider the Paths between them and the different options that you have in order to transition from one Sephirah to another. Which way do you find easiest? Which is the most difficult? Why? What do these preferences say about you?

Sometimes this reading can surprise you, especially if you first pull a card that you consider "positive" and then pull a card that you view as "negative." Perhaps it is time to reconsider and reacquaint yourself with the energies of these two cards. You might even choose one more card to reveal the best method of transition, or else do one of the divinatory spreads from the previous chapter on this specific question.

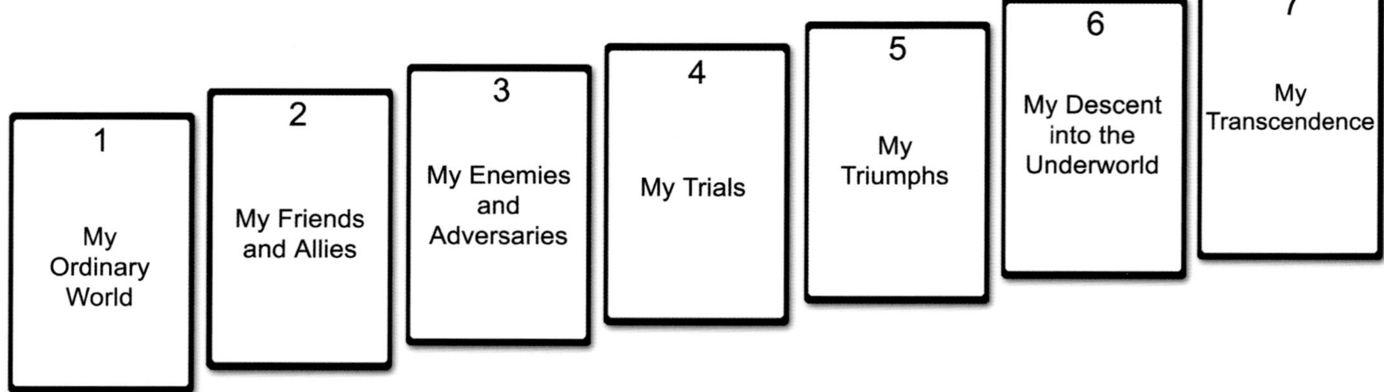

The Hero's Journey Spread

We will now consider this current lifetime. Using the entire deck, shuffle and cut the cards. Lay out seven cards to tell the tale of your own Hero's Journey:

Card One
My Ordinary World
Where do I come from? How did I begin this lifetime? What are my roots?

Card Two
My Friends and Allies
Who has helped and assisted me on my journey?

Card Three
My Enemies and Adversaries
Who has hindered or blocked me on my journey?

Card Four
My Trials
What has been my greatest challenge(s)?

Card Five
My Triumphs
What has been my greatest success(es)?

Card Six
My Descent into the Underworld
What do I still need to face?

Card Seven
My Transcendence
Where am I going?

Assigning Your Own Path's Experiment

Part One: Minor Arcana Experiment

It can be an exciting and illuminating experiment to formulate your own Tree of Life and Paths of Transformation. To begin this experiment, separate the twenty-three Major Arcana from your Tarot deck into one pile, placing the sixteen Court Cards into a second pile, and laying the corresponding Minor Arcana cards, Ace through 10, upon the table in front of you, forming the Ten Sephiroth of the Tree of Life, each Sephirah a pile of four cards:

4 Aces represent Kether
4 Twos represent Chokmah
4 Threes represent Binah
4 Fours represent Chesed
4 Fives represent Geburah
4 Sixes represent Tiphereth
4 Sevens represent Netzach
4 Eights represent Hod
4 Nines represent Yesod
4 Tens represent Malkuth

Meditate upon each of the ten piles, looking at the pictures and perhaps re-reading the introduction from Chapter Three to connect each set of cards to its corresponding Sephirah. Ask yourself the following questions about each pile:

- What do the four cards have in common?
- How are they different?
- How does each relate to its analogous Sephirah?
- What can you learn about each Sephirah by looking at its corresponding four

Minor Arcana cards?

- Which of the four cards are you most comfortable with? Which is the most difficult for you? Why? What do these preferences say about you and your relationship to the energies of the corresponding Sephirah?

Part Two: Tarot Court Experiment

Next, take your pile of the sixteen Court Cards and separate them into four piles of four: Four Kings, Four Queens, Four Princes, and Four Pages. If you recall, each of the four characters of the Tarot Court—King, Queen, Prince, and Page—symbolizes the Four Core Sephiroth of the Tree of Life.

- The four Kings are correlated with Chokmah, the Father
- The four Queens are associated with Binah, the Mother
- The four Princes are connected to Tiphereth, the Son
- The four Pages are related to Malkuth, the Daughter

These four Sephiroth—Chokmah, Binah, Tiphereth, and Malkuth (and therefore their corresponding Court Cards)—reveal the Great Work of Redemption and Transformation. To see this firsthand, place the four Kings in the Chokmah pile, with the Twos; the four Queens with the Threes in the Binah pile; the four Princes with the Sixes in the Tiphereth pile; and the four Pages in the Malkuth pile with the Tens. Ask yourself the following questions:

- What do the Kings have in common with the Twos of each suit? What does their correlation with Chokmah reveal to you?
- What do the Queens have in common with the Threes of each suit? What does their correlation with Binah reveal to you?
- What do the Princes have in common with the Sixes of each suit? What does their correlation with Tiphereth reveal to you?
- What do the Pages have in common with the Tens of each suit? What does their correlation with Malkuth reveal to you?
- Which Court Card character seems to best represent you? Why? What does its Sephirotic connection reveal about your personal emphasis/ energy/ phase of life?

Part Three: Major Arcana Experiment

Now it is time to experiment with the Major Arcana and the final Paths of the Tree of Life. If you like, you may use any prior study or knowledge that you have about the Paths, but it is unnecessary for the purposes of this experiment.

The last twenty-two Paths (excluding The Kingdom Within All card) connect two Sephiroth with each other, representing the way that must be traveled or the threshold that must be crossed in order to ascend or descend from one Sephirah to another. For this experiment, instead of accepting another's path correlations, you are going to lay each Major Arcana card between the two Sephiroth that it seems to naturally connect to you.

Have fun with this and see what you learn about the Tree of Life as a whole and each Major Arcana card in particular as you "play" with their arrangement!

For example, let us consider which Major Arcana card seems to naturally connect Malkuth to Netzach:

- In Kircher's model, these two Sephiroth are connected by The Moon.
- In Rabbi Luria's model, there is no connection between these two Sephiroth.
- In Achad's model, the energies of Netzach and Malkuth, the natural Path (or threshold to cross) are the Empress, because of her joint correlation with Netzach to Venus, as well as the Empress' emphasis upon the Earth, Motherhood, femininity, and the birthing of physical bodies.
- Which Major Arcana card would you use to connect Malkuth to Netzach? Why? What about the other twenty-one Paths?

The Tree of Life Spread

Now it is time to move beyond this current lifetime and consider your self from the eternal perspective. Shuffle and cut the entire deck, then lay down eleven cards into the shape of the Tree of Life meditate upon the insights that they reveal about the truth of your existence:

Card One
Kether
What am I outside of (or before and beyond) creation—beyond the realms of matter, energy, space, time, thought, and idea?

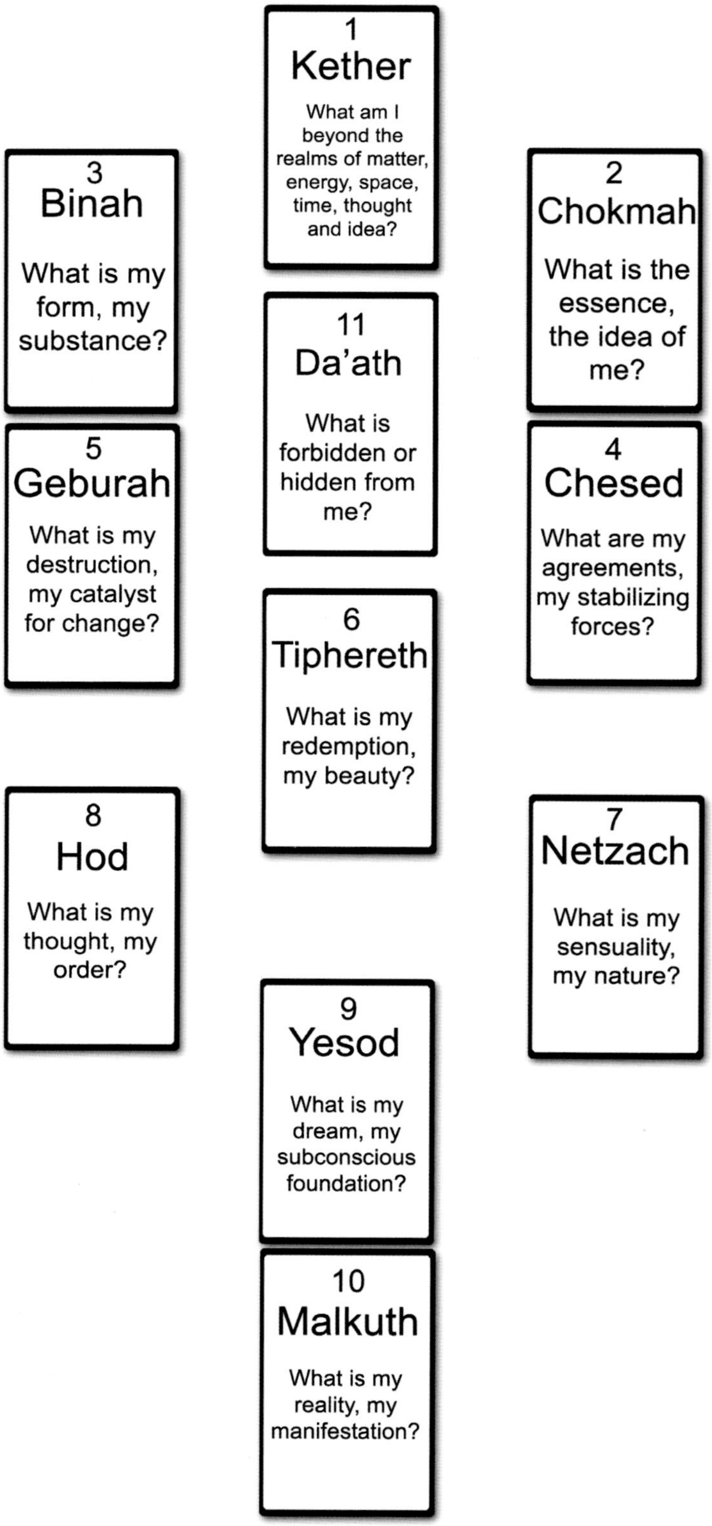

1
Kether
What am I beyond the realms of matter, energy, space, time, thought and idea?

3
Binah
What is my form, my substance?

2
Chokmah
What is the essence, the idea of me?

11
Da'ath
What is forbidden or hidden from me?

5
Geburah
What is my destruction, my catalyst for change?

4
Chesed
What are my agreements, my stabilizing forces?

6
Tiphereth
What is my redemption, my beauty?

8
Hod
What is my thought, my order?

7
Netzach
What is my sensuality, my nature?

9
Yesod
What is my dream, my subconscious foundation?

10
Malkuth
What is my reality, my manifestation?

Card Two
Chokmah
What is the essence, the idea of me?

Card Three
Binah
What is my form, my substance?

Card Four
Chesed
What are my agreements, my stabilizing forces?

Card Five
Geburah
What is my destruction, my catalyst for change?

Card Six
Tiphereth
What is my redemption, my beauty?

Card Seven
Netzach
What is my sensuality, my nature?

Card Eight
Hod
What is my thought, my order?

Card Nine
Yesod
What is my dream, my subconscious foundation?

Card Ten
Malkuth
What is my reality, my manifestation?

Card Eleven
Da'ath
What is forbidden or hidden from me?

Be prepared for some unexpected cards; give yourself time to fully take in all that the spread reveals about you. Rather than finding fault with yourself, consider the larger picture revealed by the spread. The Tree of Life spread reveals where you are right now, in all your divinity and baseness. Remember Shakespeare's immortalized advice, "To thine own self be true."

CONCLUSION

> *"It is in the hope of awakening some spark of the smouldering fire of this inner consciousness in the hearts of those who may read these lines...and from that spark enkindling a great fire that will burn up the veils which hide man from Himself—from God...to those who are slumbering contentedly, wrapped round with the delusion and dreams..."*
>
> (Achad 1999, *The Chalice of Ecstasy*, 3).

Whatever your concerns, I hope that the Tarot provides you with the tools you need to discover concise answers to your questions, as well as aids you in gaining awareness and confronting the truth of your life's circumstances. My initial goal in writing this book was threefold—to empower the individual spirit to create his or her own reality, effectively interact with the realities of others, and understand this game called Life—so that there will never be the need for my (or anyone else's) help again. Most "spiritual ad-vice" provides only temporary relief from one's suffering and misery; soon we find that the relief fails and we must, once again, seek out a "professional" or a group to assuage our pain. The avoidance of pain, or pa(y)-in, is simply the avoidance of paying our own bills—those heavenly accounts of what we owe others, the physical universe, and ourselves—and to the degree that one avoids paying creditors, she/he will ultimately experience much greater pain (remember all that compound interest!) as a result of not paying what one owes in the first place.

May the Tarot guide you towards confronting the truth of your pain, through the process of peeling back the fog and overwhelm that prevents you from achieving a perfect answer for each and all.

My final goal in writing this book (and crafting *The Kingdom Within Tarot* deck, as well) was to weave together (once and for all) what I have seen throughout my own experiences and studies, so that those who come after may discover their own truth rather than investing myriad hours into investigating the truths recorded by countless others. The irony of studying the Tarot (or any creation intending to impart enlightenment) is that, metaphorically speaking, it is simply a step ladder or set of training wheels: as soon as the individual regains the ability to see the truth, all human constructs become unnecessary and obsolete. To my delight, in the very act of birthing this project, I have found myself opening more fully and seeing more clearly than ever before.

There are as many different Paths in life as there are people, for each of us is a Star in his or her own right. As I observe those around me, it seems that much of Western society's energy today is aimed in one of two directions: the acquisition of stuff or the creation of drama. The first brings a temporary sense of security, while the second is a desperate attempt to create artificial life in order to avoid truly living. For much of humanity, Life becomes the destination of a fixed condition as they live "quiet lives of desperation" in their attempt to halt all change that doesn't fit their earthbound perspective. This comprehensive Tarot book, along with *The Kingdom Within Tarot* deck, were created to rouse those who seek eternity, but are lost in either a religion of bodies or a philosophy of minds... for eternal life can only be uncovered by the Spirit.

What do I wish for the reader, for this present age of humanity? For this succinct statement of intention, I must defer to the closing inspiration of the literary masterpiece, *The Amber Spyglass*, by Philip Pullman: rather than the never-ending search for the Kingdom of Heaven (or a return to the Queendom of Earth), I wish you the discovery of your own kingdom, within the agreed upon "Republic of Heaven".

Suppose naught, but see all!

Juno Lucina

BIBLIOGRAPHY

Achad, Frater. "Q.B.L. or The Bride's Reception: Being a Qabalistic Treatise on the Nature and Use of the Tree of Life." *The Hermetic Library*, (December 1997), http://hermetic.com/browe-archive/achad/qbl/QBL%20title%20and%20TOC.htm. Retrieved from the web on October 10, 2002.

Achad, Frater. "The Chalice of Ecstasy." *The Hermetic Library*, (January 1999), http://hermetic.com/achad/pdf/chalice.pdf. Retrieved from the web on October 10, 2002.

Achad, Frater. "The Egyptian Revival." *The Hermetic Library*, (March 1997), http://hermetic.com/browe-archive/achad/egyptian/egypt1.htm. Retrieved from the web on October 10, 2002.

Campbell, Joseph. *The Hero with a Thousand Faces*. Bollingen Series XVII. Novato: New World Library, 2008.

Campbell, Joseph, with Bill Moyers. *The Power of Myth*. New York: Anchor Books, 1991.

Crowley, Aleister. *Gems from the Equinox*. Israel Regardie. Tempe: New Falcon Publications, 1974.

Crowley, Aleister. *The Book of the Law*. York Beach: Samuel Weiser, Inc., 1976.

Crowley, Aleister. *The Book of Thoth (Egyptian Tarot)*. York Beach: Weiser Books, 1974.

Desikachar, T.K.V. *The Heart of Yoga: Developing a Personal Practice*. Rochester: Inner Traditions International, 1995.

Durant,Will. *Our Oriental Heritage. The Story of Civilization*. New York: Simon and Schuster, 1935.

Filbert, Geoffrey, C. *Excalibur Revisited: The Akashic Book of Truth*. Self-published manuscript, 1982.

Frazer, James G. *The Golden Bough: A study in Magic and Religion*. New York: Macmillan Publishing Company, 1922.

Freke, Timothy, and Peter Gandy. *The Jesus Mysteries*. New York: Three Rivers Press, 2001.

Fussell, Joseph. "The Significance of Easter." *Sunrise*, April/May, 1999.

Jung, Carl G. *Psychological Types*. Bollingen Series XX. Princeton: Princeton University Press, 1971.

Keirsey, David, and Marilyn Bates. *Please Understand Me: Character Temperament Types*. Del Mar: Prometheus Nemesis Book Company, 1984.

Korzybski, Alfred. *Science and Sanity: An Introduction to Non-Aristotelian Systems and General Semantics*. 5th ed. Brooklyn: Institute of General Semantics, 1994.

Osho. *This Very Body The Buddha*. Mumbai: Jaico Publishing House, 1973.

Myss, Caroline. *Sacred Contracts: Awakening Your Divine Potential*. Edinburgh: Harmony Publishing, 2002.

Place, Robert M. *The Tarot: History, Symbolism, and Divination*. New York: Penguin Group, 2005.

Quinn, Daniel. *Ishmael: An Adventure of the Mind and Spirit*. New York: Bantam Books, 1992.

Tennyson, Alfred L. *Idylls of the King*. London: Penguin Books, 1983.

Wilson, Robert A. *Prometheus Rising*. Tempe: New Falcon Publications, 1983.